FROM THE PEOPLE WHO STARTED IT ALL—EVERYTHING YOU NEED TO KNOW ABOUT NUTRITION

. . . Tips on growing your own herbs and a guide to using them

. . . Vitamin and mineral count of many favorite foods, such as meat, eggs, fish, vegetables, nuts, and soybeans

. . . A table showing the salt content of most common foods

. . . A special preparation chart for Chinese wok cookery

. . . An adult discussion on beverages—milk may not be as good for you as you think!

. . . A full month of healthful menus to get you on your way to natural cooking

ABOUT THE EDITOR:

CHARLES GERRAS is the executive editor of the Book Division of Rodale Press, and for nearly ten years he served as managing editor of *Prevention* magazine.

NATURAL COOKING
THE PREVENTION® WAY

Hundreds of Nutrition-Packed Recipes
from the Readers of *Prevention,*®
America's Leading Health Magazine

EDITOR
Charles Gerras

ASSISTANT EDITORS
Anna Wieder
Joan Bingham
and Joanne Moyer

A PLUME BOOK
NEW AMERICAN LIBRARY
TIMES MIRROR
NEW YORK, LONDON, AND SCARBOROUGH, ONTARIO

PLUME TRADEMARK REG. U.S. PAT. OFF. AND FOREIGN COUNTRIES
REGISTERED TRADEMARK—MARCA REGISTRADA
HECHO EN FORGE VILLAGE, MASS., U.S.A.

SIGNET, SIGNET CLASSICS, MENTOR,
PLUME and MERIDIAN BOOKS
are published *in the United States* by
The New American Library, Inc.,
1301 Avenue of the Americas, New York, New York 10019,
in Canada by The New American Library of Canada Limited,
81 Mack Avenue, Scarborough, Ontario M1L 1M8
in the United Kingdom by The New English Library Limited,
Barnard's Inn, Holborn, London, E.C. 1, England.

First Plume Printing, May 1974

4   5   6   7   8   9   10   11

PRINTED IN THE UNITED STATES OF AMERICA

Contents

Introduction

The first thing you notice about cooks who have just become conscious of nutrition is that they are bursting with questions. They want help in putting their new-found knowledge to work—without making too many waves. One housewife asks, "What can you *do* with wheat germ, safflower oil, sunflower seeds, and how can you do *without* sugar, salt or deep-fat frying?" Another writes, "My family doesn't want to nibble on watercress, washed down with herb tea— when they sit down to a meal they want a meal! What can I serve?" From still another concerned wife and mother we hear, "My husband likes pies, stews and hearty soups; my kids are always looking for something to snack on between meals. I talk so much about food values now that they think they'll have to settle for vitamin pills and canary-type portions of raw grass. Can you suggest a few sure-fire recipes that will turn my group on to healthful eating?"

Here is a book that will solve all of these problems, a book that describes a variety of ways to put the best nutrition into familiar foods such as meat loaf, pies, and omelets, and introduces healthful new recipes that add up to truly gourmet fare.

J. I. Rodale, the founder of PREVENTION magazine, was convinced from the start that appetizing, interesting, hearty foods can also be rich in nutritional values. To prove it, readers were invited to submit recipes that reflect the PREVENTION point of view, recipes containing healthful ingredients and that are cooked using techniques that best conserve nutrients. A selection of these was published monthly, providing other subscribers with new and tempting ways to introduce high-test nutrition into familiar dishes. They demonstrated fresh ideas for incorporating natural supplements— brewer's yeast, wheat germ, bonemeal, soy milk, kelp, etc.—into any course at any meal.

PREVENTION has also printed some very strong evidence indicting certain foods that seem basic to the average American menu and many of them are discussed in the pages that follow—allergies to milk; high blood pressure from too much salt; white sugar as an agent of tooth decay and hypoglycemia, and as a vitamin antagonist; bread and wheat products as a cause of constipation, colds and allergies; hopelessly nutritionless, additive-ridden, over-processed breakfast cereals; citrus fruit juices in relation to tooth enamel erosion; sugar-laden sodas and ice cream and their unhealthy effect on metabolism. These objections were taken into account, and the magazine's regular readers came up with ingenious substitutes. They found ways to make crackers and breads without using wheat; refreshing drinks for summer that make sodas obsolete; honey-sherbets that fill in for ice cream; pies and cakes that do not call for sugar or flour; "milk" made from nuts and seeds that stand-in well for the dairy product.

The result over the years, is this treasure chest of recipes that reflect the unique PREVENTION point of view—created by everyday housewives, not scientists, and served to ordinary families, not guinea pigs.

There are ideas for flavorful, vitamin-filled breakfast foods, the like of which you can't buy anywhere; mouth-watering casseroles that are completely original and packed with health values; and luscious desserts with a build-up factor that are fun to prepare and fun to eat. These hundreds of inventive cooking ideas are reinforced with tips on basic food values and interesting facts on the pitfalls of modern food processing.

To get the cook off to a good start, a month's menus are provided; they suggest every course, through three meals a day. There are special holiday ideas—Thanksgiving, Christmas and Easter Dinners, a Passover Feast and a New Year's Eve Party.

The recipes that follow prove good eating need never mean dull eating, and that nutritional foods are the best tasting of all.

C. G.

What Is Organically Grown Food?

ROBERT RODALE

Editor and Publisher of Prevention Magazine

"Organically-grown food is food grown without pesticides; grown without artificial fertilizers; grown in soil whose humus content is increased by the addition of organic matter; grown in soil whose mineral content is increased with applications of natural mineral fertilizers; and food that has not been treated with preservatives, hormones, antibiotics, etc."

That definition should leave little doubt in anyone's mind about what organic foods are. You cannot spray organic food with poisons. You can't grow it on soil that has been treated heavily with cheap artificial nitrogen to blow up the size of plants at the expense of their mineral content. You can't put organic food through a factory, stripping some of the nutrients and adding chemicals to change its color and flavor and add shelf life. Because if you do those things the food will no longer be organic.

There is no way that the American people can remain healthy in the long run without eating food that is organically grown.

That is a strong statement, but it is true for these reasons:

1. Standard commercial food has been and continues to be manipulated for the prime purpose of creating profit for processors, not nutrition for consumers. Taste, flavor and appearance are given far more attention than food value by most food marketers, because those qualities have the most sales appeal. Nutrition is still considered to be appealing to only a minority of consumers.

There is also far too much stress on quantity of food, rather than quality. Farmers are paid by the bulk amount of food they produce, not by the nutritional value they create. Food processors make matters worse by puffing some foods up with air, or by using chemical extenders and similar practices.

Furthermore, engineering of food commodities into convenience meals, through the use of extended processing and use of additives, encourages people to eat an unbalanced diet. We are so captivated by the ingenious advertising and marketing of new types of convenience foods that we are cutting our attachment to traditional meal patterns, and using new foods of questionable nutritional value that we see advertised. Many of these food items don't fit easily into the "4 food groups" which are taught as the way to plan a balanced diet. Balancing the diet therefore becomes far more difficult.

Serious disease problems are traced directly to the too-common practice of eating highly processed foods. Government surveys have shown that people in all income groups can be lacking in calcium, vitamin A, vitamin C, and other nutrients. Obesity, heart problems, and possibly even cancer have resulted from a steady diet of high-calorie, low-nutrition, processed foods.

2. Organic foods, because they are offered in natural form, usually unrefined, encourage people to return to the traditional diet patterns that were common in the days before "diseases of civilization" became so commonplace. Organic foods are made into whole grain breads, wholesome soups, stews, casseroles, and desserts packed with minerals and vitamins as well as good taste. It is difficult to eat an unbalanced diet of natural foods.

Organic foods also gradually become the tangible expression of a philosophy of natural living. You do not just eat organic foods. While you are eating them you *think* about how that food was grown in a natural way, and how it was processed in your own kitchen instead of in an impersonal factory.

A desire to learn and practice good nutrition flows naturally from the organic food experience. When you seek out food that is better nutritionally you are expressing greater respect for your body and a self-imposed obligation to do everything possible to make it healthy. Suddenly, the habit of healthful eating that is so difficult to practice when using supermarket foods becomes utterly simple and automatic.

Eating organically is the only way to prevent further degeneration of dietary habits as the result of continued introduction of junk foods into our culture. Efforts to teach people how to select a good diet from among different types of processed foods have largely failed. Unless we adopt a strong philosophy of eating that regards food as "more than bread alone," we are no match for the onslaught of persuasive advertising for foods of inferior nutritional value.

The amount of money spent on food is not by any means the primary factor influencing the value of our diets. Government studies have shown that people with high incomes tend to eat wrongly, although to a lesser degree, than people living on poverty levels.

Dedication to natural living and a natural way of eating is the best assurance that we will eat healthful foods.

3. Organically grown foods are usually of better quality than ordinary foods. I say "usually" because there is tremendous variation in food according to where it is grown, what the season was like, and how you interpret the meaning of the word quality.

For example, the organically-minded person feels that signs that insects have been nibbling at food are acceptable, and almost constitute proof that the food was not sprayed. A buyer of plastic food immediately rejects insect-marked food for visual reasons, without bothering to take a bite and discover better flavor or more nutritional value.

Why are organically grown foods of better quality? Because the grower makes efforts to replace in the soil all the needed minerals and other nutrients through the use of organic and natural mineral fertilizers. The chemical grower applies those fertilizers that will produce the greatest yield. The organic farmer is interested in yield also, but if he is sincere he will also do the things that will produce food of the greatest quality.

For almost all of mankind's history, food production has been organic in every sense of that word. Only in the past hundred years—indeed a short time in man's history—has the chemical method of farming achieved prominence. And we see now that along with a harvest of lower quality food we are also reaping sickness, pollution and environmental decay.

It is time to change, and to "go organic."

Cooking Hints

Quick Tips

• Never soak fruits or vegetables in water for more than a minute or so. Large amounts of vitamins and minerals can be lost that way.

• If you buy produce in stores, wash it as soon as you can in very cold water. Store what you will use for the next meal in a covered dish; produce that is to be kept for a few days should be dried quickly and stored in crisper bags, tightly shut to exclude air.

• Prepare salads just before serving. Keep them covered until they are eaten. Fix only enough for that meal.

• Carrots and such vegetables should be cut lengthwise so that fewer nutrients will escape, especially in cooking.

• Use as little water as possible in cooking, and save every bit of it for use in soups and gravies. Store it in a glass jar until needed, covered tightly of course.

• When cooking vegetables, have the water hot before you add them and cover tightly; reduce heat to barely simmering. Use a large utensil so that the cover will "seal," and won't be lifted by the pressure of the steam. Most vegetables can be done in 6 or 8 minutes and come out with a better flavor, better texture and more nutrition.

• Avoid using aluminum and plastic utensils in connection with food. Certain undesirable elements from these materials tend to migrate into the foods and contaminate them. Pyroceram, pyrex glass, enamelware and stainless steel are best for cooking.

• Never cook anything twice.

• Drop frozen vegetables into boiling water while they are still frozen; vitamin C is lost as they thaw.

• The big seed companies have special varieties of fruits and vegetables for freezing; buy or grow these kinds for best results.

• The addition of one teaspoon of pure cider vinegar to fruit or vegetable gelatin salads will keep them from running after being unmolded.

• Coconuts are more easily cracked and peeled if they are heated for a few minutes beforehand.

• A tablespoon of cold water in any coffee substitute about 10 minutes before serving will help to settle the grounds.

• Use a vegetable brush to remove silks from the corn.

• A slice of apple will remove the bitterness from cooked cranberries. It should be cooked with them.

• Peeling cucumbers from the blossom end will minimize the bitter taste. Grow the light green varieties for better, sweeter flavor.

• Dip dried fruits in cold water before putting through the food chopper or blender and they will be less sticky.

• Natural Easter egg colorings: boil the eggs with fresh grass for green; tumeric or onion skins for yellow; with beet juice for red. A combination of yellow and green makes chartreuse and a combination of red and yellow makes orange.

• Keep fresh fish on cracked ice rather than in ice water.

• Your own dried fruits won't get wormy if sassafras bark is sprinkled through them. (Sassafras bark tea has a most delightful smell.)

• To avoid the bother of wrapping dried herbs in cheesecloth before adding them to the cooking food, simply put them in a tea strainer and drop it in the boiling liquid.

• When you want hot plates for serving steaks or mutton, heat them in hot water rather than in the oven, as the latter may cause them to crackle.

• Popcorn will pop better if it is kept in the refrigerator or freezer to be brought out just before popping.

• Baked potato skins will be soft and tender for eating if the scrubbed potatoes are brushed with cooking oil before they are put in the oven. Prick each potato with a fork several times. This helps to make them mealy.

• Boiled rice won't burn on the bottom if you oil the pan first. Cook at low heat, and steam the last 10 minutes.

• Leftover roasts will not dry out if wrapped in a wet cheesecloth and placed in a tightly covered dish in the refrigerator.

• In the case of detergent burn on hands, wet them with a mixture of vinegar and rose water. The latter is available from most any drug store. After this has soothed, then use any hand lotion.

What About Cooking Temperatures?

We asked a knowledgeable biochemist what the cooking temperature is at which the fats in meat or other foods may become dangerous. (Too great a heat can produce harmful compounds in fats—indeed, these compounds have been shown to be cancer-causing.) He answered that the way you do your cooking controls the results and an infinite variety of circumstances may be involved.

Let's say you're broiling a steak. If you like it rare you may broil it for a short time beneath a fairly moderate flame and the temperature may be so low as to leave the entire inner part of the steak completely raw. On the surface of the steak you may have achieved a temperature high enough to form chemical substances dangerous from the point of view of health. If you broil the steak at high enough heat to char it, then you have certainly created substances that are suspected of being quite dangerous from the point of view of health. But, of course, the same is true of a burnt crust of bread, toasted to that temperature.

If you put a roast in the oven to cook, some of the same problems appear. Searing the roast at a high temperature before putting it in the oven may produce dangerous fatty substances on the surface of the roast. But, if you like to roast at a moderate temperature, the inside of the meat may be just warmed by the time you are ready to serve it. If you enjoy eating the charred parts of the roast and avoiding the softer part of the meat, you will be more likely to get a dangerous substance.

The length of time you cook the food is also involved. This is especially easy to observe in cooking bacon or some equally fatty meat. Up to a certain point the meat cooks slowly. But, suddenly, almost in a moment, it burns and chars. This is the point at which the dangerous temperature was reached. But you can cook bacon slowly for a much longer time and get a little or no burning, which seems to indicate that no danger is involved. Still, cooking at fairly high heat over a very long period of time may result in a final temperature high enough to do some damage.

If you cover something which is cooking on the stove, you increase the amount of heat to which the food is exposed. Leaving the cover off allows some of the heat to escape. Turning the slices of whatever you are cooking reduces the amount of heat to which they are exposed, so they are much less likely to burn or char.

The size and original temperature of the food you are cooking also influence the result. Foods chopped fine cook much more quickly than large pieces because more total surface is exposed to heat. So it seems less likely that you would reach dangerous temperatures cooking something like ground meat or chopped vegetables which can be tossed quickly in a skillet. On the other hand, if you cook a meat loaf until the outside is burned in order to make certain that the interior is fully cooked, you have certainly created some undesirable fatty substances on the surface of the loaf.

Deep fat or French frying is problematic from several points of view. You don't want the food fried to be fat-soaked and soggy, so you keep the fat at a very high temperature, that way the food will be coated with a crisp layer of fat. Undoubtedly even this fat has been raised to a temperature high enough to be unhealthful.

Then, too, since so much fat is used in French frying there is a tendency to use the same fat over and over, keeping it (often unrefrigerated) between fryings. Not only does the unchilled fat become rancid, but in the heating and re-heating, there is certainly a degeneration of the fatty substances into compounds that are bound to be harmful. For deep fat frying, many people use hydrogenated fats (solid at room temperature like lard, butter or commercial shortening) which are deficient in unsaturated fatty acids.

If you are going to use fats in cooking—and we think it is permissible to a limited degree—use oils that are liquid at room temperature—olive oil, corn oil, cottonseed oil, peanut oil, sunflower seed oil, etc. Cook foods for as short a time as possible at as low a temperature as possible. The shorter the cooking time, the higher the temperature may be, within limits. And the longer the cooking time the lower the temperature should be—again, within reason.

In general, what we are recommending is braising—that is, cooking the food first in a little oil to prevent it from sticking to the pan. By so doing the food is coated with enough oil to prevent it from losing valuable vitamins and minerals throughout the rest of the cooking process. Then you can put a lid on the utensil and turn the fire quite low to complete the cooking economically and healthfully. This kind of fat-cookery should not produce dangerous by-products.

Food Seasoning

There Are Natural Substitutes for Salt

Food Seasoning—Most health authorities agree that excessive salt intake is bad for anybody. How much is too much? The addition of salt in any amount to food is considered by some physicians to be unwarranted, even dangerous, particularly where circulatory or kidney problems are involved. In general, people find the adjustment to a salt-free diet easy enough once they've made up their minds to stick to it. For others the loss of salt seems to take all of the joy out of the food they eat. They complain that it's flat and uninteresting. They continue to salt their food even in the face of a physical condition that can be seriously affected by this practice.

Several check points for those anxious to maintain a diet free of salt: For one thing, both butter and margarine are usually sold with salt added; ask for the unsalted varieties. Nearly all canned foods contain salt, as do some frozen foods; check for the ones that don't. Of course, garlic, celery and onion salts contain huge amounts of sodium. Also be on the watch for sodium in the list of ingredients on labels of flavor improvers. Special foods designated as salt-poor should be checked for just how much salt they do contain. Often "salt-poor" is still too "salt-rich" for some people.

A resourceful cook can use herbs and spices to create new flavors that will make the dieter forget that he ever used salt to bring out flavor.

Take garlic, for example. Cultivated for thousands of years, it was known as a food and medicine by every ancient race. In France today, minced garlic is served in a mayonnaise sauce as a tonic. Nearly every meat, many vegetables and of course, salads are vastly improved by garlic.

Salt Content of Some Common Foods

Meats:			Salt in Grams
Bacon	3	slices	1.200
Beef	1	serving	.057
Chicken	1	"	.048
Duck	1	"	.040
Goose	1	"	.060
Ham	1	"	1.6 to 2.0
Lamb Chop	1	"	.057
Lamb Roast	1	"	.067
Turkey	1	"	.040
Veal Roast	1	"	.057

Fish:			
Bass	1	serving	.069
Cod	1	"	.066
Haddock	1	"	.057
Mackerel	1	"	.076
Oysters	1	"	.050
Salmon (canned)	1	"	.059
Trout, shad	1	"	.061

Dairy Products:			
Cheese (American)	1	inch cube	.164
Cheese (cottage)	2	tablespoons	.280
Cheese (cream)	¼	cake	.250
Eggs	1	whole	.088
Buttermilk	½	cup	.160
Milk, whole	½	cup	.175
Milk, powdered	2	tablespoons	.080

Fruits:			
Apple, baked	1		.008
Apricots, fresh	3		.003
Banana	1	small	.206
Cranberries	⅔	cup	.015
Figs, fresh	1	large	.005
Grapefruit	½	small	.008
Grapes	24		.010
Grapejuice	½	cup	.003
Muskmelon	½	cup, cubes	.030
Oranges	1	medium	.010
Peaches	1	medium	.010
Pears	1	medium	.020
Pineapple	1	slice	.080
Prunes	6	medium	.019
Rhubarb	¾	cup	.059
Strawberries	¾	cup	.010
Watermelon	1	serving	.010

Vegetables:			Salt in Grams
Artichokes	1	medium	.018
Asparagus	10	stalks	.060
Beets	⅔	cup	.100
Brussels Sprouts	⅔	cup	.070
Cabbage	⅔	cup	.020
Carrots	¾	cup	.060
Cauliflower	½	cup	.060
Celery	¾	cup	.060
Corn	¼	cup	.020
Cucumber	10	slices	.050
Eggplant	½	cup	.040
Endive	10	stalks	.275
Greens, dandelion	½	cup	.168
Lentils	¼	cup	.030
Lettuce	10	leaves	.120
Lima beans	¼	cup	.030
Peas	¾	cup	.006
Peppers	2	medium	.020
Potato	1	medium	.160
Pumpkin	½	cup	.060
Spinach	½	cup	.120
Squash, summer	½	cup	.010
String beans	⅔	cup	.040
Tomatoes	1	medium	.060
Turnips	½	cup	.070
Radishes	5	medium	.024
Watercress	10	pieces	.025

Cereals:			
Bread, graham	1	slice	.230
Bread, white	1	slice	.130
Cornbread (without salt)	1	piece	.001
Farina, cooked	¾	cup	.038
Macaroni	½	cup	.024
Oatmeal	½	cup	.033
Shredded wheat	1	biscuit	.034
Rice	½	cup	.027

Nuts:			
Almonds	14		.009
Peanuts	9		.010
Pecans	12		.024
Walnuts	3		.010

Several hours before roasting or broiling a chicken rub crushed cloves of garlic both on the inside and outside flesh. Leave the chicken at room temperature for at least a half hour to allow the flavor to penetrate thoroughly.

A roast leg of lamb is never complete without a generous rubbing with cut garlic cloves before cooking. Its pungency blends extremely well with the mild yet distinct flavor of lamb. When roasting beef, use garlic with the less tender cuts. Really fine prime rib roasts, however, need very little seasoning—a sprinkling of paprika and a trace of garlic, if wanted.

A long-standing rule in making appetizing salads is to rub your wooden salad bowl with garlic. For a more penetrating flavor suspend two halves of a cut clove in salad dressing—a 3 to 1 mixture of olive oil (the finest you can get) and red wine vinegar. It is easy to make up a good-sized batch of dressing to have on hand at all times.

Sometimes a housewife is tempted to by-pass fresh garlic for garlic powder. Not only is she cheating herself of food value lost in the drying process, but also of the full, rich garlic flavor. It simply is not the same.

For a new taste in asparagus, sprinkle the stalks and tips with nutmeg before serving.

Cucumbers take on a new flavor when sliced very thin and marinated in tarragon vinegar before serving.

For other ways of serving salt-free vegetables try: green beans seasoned with nutmeg or savory; onions boiled with clove and thyme are new-tasting; unsalted peas will taste more interesting if they are sprinkled with chopped or powdered mint. Add bay leaf, sweet paprika, rosemary or oregano to goulash or stew. Rub lamb chops with freshly ground pepper or ginger before broiling; a roast of beef treated the same way before cooking with a large bay leaf in the roasting pan will be a pleasant surprise. When it's veal chops, rub them with saffron and ground pepper before simmering them in oil, to which you've added a little water; as for veal stew, it will take nicely to onion, bay leaf, powdered mace and celery leaves for added flavor.

Grow Your Own Herbs

The skillful use of herbs can bring a new kind of taste enjoyment to almost everything you prepare in your kitchen. It goes without saying that you get the most flavor and most enjoyment from herbs if you can go out into your own organic kitchen garden, snip them and savor their fresh tangy and distinctive aromas before you add them to the soup, stew, omelet or salad.

If you have a backyard, by all means reserve some space for an herb garden.

But even if you have no backyard, you can still enjoy the subtle flavors of home-grown herbs and the joy of growing your own. Try a window box on your terrace or on your windowsill. Most plants do best in a sunny exposure, but many will do equally well in a fairly light place.

The succulent varieties require large amounts of water and care should be taken that they never suffer from lack of moisture. Placing the pots on water-covered pebbles will increase humidity and prevent excessive drying. If you spray the tops with tepid water once a week, you will keep them dust free and healthy.

A quick grower like chives can be started in the same pot in which it will remain. Sow thickly in light, alkaline soil, and within a few weeks the grass-like spikes will be almost ready for cutting. Keep slightly on the dry side, watering only when fairly dry to the touch.

Starting parsley takes a bit more care. First, soak the seeds overnight in lukewarm water before planting in pots. They sometimes take two or three weeks to germinate if you don't dunk them first. The soaking seems to soften up the seed coat.

Dill, sweet basil, thyme and other herbs get the best start if sown first in seed pans or flats. As soon as the seeds have been planted and the soil tamped down, cover with a glass plate to keep the humidity high, then shade with a newspaper until the seedlings show themselves above the ground. Transplant into small pots when about two inches high.

Should you want to start the seeds in a clay pot, you might try the following arrangement: Fill the bottom of a large clay pot with stones and then a layer of sphagnum moss or peat moss, whichever is on hand. Insert the smaller seeded pot into the larger one, filling in the sides with more of the moss. This double pot arrangement keeps the soil reasonably moist but not dank, which encourages bacteria. Don't water the top of the plant part unless you apply it very gently with a syringe. The better method is to water from below through the moss and the larger pot.

With plenty of sunlight, you should have no trouble in growing any of these herbs. Place at a bright window, preferably with a southern exposure, counting on a good six hours of full sun. Don't bother with a northern exposure or you won't have a bit of luck with your plants. Many times an east or west window works out well.

Thyme must have a hot sun; the mints will get along in some shade, so they can be relegated to a spot farther from the window. A cool room averaging 55 to 60 degrees during the day is ideal for herbs. A cool sun porch is usually the answer for most people whose home temperature rarely drops below 70 degrees. Plants will survive in warmer temperatures, however, but ordinarily will not grow so robust.

What should you grow in your kitchen windowbox? Parsley is the headliner and one of the loveliest plants that can be grown. It is as green and graceful as a fern, will grow even in poor light, is rich in chlorophyll, and, according to the old herbals, it "multiplieth greatly a man's blood and comforts the heart and the stomach."

Chives are the next most widely grown window herb. Valued for the delicate onion-like flavor which they impart to foods, they are also decorative when chopped fine and sprinkled on salads or other dishes. Produce departments of markets frequently offer pots of chives; these invariably need repotting, as they have been jammed into their containers bare-root to lessen shipping weight.

Pepper grass or garden cress, as it is sometimes called, is a quick growing plant much used for salads and as a garnish. Seeds should be sown rather thickly on damp sphagnum and within six to eight weeks will give plants large enough for cutting.

Mint is an old favorite as good for nibbling as it is in cooking or used in food drinks. Plain broiled potatoes or carrots rate a gourmet's applause when sprinkled with fresh chopped mint.

Sorrel makes a rather attractive plant, and has much the same sour flavor as pepper grass. It is a long-lived perennial and will stand frequent and severe cutting. Sweet marjoram, sweet basil, rosemary, savory, oregano, thyme, bay, lemon verbena and ginger are other good herbs for your window garden.

Here is a guide to herb use which you will find helpful:

Basil with all tomato dishes; try it also in soups, salads, egg and cheese dishes.

Caraway with baked apples, bread, cookies and cheese.

Celery, freshly dried leaves for giving good taste to many foods.

Chervil, a popular French herb similar to parsley, which is fine in all soups and salads.

Dill, which besides being used in pickling, is very tasty in dried green leaf form in potato soup and fish sauces.

Fennel for flavoring breads, cookies, fish sauces, chowders, and the tea which is a common beverage among Europeans as a digestive aid.

Coriander, one of the ingredients in curry powder, used in breads, cookies, pies and soups.

Marjoram for lamb, string beans, lima beans and as an excellent salad herb.

Parsley, called an indispensable seasoning, for use with vegetables and in all salads.

Peppermint as a refreshing tea and on fresh fruits, melons, etc.

Rosemary for all chicken dishes, gravies; also good with lamb and beef.

Sage to go with pork, cheese and egg dishes.

Savory to add life to string beans and any beef recipe.

Spearmint for mint sauce, relish and vinegar, as well as on several vegetables, fruits and in beverages.

Tarragon for the best vinegar, French dressings, omelet, fish and cheese plates.

Thyme, a favorite in lamb and beef; an important poultry herb.

Breakfast Foods

Wheat Germ: A Wonderfully Good Food

No matter how attractive the package or the premium offered, don't be misled into counting on cold, processed cereals to add anything nutrition-wise to your diet. These cereals are almost entirely devoid of food values, loaded with harmful additives and in many cases coated with unhealthy sweeteners.

What if your family absolutely refuses to relinquish their boxed cereal? We suggest taking it away from them so gradually that they won't know what happened. Wheat germ is your best ally in an operation like this. Add a little to the bowl of packaged cereal tomorrow morning. Nine chances out of 10 no one will notice. In a month or so begin adding a little more. And a little more. This will mean a little less of the packaged cereal. In due time, suggest hot cereal for breakfast, and make the hot cereal whole grain. You may still add wheat germ.

Why all the enthusiasm for wheat germ? Why should we, while cautioning against getting too much of cereal foods, recommend wheat germ in the highest possible terms?

In some cases the most valuable part of the cereal is available as a separate food. The germ of the cereal contains practically all of the nutriment except starch. The rest of any cereal kernel consists mostly of starch. This makes wheat germ a peculiarly valuable food in which protein, minerals (especially iron), the B vitamins and vitamin E are concentrated. There are 24 grams of protein in one-half cup of wheat germ. There are only about 3 grams of protein in more than a cup of processed cold cereal.

Like all worthwhile fresh foods it spoils easily. Once it is removed from the wheat, it deteriorates rapidly, and the fats it contains become rancid. This destroys vitamin E. So you must treat wheat germ as you would any other perishable food. It should be refrigerated at all times, and it is best to buy a small quantity at a time. Usually, wheat germ is vacuum-packed which means there is no air inside the package to permit any rancidity or spoilage. Once this vacuum seal has been broken, it's into the refrigerator with the wheat germ!

Wheat germ is good just because this superlatively fine food is so inexpensive and can be used in so many ways. Once you and your family have come to like the taste, you can add wheat germ to almost any dish and bring up its nutritive value like magic.

What is the difference between wheat germ and wheat germ oil? Just the same difference there is between peanuts and peanut oil, or corn and corn oil. Wheat germ oil is pressed out of the germ. It contains all the fat-soluble vitamins that are in the germ but not the protein or the water-soluble vitamins like the B vitamins. Of course, wheat germ flakes like the kind you buy have not had the oil removed from them. It is still there for your benefit.

By the same token, of course, wheat germ oil is far richer in the fat soluble vitamins than wheat germ flakes could be, for these are concentrated in the soil. So you will get more vitamin E and the unsaturated fatty acids in the oil.

Most people prefer the taste of the toasted germ. Raw germ has more in the way of vitamins, for some of the very sensitive B vitamins are destroyed by heat. However, if you buy raw germ and then don't like the taste of it, you can toast it yourself in a very slow oven, spread out on a large pan. You will lose very little vitamin content. If your family will eat more of it willingly if it is toasted, then toast it.

It goes well with almost anything. It is particularly useful as a substitute for bread or cracker crumbs—in meat loaves, casseroles, cutlets, things of that kind. Many people use it in salads as well or sprinkled over fruits or berries for dessert. It is perfectly acceptable as a breakfast cereal all by itself or with fruit or yogurt. And of course, you can add it to any kind of bread, pancakes or waffles you are making, with no change in the recipe except that you may need more liquid.

Are vitamins lost during cooking? Yes, and for this reason we advise eating it as it is, and not cooking it. But if you want to enrich cooked foods, then the wheat germ must be cooked, too. And you do not lose any more vitamins out of the wheat germ in cooking than you lose out of liver or eggs when you cook them.

Cereal Recipes

Buckwheat Delight

Here's a breakfast dish that's festive enough to double as dessert. To 2½ cups boiling water add ½ cup buckwheat groats. Sweeten to taste with honey and add raisins and chopped dates. Boil for about 12 minutes. When almost finished, stir in ½ cup shredded coconut.

This is delicious served hot or cold. Serves 4.

All-In-One Breakfast or Brunch

Soak ½ cup corn meal in 3 cups water overnight. In morning bring to boil and add 2 or 3 finely chopped apples. When thoroughly cooked remove from fire and stir in 2 eggs. Serve at once with honey.

Raisins and dates and nuts can be added, if desired. Serves 2.

Scrapple

2 cups corn meal
1 cup wheat germ
1 cup meat or vegetable broth
1 teaspoon chopped onion
1 cup home-canned tomatoes

¾ cup peanut butter
1 cup ground leftover beef, chicken or lamb
seasoning to taste

Mix corn meal and wheat germ with broth and cook in top of double boiler until mixture is thick. Add onion and cook 10 minutes. Add tomatoes and meat. Dilute ¾ cup peanut butter with small amount of hot water and add to the other mixture. Add seasoning. Put into a dish and let set in ice box over night. Slice and brown. Serves 6.

Holiday Scrapple

This is a great way to put the remains of the holiday bird to good nutritional use. Makes a wonderful high protein breakfast that the children can easily heat and serve themselves. If your children are accustomed to putting syrup on their scrapple, give them pure maple syrup or raw honey.

2 cups corn meal
1 cup wheat germ
1 cup chicken or turkey broth
1 teaspoon chopped onion
1 cup chopped celery
2 tablespoons chopped green pepper

1 cup canned tomatoes
2 cups ground cooked chicken or turkey
¾ cup ground almonds mayonnaise
seasoning to taste

Mix corn meal and wheat germ with broth and cook in top of double boiler until mixture is thick. Add onion and cook 10 minutes. Add celery, green pepper, tomatoes, and chicken or turkey. Mix almonds with a little mayonnaise and add to the chicken or turkey mixture. Add sea salt or kelp to suit taste. Put into an oblong dish and place in refrigerator for a few hours or overnight. Slice and brown. Serves 4-6.

Hi Protein Breakfast

Put one tablespoon millet meal and ⅛ teaspoon kelp in a small sauce pan. Add ⅓ cup cold water and one beaten egg.

Cook on low flame till it comes to a boil and cook two minutes. Add one teaspoon honey. Makes a delicious breakfast.

Apple Muesli

Whiz up ½ cup rolled oats in the blender, or chop fine. Add 2 cups water, cover and let stand overnight. In the morning, scrub 4 unsprayed apples, core and grate into the oatmeal mixture. Add honey or maple syrup or blackstrap molasses, or a combination of all three. Serve in oatmeal dishes with rich nut milk and a sprinkling of chopped sunflower seeds. Serves 4.

Oatmeal With Rice Polishings

Use the old fashioned large rolled oats. Put them to soak the night before in cold water, and cover the cooking dish tightly. In the morning, bring them to the boiling point and cook about 30 seconds, stirring all the time. Now add your supplements and dish up the oatmeal. On the top of each dish, put about 2 tablespoons of raw rice polishings, which is a very pleasant-tasting addition to any breakfast cereal. You obtain the full value of the rice polishings by eating them raw.

Baked Breakfast Rice

Full of nutrients and a nice change in the morning menu.

2 cups cooked brown rice	1½ cups soy milk
1 cup raisins	

Mix all ingredients. Pour into deep casserole dish. Cover. Bake for 45 minutes at 325°. Serve hot with honey and additional soy milk. This dish may be prepared in the evening and refrigerated overnight. Slip the casserole into the oven upon arising and breakfast is ready when the family is. Serves 4.

High Protein Cereal

Grind in a nut grinder the following seeds in the proportions suggested below:

4 parts sunflower seeds	2 parts unblanched almonds
2 parts pumpkin seeds	1 part carob powder
2 parts roasted soybeans	

Mix thoroughly and store in refrigerator. Serve with fruit: bananas, berries, prunes, etc. or: fruit juice, or nut milk. Can also be served over salads.

No-Sugar Cereal

The night before, put the following to soak in cold water:

½ cup chopped sunflower seeds	½ cup buckwheat groats
½ cup large rolled oats	1 cup unsprayed-unsulphured
½ cup millet	raisins or dried prunes

In the morning, put the cereal (adding more water if needed) on a moderate heat and bring to a boil. Serve with nut milk. It needs no sweetener as the fruit takes care of that. Serves 4.

Hot Cereal

1 cup soya grits or granules   1 cup large rolled oats
1 cup millet   1 cup barley
1 cup chopped sunflower seeds

Mix these together and keep them in a closed container. At night, take out enough for your family's breakfast, add raisins, figs or prunes and water to cover. Keep in a covered saucepan overnight, and bring to the boil in the morning, then simmer 2 minutes. Serve with nut, banana or coconut milk and honey if desired.

Delectable Breakfast

This is especially delicious when topped with yogurt.

1½ cups raw grated organic   1 cup of previously mixed dry
    apples   ingredients

One cup each of soy lecithin granules, wheat germ, sesame or sunflower meal, brewer's yeast powder, and unsweetened coconut. This mixture should be kept in a tight jar in the refrigerator. Use as desired on fresh raw fruit.

Pancake and Waffle Recipes

Artichoke (Jerusalem) Pancakes

These are made like potato pancakes and taste about the same. Scrub the artichokes and leave the skins on if they clean up nicely. Grate them fine, and add about 3 eggs to each 1½ cups of grated pulp. Add sea kelp to taste and arrowroot flour to thicken to pancake consistency. Bake on a moderately heated griddle, lightly oiled. Sprinkle with sesame seeds while the first side is browning for extra flavor and vitamin and mineral content. Serves 4-6.

Barley Pancakes

Pour ½ cup warm water into a mixing bowl. Add 2 tablespoons of baker's yeast, 2 tablespoons of honey and let rise for 30 minutes, in a warm place. Add:

2 eggs
1 cup barley flour
1 cup soy milk

2 tablespoons vegetable oil
1 cup raw wheat germ

Mix well and bake on a moderately hot griddle until done. Spread with cashew butter and top with honey. Delicious with soft boiled eggs. Serves 4.

Old Fashioned Buckwheat Pancakes

½ cup powdered whey
1 cup warm water
1 package yeast
1 beaten egg

2 tablespoons cooking oil
1 teaspoon sea salt
½ cup pure buckwheat flour
½ cup wheat germ flour

Dissolve the powdered whey in the warm water, then add the yeast and let stand for 10 minutes. Add the other ingredients, and let it stand at room temperature for several hours. Bake. This recipe will make about 10 pancakes.

Buckwheat Pancakes

4 eggs, separated

Beat the egg whites and set aside. Put the yolks in a very large bowl because they expand greatly as the ingredients are added. (An electric mixer is needed for this recipe in order to get the thickening during the beating process.) Start the egg yolks under the beaters and beat at medium speed and add these ingredients gradually and in the order given:

½ cup boiling water
4 tablespoons cooking oil

1½ cups hot potato water
1 teaspoon sea kelp

As you add the hot water, oil and hot potato water to the beating mixture it expands and rises. You should have nearly 2 quarts of batter by this time. Now fold in:

1 cup sifted buckwheat flour   ½ cup sifted wheat germ flour
                                      (or corn flour)

Next, fold in the egg whites which were beaten stiff when you started out. Bake the usual way. You should have around 3 quarts of batter and any that is left over can be refrigerated and used later.

Best Buckwheat Pancakes

3 eggs, separated   2 cups soya milk
3 tablespoons cooking oil   1 cup soya powder or flour
1 teaspoon sea kelp   1 cup buckwheat flour

Beat the 3 egg whites stiff and set aside. Put the egg yolks, oil, kelp and milk under the beaters, beat lightly while you sift the flours together. Add and beat, then fold in the beaten egg whites and bake as usual. Makes about 10.

Carrot Pancakes

1 large carrot   1 tablespoon wheat germ
1 large potato   1 teaspoon soya flour
1 small onion   sea salt to taste
1 large beaten egg   a dash of basil

Cut carrot on a shredder. Cut potatoes in small pieces. Cut onion fine.

Put in blender, then add other ingredients and mix.

Use unsaturated cold-pressed oil in large skillet. Drop by tablespoons into oil and sauté, but with very low heat or pancake will scorch.

These cakes are very good for breakfast instead of bread. Serves 2.

Vegetable Pancakes

2 cups grated uncooked
  potatoes
2 cups grated uncooked carrots
2 eggs, beaten

2 tablespoons brown rice flour
1 tablespoon finely chopped
  chives
1 teaspoon sea salt

Combine all ingredients. Brown both sides on oiled skillet, using enough vegetable oil so that it bubbles up around the edges of the cakes. Serves 4.

Corn-Apple Pancakes

1 cup organic apples, chopped
  small or grated
1 cup cornmeal, yellow
  stoneground
1 teaspoon kelp

2 eggs, separated
2 tablespoons oil
1 tablespoon honey
1 cup soya milk

Grate apples, set aside. Beat egg whites stiff but not dry. Put yolks in another bowl, stir in honey, oil, and soya milk. Add cornmeal and kelp and stir till just smooth. Add apples. Fold in egg whites carefully. Bake on oiled griddle or skillet. Serves 2 or 3.

Corn Chapatties

2 cups yellow cornmeal
2 tablespoons cooking oil

1½ cups hot water

Pour the hot water over the other ingredients and blend. Then shape them into thin patties or wafers in the hands. Bake slowly on a hot griddle or skillet, turning once. The griddle should be slightly oiled and the chapatties allowed to cook slowly on each side.

Corn Fritters

Have 6 ears of fresh, uncooked corn. Slit grains with a fork and scrape corn from cob. Beat 2 whole eggs and mix with the milky corn. Season to taste. If it seems too soft, add a little wheat germ. Bake like griddle cakes. Serve with honey or maple syrup. Great for breakfast or side dish with dinner. Serves 6.

Mexican Tortillas

2 beaten eggs	2 tablespoons cooking oil
1 teaspoon sea kelp	1 cup yellow cornmeal

Add enough hot water, little by little while beating, to make a medium batter, as you would for pancakes or waffles.

Heat a griddle or heavy skillet medium hot and drop the batter in small amounts, flattening each cake with the bowl of the spoon. Turn and bake on the other side and stack them.

Tortillas

The dictionary says a tortilla is a flat corn cake baked on a hot iron. So here is a flat corn cake baked on your griddle.

3 eggs	1 cup cornmeal

Blend until thick and add:

1 cup hot water

Spoon on hot griddle. Brown on both sides. Stir batter each time before spooning on griddle. These can also be eaten as pancakes.

All-Corn Waffles

4 small eggs, separated	1½ cups nut milk or tahini milk
2 tablespoons oil	2 cups sifted corn flour

Blend the 4 egg yolks with the oil, add the milk gradually, then sift in the flour. The reason we stress sifted corn flour is because 2 cups of unsifted flour makes 3 cups of sifted corn flour, thus throwing the recipe off.

Beat the egg whites beyond the frothy stage but not stiff. Then mix them into the batter and beat it until it is very light, and has increased in bulk about one-third. Bake the usual way for waffles. Serve with honey or maple syrup. Makes about 6.

Matzo Meal Pancakes

4 eggs, separated
⅔ cup water or soy milk
⅔ cup Matzo meal

1 teaspoon sea kelp
1 tablespoon honey (optional)
1 tablespoon cooking oil

Beat the egg whites stiff and set aside. Beat the egg yolks light, add milk, then kelp, honey and oil. Fold in the meal, then the egg whites and bake on an oiled griddle or in a heavy skillet.

Serve with poached eggs which have been seasoned with sea kelp and paprika. Serves 4.

Oatmeal Pancakes

2 cups soy or nut milk   2 cups fine oatmeal

Scald the milk and pour it over the oatmeal. Blend thoroughly and cool. Then add the following ingredients:

2 egg yolks   ½ teaspoon nutmeg
1 teaspoon honey

Blend together, then add the 2 egg whites which have been beaten fluffy but not stiff. Fold them in carefully and bake the pancakes on a moderate griddle which has been oiled. Serves 6.

Pecan Maple Waffles

1 cup oat flour
¼ cup pecans, ground fine
¼ cup pure maple syrup
¼ teaspoon lecithin granules
1 teaspoon sea salt

1 tablespoon sunflower seed oil
⅓ cup soy milk plus
  1 tablespoon
1 tablespoon safflower oil

Beat lecithin into soy milk. Add sea salt, oil, maple syrup and stir well. Add pecans and oat flour. Beat well. Set aside for 15 minutes. Drop off spoonfuls onto hot waffle iron. These are crisp and can be eaten like crackers. Serves 4.

Peanut Pancakes

1 cup pumpkin and/or squash seed milk	½ cup rice polish or wheat germ flour
2 egg yolks	½ teaspoon sea kelp
2 egg whites beaten stiff	½ teaspoon honey or blackstrap molasses
1½ cups peanut flour	

Beat the egg whites and set aside, then beat the egg yolks, kelp and sweetening (optional). Add the flour and blend, then fold in the beaten whites last. Bake on a very moderate griddle and slowly, as peanut flour browns quickly. Serves 4-6.

Peanut Waffles

2 cups soy or tahini milk	3 cups unsifted peanut flour
4 egg yolks	1 cup wheat germ
2 tablespoons cooking oil	1 teaspoon sea kelp
½ cup finely chopped peanuts	

Blend all ingredients. If you use soy milk, use either instant or regular powder and make it according to directions on the can. Add:

4 stiffly beaten egg whites

Fold these in carefully. Bake on a moderate, well-oiled iron. Avoid high heat as peanut flour burns easily. Serves 6-8.

Potato Pancakes

4 cups grated raw potato	2 tablespoons potato flour
3 beaten eggs	2 tablespoons wheat germ flour, or enough to make a rather thick batter
2 teaspoons sea kelp	
1 tablespoon cooking oil	

Using a tablespoon of batter for each pancake, drop on a hot, oiled griddle, and bake until browned on both sides. Add whatever supplements you need to the batter. They may be varied by the addition of chopped nuts or sunflower seeds, or the batter may be sprinkled with sesame seeds immediately after it is poured on the griddle. Serves 4.

Potato Flour "Noodles"

3 eggs
3 tablespoons water

3 tablespoons potato flour
⅛ teaspoon sea salt

Beat eggs, add water, salt and flour. Blend well; it makes a thin batter. Heat a small frying pan (6 or 7 inches) brush with peanut or safflower oil. Pour 1 tablespoon of the batter in a thin stream starting at the center and tilt the pan to distribute evenly.

Cook over moderate heat on both sides till lightly browned. Turn on a towel. When cool, roll up each pancake and cut very thin. Delicious with chicken soup. No additional cooking needed. Serves 4.

Extra Special Pancakes

2 cups grated raw potatoes
1 cup grated carrots
1 medium onion, grated
1 cup grated apple
4 tablespoons soya flour

2 or more tablespoons wheat germ
1 or 2 tablespoons honey
1 teaspoon kelp
2 eggs, unbeaten

Put all in large bowl, mix well. Bake on oiled griddle or skillet— using more oil than usual for pancakes—until nicely browned and crisp. Serve with honey. Serves 6.

Brown Rice Griddle Cakes

3 eggs, separated
2 cups nut or soy milk
1 tablespoon sea kelp
3 tablespoons cooking oil

1 cup brown rice flour
1 cup rice polishings
½ cup soy flour

Beat the egg whites very stiff and set aside, then put the other ingredients in a mixing bowl and beat them about 3 minutes as rice flour needs much beating. Fold in the egg whites and bake on griddle. A bit of honey may be added if desired. Makes 8 or 10.

Seed Pancakes

Beat the whites of three eggs until stiff. Next add the yolks and beat well.

Add three tablespoons sunflower seeds and three tablespoons pumpkin seeds ground finely in seed grinder. Cook as for regular pancakes. Use two spoonfuls of mixture to make one pancake. Serves 3 or 4.

Soy-Corn Flour Waffles

2 eggs, separated
2 cups soy or nut milk
1 teaspoon sea kelp
1 cup sifted soy low-fat flour

1 cup sifted corn flour
1 tablespoon sunflower seed
  meal
4 tablespoons cooking oil

Beat the egg whites very stiff and set aside. Beat the other ingredients well, fold in the egg whites and bake in waffle iron until crisp. This will make 5 or 6 waffles on round iron.

Soybean Waffles

2 eggs, separated
2 cups soy milk
2 tablespoons soy oil

1 teaspoon sea kelp
1 cup lo-fat soy flour
1 cup wheat germ flour

Beat the egg whites stiff and set aside. Beat the other ingredients, fold in the egg whites and bake until crisp on a hot waffle iron. This will make 5 or 6 waffles.

Wheat Germ Pancakes

2 cups nut milk
4 egg yolks
2 tablespoons cooking oil
2 teaspoons sea kelp

1 teaspoon honey (optional)
2 cups wheat germ
1 cup brown rice flour

Beat the egg yolks, then add the milk and flour. Beat well, and fold in the stiffly beaten whites of the 4 eggs just before baking. This recipe makes about 16 pancakes. Serves 6 or 8.

Zucchini Pancakes

2 or 3 zucchini squash
1 egg
3 tablespoons soy flour

½ onion chopped (if desired)
½ teaspoon sea salt or kelp
¼ cup cold-pressed oil

Grate zucchini. Add beaten egg, soy flour, chopped onion and salt. Mix together. Heat oil in skillet. Form small pancakes and brown slightly on both sides about 5 minutes. Serves 4.

The Egg Is a Masterpiece

Eggs are high in quality—protein, vitamins and minerals. They have to be. Remember, the actual substance of the eggs we eat has been carefully compounded by nature to nourish an unborn chick to maturity. The proper food elements necessary to do this job are packed conveniently in a package you can hold in your hand. Eat several eggs a day, and you are treating yourself to nutritional excellence that is impossible to duplicate. Eat 100 grams of any other protein food—meat, milk, soybean, wheat, nuts—and they will all fall short of the same amount of egg in the essential amino acids they give you.

The white of an egg is about 10 per cent protein, the yolk about 16 per cent. Between them, these 2 parts of the egg are rated as having the best distribution of 17 amino acids. The amino acids combine to form protein, and protein is transformed by the body into eyes, nerves, skin, liver, brain—in fact, every organ we have is tissue made of protein.

Not every type of protein will make good tissue. It takes "high-quality" protein, a food containing all the essential amino acids in proper proportion. These complete proteins appear in foods from animal sources. Meat and fish offer complete protein, but eggs offer more and better value for building and maintaining body tissue than any other food.

Except for vitamin C, eggs contain just about anything we need in the way of nutrition. They have enviable stores of the B vitamins, and also vitamins A and D.

Their Vitamin and Mineral Content

Here is the vitamin and mineral content of 100 grams of eggs—which is about two medium sized ones:

Vitamin A	1140 International Units
Vitamin D	50 units
Vitamin E	3 milligrams
Vitamin B	
Thiamin	120-150 micrograms
Riboflavin	340 micrograms
Niacin	.1 milligram
Pyridoxine	22 micrograms
Pantothenic acid	800-4800 micrograms
Biotin	9 micrograms
Calcium	68 milligrams
Phosphorus	224 milligrams
Iron	2.52 milligrams
Copper	.23 milligrams
Magnesium	.03 milligrams
Chlorine	106 milligrams

Some generations ago, it was a common practice to eat ground eggshells. Not a bad idea. The shell, which consists largely of calcium, magnesium and phosphorus, can be dried and ground fine enough to eliminate any objectionable grittiness. The powder then makes a nutritionally superb addition to a fruit or vegetable drink.

Eggs contain plenty of cholesterol, and we tend to forget that the body needs this compound. In the wake of the scare concerning the part cholesterol might play in causing heart disease, some people cut eggs from their diet. Even some doctors forbade their patients to eat eggs. After over a decade of discussion it has become apparent to most researchers that the amount of cholesterol intake from foods is not so important as how the body handles cholesterol once it has been ingested. The body has tools for this. Chief among them is lecithin, a natural compound which acts to keep unused cholesterol particles in suspension in the bloodstream. In this state cholesterol keeps moving along with no opportunity to group into the large, clogging masses that can cause trouble. Eggs offer the body large amounts of lecithin and B vitamins to help process any cholesterol the egg contains. Choline, methionine and threonine, other important cholesterol regulators, are richly present in eggs.

In all of the material we have seen on eggs, stress has been laid on their freshness. One reason is that each passing day means a lessening of nutritional value, as well as a change in an egg's taste and smell. There is no way for most of us to tell how long an egg has been around until we break it. When we buy them in a carton, we must trust the marking. If it's marked AA, it should be of the highest quality, with a clean, firm thick shell, and a yolk that will stand round and full when the egg is broken. Grade A is a step below this, but considered good quality and fine eating at a few cents cheaper cost. When an egg is Grade B, it is best used as an ingredient in custards, casseroles, and the like, not to be served alone.

When eggs are kept cold, their losses in taste and nutrition are minimized, hence cold storage for surplus eggs. Hundreds of thousands of crates are stored in this way, and you really can't be sure that the carton of AA eggs you buy is not a cold storage product unless you buy direct from the farmer. The grade label might guarantee the quality of the egg, but tells you nothing about how old this "quality egg" might be.

Somewhere the impression has been created that eating a raw egg might be more healthful than eating a cooked one. A cooked egg is as rich in nutrition as a raw one—and safer. It has been discovered that large amounts of raw egg white given every day can cause illness. This offending element, avidin, is neutralized in cooking.

We believe that fertile eggs, that is, eggs produced by hens who have the opportunity to fraternize with a rooster, are better for you than infertile ones. We believe, too, that the hen who has a chance to peck and scratch in a barnyard produces a better egg than the hen confined to a perch in the chicken house all her life.

Fertile eggs are also more flavorsome than unfertilized ones. A flavor comparison at breakfast some morning, with one of each egg on your plate, will convince you of the fertile egg's superiority. To get fertile eggs you'll have to check around for a farmer who raises chickens in this natural way. Such non-commercial operations are rare, but worth the hunt.

You might not be able to get everything you want in every dozen of eggs you buy, but there are simple rules to follow that will help you to get your money's worth.

Buy from a reliable supplier.

Buy the best eggs you can afford.

Buy by grade only (unless you know the source personally).

Store eggs in a cold place.

Serve eggs often with the assurance that no food could supply your family with so much food value so easily, so cheaply and so enjoyably.

Egg Recipes

Eggs Foo Yung

Put a heavy type skillet to heat.

Under the beaters, put 6 eggs, 6 tablespoons of water, 1 tablespoon sea kelp, and beat thoroughly. Then add 1 cup freshly sprouted Mung beans and 1 teaspoon fennel seeds.

Cover the bottom of the skillet with cooking oil. Pour in the batter and turn the heat down. Cook about a minute, then cut in quarters and turn each section and brown on the other side. A minute of medium heat per side will just about do it if the skillet is preheated. Serves 4.

Deviled Eggs

Hardboil the required number of eggs, put in ice cold water then shell and slice lengthwise. Remove the yolks, add mayonnaise, minced onion, ¼ teaspoon of cumin to each 4 eggs, and when they are seasoned add sea kelp to taste. Put the mashed mixture back in the whites and arrange them nicely on salad greens and garnish with paprika. Keep refrigerated with a tight covering over them until serving time.

Fruit Omelet

4 eggs, well beaten
1 cup shredded raw apple

¼ cup tomato juice
1 tablespoon vegetable salt

Beat eggs until light, then beat in other ingredients. Pour into well oiled baking dish and bake in a moderate oven (375° F.) about 15 minutes or until brown. Serves 2-4.

Baked Herb Omelet

6 eggs, separated
2 tablespoons cold water
½ teaspoon sea salt
1 tablespoon brewer's yeast
1 teaspoon minced chives

¼ teaspoon marjoram
¼ teaspoon chervil
2 tablespoons peanut oil (cold pressed)

Beat yolks until lemon colored. Combine remaining ingredients except egg whites, add to yolks and mix thoroughly. Beat egg whites until stiff and fold gently into yolk mixture. Turn into oiled pie plate and bake at 350 degrees for 15 minutes. Serve immediately upon removal from oven. Serves 4.

Eggs Minnetonka

2 eggs
4 teaspoons water
1 teaspoon parsley flakes

2 or 3 dashes paprika to taste
2 or 3 dashes garlic powder to taste

Break eggs into small bowl and add other ingredients. Beat until well blended. Pour mixture into pan in which oil is heated. Stir eggs occasionally, cooking until they reach desired consistency. Serves 2.

Herbed Omelet

Take required number of eggs for your family. Beat the whites very stiff. To the yolks, add for each yolk:

1 tablespoon cold water   ¼ teaspoon minced herbs
  pinch of paprika

Beat this mixture until herbs are reduced and yolks are yellow. Fold it into the beaten whites, blend carefully. Pour the mixture into an oiled skillet, the heavy type like enameled iron, which has been heated moderately hot. Cook over low heat until the omelet is puffed and brown on the bottom, then transfer it to a 350 degree oven. Bake for another 5 minutes and serve hot.

Italian Style Eggs

4 eggs   3 tablespoons olive oil
4 chicken livers   ¼ cup warm water
1 tablespoon tomato paste   4 tablespoons light cooking
1 tablespoon chopped onion,   wine
  leeks or chives   season to taste

Sauté the halved chicken livers and onions in the heated oil for 5 minutes. Add the tomato paste which has been diluted by the warm water, add seasoning, and cook slowly for 5 minutes. Add wine and stir. Break and add each egg slowly so as to not break the yolk. Cover the pan and allow the eggs to poach till whites are firm. Serves 4.

Kidney Omelet

4 eggs   bacon as desired
2 veal kidneys, cored and cut   1 tablespoon cold pressed oil
  into small pieces

1. Grill the bacon. Drain and set aside, covered, on a warmed plate.

2. Pour away all bacon fat, except for about 1 tablespoon. Sauté pieces of kidney in the hot bacon fat for about five minutes, then set them aside.

3. Break the eggs into a medium-sized bowl. Season to taste. Beat the eggs with a wire whisk or fork until yolk and white are just blended.

4. Warm a 10-inch omelet pan, coat bottom of pan with oil and heat till sizzling.

5. Pour in the eggs. They will start setting immediately. Add the kidneys. Tipping the pan away from you, lift the partially-set eggs on the raised side and then tip the pan towards you to let the runny part move into the space you have made. When all the egg mixture except the surface has set (the surface should have the consistency of custard), the omelet is ready. Fold it in half with a spatula and roll it onto a serving platter. Garnish with strips of crisp bacon.

Variations:

Mushrooms and onions, finely chopped, can be added to the filling. Use only one kidney if you do this because an omelet should never be "bursting at the seams" with filling.

Chopped green pepper complements both kidney and eggs very nicely.

Some fresh herbs may be added to the egg mixture.

The omelet may be garnished with mushroom caps instead of bacon. Serves 2.

Mung Bean Omelet

Put a heavy iron type skillet on to heat. Chop 1 cup of Mung bean sprouts fine while 6 egg whites are beaten frothy. Now add 1 tablespoon sea kelp and ⅓ cup cold water to the whites and beat them until they are stiff. Set aside and beat the 6 yolks until they are thick, add the sprouts and blend together. Pour 1 tablespoon of salad oil in the hot skillet. Fold the egg yolk-and-sprout mixture into the whites and pour it gently into the hot skillet. Spread, reduce heat and cook gently until the bottom of the omelet is browned. Set the skillet in the oven to finish browning on the top. Then loosen the sides with a metal spatula, cut across the omelet, fold one half over the other, slip to a warm plate and serve hot. Sprinkle the top with fresh parsley and herbs if desired. Serves 4.

Poached Eggs Italiano

Poaching sauce
1½ quarts home canned tomatoes
2 tablespoons olive oil
1 large onion chopped

2 cloves garlic minced
2 basil leaves
1 teaspoon oregano
sea salt to taste
4 eggs

Heat olive oil in skillet, add garlic and onion, cook until tender. Add tomatoes, basil, oregano and sea salt to taste and cook for 20 minutes.

Add the 4 eggs and cook till set, about 5 minutes.

Serve eggs with some sauce and brown rice to soak up sauce. Makes an excellent lunch. Serves 2.

Scrambled Eggs in Asparagus

Cut cup of asparagus in inch lengths and simmer, with sea kelp, until tender, probably 5 minutes. Break in 1 egg per person, cutting through them as they simmer until you have them scrambled as you like them. Season again and serve.

Muffin-Poached Eggs

For a treat, the eggs may be poached in muffin tins which have been well-oiled so that they come out easily. Arrange the muffin-shaped eggs on a platter. Garnish with paprika.

Polynesian Scrambled Eggs

Note: The ingredients are based on one egg per person.

1 egg
1 tablespoon unsweetened pineapple juice or coconut milk
1 teaspoon powdered soya

1 teaspoon crushed unsweetened
   fresh pineapple
1 teaspoon grated unsweetened
   fresh coconut
   dash of kelp

Scramble the eggs in the usual way by beating well, then blending in the pineapple or coconut juice, soya powder and kelp. Add coconut and pineapple and put in a well-oiled skillet over a medium flame, stir until of right consistency. Sprinkle each serving with sesame seeds. Serve immediately.

(This recipe can be made in a double boiler for those who prefer their eggs scrambled that way.)

Scrambled Eggs and Mushrooms

Take a cupful of fresh washed mushrooms to each 4 eggs. Chop fresh chives or a green onion, kelp and ¼ teaspoon of marjoram into the mushrooms while you heat ½ cup soy milk. Now drop the whole eggs and seasoned mushroom mixture into the simmering soy milk and cut through the eggs with a spoon as the mixture cooks. Do this until the eggs just "set" and quickly remove from the fire. Serve very hot. Serves 4.

Spanish Omelet

Beat 4 eggs very light, then add these ingredients which have been chopped fine:

1 cup fresh mushrooms	½ green bell pepper
1 small onion	1 teaspoon sea kelp added last
½ red bell pepper	

Heat a large iron-type skillet medium hot, brush with oil, pour in the mixture, brown on the bottom, turn and reduce heat until browned on other side. Cut in portions and serve very hot. Serves 4.

Swiss Eggs

6 eggs	¼ teaspoon sea salt
1 cup tomatoes (home canned)	1 tablespoon soy oil
1 small onion	

Beat eggs together until mixed. Cook onion and tomatoes with oil before eggs are added. Add eggs, cook slowly and stir. Serves 4.

Sunflower Seed Omelet

Heat a heavy skillet (preferably iron covered with enamel).

4 eggs beaten very light	½ teaspoon sea kelp
1 cup sunflower seed meal	½ teaspoon caraway seeds

Blend ingredients. Oil the hot skillet, pour in the mixture, let brown on bottom, cut in quarters, turn and brown on the other side. Serves 2-4.

Appetizers and Relishes

The Key to Zestful Appetizers

A good appetizer is an interesting and nutritious prelude to dinner. The right choice will add zest to an already well-balanced menu.

Right before mealtime, when everyone is hungry, serve a combination tray of raw zucchini, carrot sticks, celery, turnip slices, pickles (beet or cucumber) or red cabbage wedges. You're presenting the family with a valuable pick-me-up that can do wonders for them.

Carrots are mineral-rich and high in carotene, a substance the body transforms into vitamin A. Vitamin A strengthens the body's defenses against infectious organisms and works toward better vision.

Celery, rich in vitamin A and the B complex, is a good source of vitamin E. There is ample evidence that vitamin E is the nutrient that is important in maintaining healthy muscles—and don't forget the heart is a muscle! Ample vitamin E also acts to protect the body's store of vitamins A and C.

Raw cabbage is rich in calcium and phosphorus. It is high in vitamin C and vitamin K, the blood clotting vitamin.

Bear in mind that every cut surface means loss of vitamin C, so wait to slice raw vegetables for appetizers until just before serving. Set them out alone, in combinations, or try using them in these recipes. Soon you will find that some of the most healthful foods there are have become family favorites.

Raw Apple Relish

4 sour apples, cored but not
   peeled
2 green peppers
2 stalks celery

1 small onion
⅓ cup honey
⅓ cup diluted pure cider
   vinegar

Grind the apples and vegetables, then add the honey and vinegar. Keep in a covered dish in the refrigerator.

Raw Beet Relish

2 cups fresh, uncooked ground
   beets

2 tablespoons honey
2 tablespoons pure cider vinegar

Scrub beets thoroughly and only peel the stem and root end. Mix vinegar and honey till well blended, pour over ground beets. Refrigerate awhile till flavors penetrate the beets.

More or less of the honey mixture can be used according to individual taste. Serves 4.

Carrot Relish

Put through the medium knife of the food chopper:

4 carrots
½ red bell pepper

1 stalk celery
1 small onion

The vegetables should be ground medium fine. Now add 2 tablespoons of honey and 2 tablespoons of pure cider vinegar and keep refrigerated and covered tightly until used up. Makes about 1 pint.

Corn Relish

4 cups fresh raw corn
3 cups chopped celery
2 cups chopped cucumbers

1 cup chopped peppers (green)
1 cup chopped peppers (red)
1 large chopped onion

Cut the corn off the cobs and put the vegetables through the coarse knife of the food grinder. Combine and add:

½ cup sea kelp
¼ cup turmeric
¼ cup celery seeds

3 cups honey
3 cups pure cider vinegar

This can be boiled and canned for winter use; it can be frozen for a short time, or it can be stored in the refrigerator if it is eaten in a short time. Makes about 4 pints.

Christmas Relish

Put 1 beet and 1 cup of cranberries through the food chopper, saving all juice for blender drinks. Add 3 tablespoons honey and ½ teaspoon mace.

Spiced Cranberry Relish

1 pound fresh cranberries
1 medium eating apple, peeled and cored
1 cup unsweetened crushed pineapple, or pineapple tidbits, drained

1 teaspoon ground cinnamon
¼ teaspoon powdered ginger
¼ teaspoon ground cloves
1 cup honey

Put the cranberries and apple through your food chopper. Add the drained pineapple and spices. Blend thoroughly and then blend in the honey.

Store it in a covered dish in your refrigerator for at least 6 hours before serving.

Cranberry Relish

Pick over and wash cranberries, put through food chopper, using fine cutter, mix in with half as much fully ripe mashed bananas. Sweeten with honey, beat well.

The flavor is improved by permitting it to blend for an hour or so before serving.

Chopped Relish

If you want just the chopped cranberries that you used to run through a food chopper, all you do is throw as many as you want, fresh or frozen, into the blender and chop them to the fineness desired. You might have to stop and push down the sides with a rubber scraper until they are chopped, depending on your brand of blender. If you want to add other fruit, chop that separately, then add it to the cranberries. If it is quite a dry fruit, add honey to it in the blender. It will go easier. And you have to sweeten the cranberries to taste anyway. Stir it all together and set into the refrigerator.

Cranberry-Apple Relish

1 pound fresh cranberries
5 pounds apples (preferably mixed—McIntosh, Cortland, yellow Delicious, etc.)

2 cups pineapple juice or apple juice
1 teaspoon cinnamon (optional)

Place in large soup pot washed and picked-over berries, sliced apples, juice and simmer about two hours. Add cinnamon the last half hour.

Relish can be stored in refrigerator for several weeks.

Instant Relish

Chop equal parts of frozen or fresh pineapple and raw cranberries. Add raw honey to taste.

Cooked Cranberry Sauce

Cranberries should be eaten raw, but if the folks rebel and want "cranberry sauce" then cook the cranberries gently with an apple or two in a small amount of water, tightly covered and simmer until they stop "popping." Then cool and strain them before adding the honey. We should always cool cooked fruits before adding honey, as the heat destroys the enzymes in it. Both fruit and honey should be eaten raw for this reason.

Eggplant Relish

1 large eggplant	2 cups boiling water
3 large stalks celery	1 medium onion
1 teaspoon leaf oregano	½ bay leaf

Peel eggplant and cut into 1-inch cubes. Cut celery in 1-inch cubes. Slice onion. Place eggplant, celery, onion, oregano, and bay leaf into boiling water and boil 5 minutes. Drain thoroughly, remove bay leaf and marinate several hours or overnight to blend flavors.

4 tablespoons oil and 3 tablespoons cider vinegar may be used as marinade. Serves 6.

Pepper Relish

1 cup chopped red peppers	1 cup honey
1 cup chopped green peppers	1 cup vinegar
2 cups chopped cabbage	1 teaspoon celery seeds
½ cup chopped onions	

Sea kelp may be added if desired. Keep refrigerated.

Spanish Relish

Two cups thinly sliced cucumbers, ½ cup each chopped *bell pepper, tomatoes* cut in small chips and minced *onion*. A few minced *nasturtium* leaves or chopped green nasturtium seed pods will add a peppery flavor, if liked, or a tablespoon grated horse radish if the nasturtiums are not available. These ingredients are juicy and very little dressing is required. Makes about 1 quart.

Spiced Apple Halves

Make a thin syrup of ½ cup honey and 3 tablespoons hot water, then add just enough beet juice to color. Cook 6 apple halves in this mixture, adding cinnamon during the cooking. Remove the apples to a serving dish, strain the syrup over them and let it jell by putting in a cold place before serving. Serves 3.

Guacamole

2 ripe avocados, peeled	½ teaspoon chili powder
1 small onion, grated	2 tablespoons catsup, home-
3 tablespoons freshly squeezed	made (optional)
lemon juice	¼ cup mayonnaise
½ teaspoon kelp	

1. Mash the peeled avocado in a bowl with a fork until smooth; or cut the avocados into small pieces and place them with all ingredients except mayonnaise in a blender. Blend until almost creamy—do not blend too long as the mixture will not keep its shape.
2. If guacamole is prepared using a fork, season with grated onion, lemon juice, kelp, chili powder, and catsup. Mix well.
3. Cover mixture with a thin layer of mayonnaise to keep from becoming dark; refrigerate, covered, until ready to serve.
4. Just before serving, stir mayonnaise into mixture. Stir well. Serve on crisp lettuce leaves as an appetizer; garnished with fresh cherry tomatoes or tomato quarters, celery sticks, cauliflower pieces and Swedish crisp crackers.

Yield: about 2 cups.

Red and Green Hors D'Oeuvres

Halve several avocados, pit and dig the pulp out of them. Save this for the dip. Fill the halves with radishes, green onions, Pascal celery, and beet and cucumber pickles.

The dip is made as follows—Mash the avocado pulp and add minced onion, herbs and strong cider vinegar until you get just the wallop you want. Put the dip in a little red bowl in the middle of a tray or platter, and arrange the avocado boats of raw vegetables around it. Garnish the tray with parsley and wintergreen berries if possible.

Pickled Wax Beans

Heat 1 pound wax beans to the boiling stage, making sure that there is at least ½ cup of liquid on them. Stir up a sauce of 1 tablespoon each of cooking oil, arrowroot flour and pure cider vinegar.

Pour this on the simmering beans and stir and cook until the sauce is thickened. Serves 4.

Greenbean Appetizer

1 pound cooked fresh green beans	2 hard cooked eggs sea salt to taste
1 green pepper, diced	2 tablespoons homemade mayonnaise

Run cooked beans through a food chopper with the pepper and cooked eggs. Add sea salt to taste. Stir in homemade mayonnaise. Serves 4.

Zesty Beets

Beets are a good source of the B vitamin cholin and the vitamin-like substance betain, which is a good aid to digestion. They are also rich in trace minerals. These "zesty beets" are a good between-meal pick-up and an appetizing side dish for fish or meat dinners.

3 cups cooked, shredded beets	½ teaspoon sea salt
1 teaspoon onion juice	1 teaspoon honey
2 tablespoons lemon juice	½ cup yogurt

Slip peel off the cooked beets after cooling. Shred into serving bowl.

In blender mix the yogurt, onion juice, lemon juice, honey and sea salt. Pour over beets and serve warm, or chill if desired. 4 to 6 servings.

Beet Nests

Thin the beet rows, pulling them when the young beets are less than an inch through. Cook until tender, then cut the baby beets from the tops and skin them. Chop the leaves, pack in glass jars and put the baby beets on top. Dress with salad oil, honey and pure cider vinegar. Cover tightly.

Stuffed Celery

Select stalks of celery having a deep curve. Fill with a mixture made as follows: Into a bowl put two tablespoons peanut butter, one tablespoon very finely minced parsley and one tablespoon tomato pulp. Mix well together. If desired, a little minced onion may be added.

Eggplant With Onion

Put 1 chilled unpeeled eggplant, cut into ½ inch or 1 inch slices, into 3 tablespoons boiling water and 1 teaspoon vinegar. Cover, heat quickly, and simmer 15 minutes; add 1 grated onion.

Chop eggplant, season with fresh peppercorns. Garnish with parsley. Serve hot or chilled as a relish. Makes about a pint.

Garbanzo Delight

A hearty lunch pail dish that will "stick to the ribs" is cold boiled garbanzos. Simply fill small glass dishes with the cold garbanzos and pour 1 tablespoon of pure cider vinegar over the top of each dish and put on the cover. At noon they are flavored perfectly with the sour vinegar and are truly a delight.

Mushroom Appetizers

Select a tightly covered pint jar. Fill with washed and quartered mushrooms, raw. Add 2 tablespoons vinegar, and your favorite seasonings, such as: ½ teaspoon celery seed, ¼ teaspoon each of thyme and oregano. No salt is necessary.

They will in three days be transformed to a delicious appetizer.

Pickled Mushrooms

If you know your mushrooms and can identify the edible ones, gather more than you can eat and pickle the surplus for all-year enjoyment.

2 cups small whole mushrooms (cut larger mushrooms in pieces)
1 teaspoon sea salt
1 bay leaf

1 clove garlic (minced)
cider vinegar (enough to cover ¾ to 1 cup mushrooms)
1 teaspoon fennel seed

Sprinkle sea salt over mushrooms. Heat vinegar and fennel. When mixture simmers, add the mushrooms, bay leaf and minced garlic. Simmer five minutes. Pour into hot sterilized jars. Makes about one pint. Nice to serve with meat instead of relish or pickles.

Mushrooms A La Grecque

1 pound small mushrooms
⅓ cup olive oil
2 tablespoons cider vinegar
1 clove garlic, finely chopped

½ teaspoon kelp
few sprigs parsley, chopped
pinch of thyme, basil, or oregano

Rinse mushrooms quickly in cold water and drain well. Heat oil and vinegar together with other ingredients, except mushrooms, to boiling point. Cover and simmer gently for 5 minutes. Add mushrooms and cook 5 minutes longer. Chill mushrooms in this sauce. Use in relish tray or as a salad ingredient.

Note: Asparagus, cauliflower, artichoke hearts and zucchini can be treated in this fashion.

Red and Green Pickles

Again use a sectional dish if you have one, with beet pickles on one side and cucumber pickles on the other. A good substitute dish can be made by setting 2 bowls on an oblong tray or small platter. Then garnish with parsley and tiny circles of red pepper to represent holly and berries.

Raw Radish Dip

In blender:

½ cup cider vinegar   ½ cup honey

Add radish pieces to running blender until it is half full of radishes —turn on and off until radishes are shredded as fine as desired. Serve at once or refrigerate. Keeps well as a raw relish.

Vegetable Tray

This tray should hold raw vegetables such as carrot sticks, celery, raw turnip slices, cucumber slices from the freezer which are just barely thawed, red cabbage wedges, and Bermuda onion rings. The latter are made pretty by dropping them in a can of homemade beet pickle juice several days in advance. You can make a dip by mashing a very ripe avocado, adding homemade mayonnaise, grated onion and vinegar to thin slightly.

Harvest Vegetable Tray

On a fancy tray or platter, arrange several "shocks of corn" by standing short stalks of celery together, tying below the leaves, then spreading the stalks at the bottom. Cut carrots into inch chunks and lay among the "shocks" to represent pumpkins. Let the children fix this "harvest" tray and they can doubtless come up with other original ideas, even to vegetable "animals."

Zucchini Appeteasers

Fresh-gathered organically-grown zucchini (up to 8 inches in length), sliced one-quarter inch thick, provide the basis for a variety of appetizers that even weight-watchers can enjoy. Sprinkle them with soybean grits (or any protein derivative) or with sesame seed, or finely-ground nuts, sometimes spreading them first with homemade yogurt. Spread them with nut butters and add either chopped parsley, chives, or bell pepper. The garden-freshness of raw zucchini is a good contrast to avocado paste, hard-cooked egg, bean paste, or any salad mixture of fish or fowl.

Soups, Stews and Casseroles

Hearty Nourishment

Add almost endless variety to your choices of soups and stews by experimenting with some of the following recipes. Don't forget the superior value of raw vegetables over canned, dried or frozen and use the raw variety whenever you can. To make a raw vegetable soup taste like it's been cooking for hours, sauté about two table-spoons of onion in a small amount of oil until the onion is golden, then blend it with other ingredients.

Recipes for Soups and Stews

Stock

Keep the water from potatoes and all vegetables in a covered jar in the refrigerator. You can drop an onion and a few fresh leaves from basil and marjoram in it and leave them in a few days for added flavor. Use this water to add to gravies, for raw soups, and in many such places. It is precious as it sometimes holds the best part of the vegetables' minerals, which come out during the cooking. Keep every drop of vegetable cooking waters in a tightly-covered glass jar, and well-refrigerated.

Barley Soup

4 medium potatoes with skins, cut in half	4 medium carrots
	1 teaspoon sea salt
1 tablespoon oregano	1 stalk celery
2 quarts water	6 small onions
1 cut up chicken	¼ cup barley

Cook chicken, barley, oregano, water, sea salt 45 minutes. Then add rest of ingredients. Cook until chicken is tender. Serves 6.

Bouillabaisse

Heat a heavy-type cooking utensil, add 1 tablespoon of oil and turn the heat down. Keeping the cover on to provide steam for the simmering, add the following vegetables as fast as you get them prepared:

2 small onions, sliced
1 clove garlic, minced
1 carrot, diced
½ green pepper, slivered

1 tablespoon fresh thyme (or 1 teaspoon dried)
1 bay leaf, crushed
1 cup home-canned tomatoes

Simmer this sauce until the carrot is nearly done, then add the fish chunks. The sauce will only come up about a quarter of the way on the meat, so the fish needs to be turned occasionally.

2 pounds fish

You can use any of these: shad, tuna, whitefish, salmon, haddock, cod, abalone, bass, flounder, Finnan haddie, pike, pickerel, sturgeon, herring, halibut and many other varieties.

Use fillets and cut them in bite-size chunks, or cut big slabs through such fish as pickerel or pike and leave the bones in.

If you use small fillet chunks, simmer 10 minutes, but if you use large steak slabs of fish with bones intact, then simmer for 20 minutes, moving the meat to the bottom occasionally. Season with sea kelp when partly done. Serves 6.

Cauliflower Soup

1 head of cauliflower (cooked)
3 cups boiling chicken broth
2 tablespoons minced onion
2 tablespoons minced celery leaves

2 tablespoons water
2 egg yolks
dash of sea salt

Divide cauliflower into flowerets, place cauliflower and 2 cups of chicken broth in blender until it is pureed. Cook onion and celery leaves in sunflower oil until tender and golden; stir while cooking.

Add remaining cup of chicken broth into pureed cauliflower. Stir in egg yolks and water beaten together. Heat through but do not boil. Serves 6.

Chestnut Soup

½ pound chestnuts, shelled and peeled
1 quart vegetable or chicken broth
3 tablespoons soy oil

1 small carrot, grated
1 small turnip, grated
1 tablespoon grated onion
½ teaspoon sea salt—if desired

Chestnuts are simmered in broth until tender. After draining broth into another container, mash the chestnuts, and add grated carrot, turnip, and onion. Stir in soup and salt. Simmer 15 minutes gently. Serves 4.

Persian Chicken Soup

1½ pounds cooked chicken
1 chopped onion
1 bay leaf

sea salt to taste
6 peppercorns
1 stick cinnamon

A 4-pound chicken is cooked in 2 quarts boiling water, with above ingredients, usually leaving 1½ pounds of meat after removal from bones. 1 cup rice is then added to the broth and boiled ten minutes, with 1 cup seedless raisins, 2 tablespoons soy oil, and the cut up chicken. They are cooked together for ½ hour, and broth is lessened. Served in tureen with ¼ cup slivered almonds sprinkled on top. Serves 4.

Chicken Gumbo

4 cups chicken broth (have it boiling)
2 cups okra cut in ½ inch pieces
2 basil leaves

2 sprigs of savory
½ cup brown rice
1 small onion chopped

Simmer about 15 minutes, then add these ingredients and simmer until rice is tender:

2 tomatoes, quartered
1 cup chopped mushrooms
1 ear of corn, cut from cob

¼ cup chopped red or green pepper
sea kelp to taste

Serves 8.

Chinese Soup

2 teaspoons corn oil (cold-pressed)
½ cup sliced dark green celery
½ cup sliced fresh mushrooms
4 water chestnuts, diced

½ cup bean sprouts
½ cup diced cooked chicken
6 cups fresh chicken broth
1 egg, beaten

Heat oil in a saucepan; add celery and mushrooms and cook 2 minutes. Stir in water chestnuts, bean sprouts, chicken and broth; cook over low heat for 10 minutes. Add egg gradually, mixing steadily to prevent lumps from forming. The soup will have ribbons of eggs in it. Serve immediately upon removal from heat. Serves 6.

Christmas Soup—Finnish-Style

2 cups whole yellow peas, washed
1 pound fresh ribs, cut up
5 or 6 whole allspice

2 teaspoons sea salt
1 medium onion, finely diced
1½ quarts water

Place ingredients in large covered kettle. Simmer slowly for 3 or 4 hours until done. Serves 4.

Corn & Bean Soup

Add 1 beef bone to a quart of water with the following ingredients:

1 small onion
1 celery stalk, chopped
kernels from one ear of corn
½ cup pea beans which have soaked overnight

½ teaspoon celery salt
parsley
pinch of dill

Simmer 'til done. Serves 4.

Cucumber Soup

2 hard boiled eggs, chopped
⅓ cup chopped nuts
2 pints soy yogurt
½ teaspoon kelp
1 small onion, finely chopped
1½ cups diced cucumber

Beat yogurt with fork until smooth. Stir in remaining ingredients. Refrigerate. Serves 4.

Iced Cucumber and Mint Soup

1 small bunch onions, sliced
4 cucumbers, sliced
3 cups water
  season as desired
6 tablespoons rice flour
3 tablespoons chopped fresh mint
1½ cups soy yogurt

Simmer sliced cucumbers and onions. Blend with rice flour and water. Strain. Place in a cold pan and add the chopped mint. Add yogurt in a bowl standing on cracked ice. Garnish with shredded cucumber and mint before serving. Serves 6.

Raw Fruit Soup

Liquefy the following and serve in sauce dishes:

1 banana
½ cup pignolias (or any nuts)
¼ cup sesame seeds
6 stemmed figs
1 stalk rhubarb
½ cup fresh coconut chunks
2 cups water or fruit juice

Use enough liquid to make a fruit soup or mush, and add honey if desired. Serves 2.

Gazpacho (uncooked)

1 clove garlic
1 green pepper, cut up
1 Spanish onion, cut up
½ cup mixture of chives, parsley, basil, thyme, tarragon, chervil
1 pint chicken stock
1 pint meat stock
1 pint tomato juice
  juice of 2 lemons
3 tablespoons oil
1 cucumber, peeled and diced
1 tomato, chopped
1 teaspoon sea salt

Blend garlic, pepper, onion, herbs and stock in blender until smooth. Add rest of ingredients. Blend thoroughly. Chill at least 8 hours before serving. Serves 6.

Irish Soup

2 quarts water (add extra
    water as it cooks if necessary)
2 pounds lean boiling beef
½ cup split peas
½ cup barley
1 medium onion, sliced fine
1 large carrot, sliced fine

1 medium turnip, diced
1 stalk celery cut fine
1 teaspoon sea salt
2 cups finely shredded green
    cabbage
6 boiled potatoes—one for each
    person

Put meat and water on to cook. Simmer for 1 hour, then add peas and barley and cook for another hour. Then add other vegetables except cabbage and simmer for another 45 minutes. Add the cabbage and cook for another 15 minutes. Add whatever seasonings you prefer. Have potatoes boiled separately. To serve put a potato in each soup plate, then some of the meat; lastly pour the broth and vegetables over all. Serves 6.

Irish Stew

Cook spring lamb until tender, seasoning with bay leaves, thyme and sea kelp during the cooking. Add dried summer savory, and the following vegetables and simmer until the vegetables are tender: (Serve in soup bowls.)

1 potato per person

1 onion, stalk celery, 1 turnip
    and 2 carrots per 3 persons

Season again just before serving.

Julienne Soup

2 pounds lean beef shank
2 quarts water
2 turnips
2 onions
3 tomatoes

2 carrots
    small stalk of celery
1 cup peas
    small head cabbage

Simmer beef in water for four hours. Take a tablespoon of oil, put in pan and add vegetables which have been cut in long strips, and sauté to light golden brown. Then add to broth and simmer for a few minutes. Serves 8.

Lamb Mushroom Soup

1 or 2 lamb bones	1 small onion, sliced
½ dozen mushrooms, sliced	1 celery stalk, sliced
1 cup tomatoes (home-canned)	enough water to cover

Simmer until done. Season to taste. Serves 2.

Hot Lettuce Soup

Mix any leftover chicken broth from cooked-up chicken. Heat very hot and for each serving put these ingredients in the blender:

½ cup fresh lettuce	1 green onion or 3 chives
2 sprigs marjoram or thyme	

Put the greens in the blender first, and pour the hot broth in gently, so as not to break the glass. Whiz until you have a thin, light-green liquid. Serve at once.

Lentil Porridge

1 cup lentils	1 bay leaf
½ cup millet	1 teaspoon kelp
1½ quarts water	2 teaspoons celery seed powder

Wash lentils. Put all ingredients in pot and bring to boil, then simmer one hour. When finished add broth seasoning and cooked vegetables such as carrots, peas, beans, etc. Serves 4.

Lentil Soup

1 cup (untreated) lentils
1 onion (medium size)
½ cup celery leaves
½ cup parsley

2 tablespoons soya oil
¼ teaspoon sweet basil
kelp or sea salt to taste

Wash lentils and soak in 1 quart water 2 hours. Chop onion, celery leaves and parsley very fine. Add vegetables and soya oil to lentils. Cook in water in which they were soaked. Simmer until tender. Add seasoning and simmer 5 minutes. Serves 4.

Back Stove Lentil Soup Pot

1 cup lentils
bones of turkey, goose or
chicken
2 quarts water
1 carrot, sliced

1 tablespoon parsley
bit of bay leaf
½ teaspoon savory
½ cup diced celery
1 onion, sliced

Cover bones of leftover fowl with 2 quarts water, vegetables, and lentils. Simmer gently until soft. Drain, remove bones and press lentils through sieve. Simmer again gently about ½ hour. Serves 4 to 6.

Lentil Stew—Lebanese

¾ cup lentils
1 cup chopped celery
1 cup cut carrots
1 medium sized onion, diced

4 tablespoons cold-pressed oil
3 cups water
1 teaspoon sea salt

Sauté celery, carrots, onion in oil, slowly and for just a minute. Add lentils and salt and sauté together for another minute. Add water, bring to a boil. Turn heat low, let simmer for about ¾ to one hour. Serves 6.

Minestrone

1 quart vegetable stock
½ onion, sliced
1 good sized potato, sliced
½ cup kale, chopped

1 cup brown rice
¼ cup green beans, cut up
1 cup tomatoes

Season to taste with sea salt and garlic. Simmer about 40 minutes.
Serves 4.

Mulligan Stew

4 cups soup stock with bits of
  meat in it
1 cup diced carrots
½ cup chopped onions

2 stalks celery and leaves
1 cup diced potatoes
1 diced turnip
1 tablespoon sea kelp

Put 1 teaspoon each of dried marjoram, savory and thyme in a
cheesecloth and cook in the stew, discarding when done.
Simmer the above ingredients for 15 minutes, then add:

2 cups young peas

Simmer until the peas are tender. Serves 4.

Mushroom Soup

2 cups fresh mushrooms
1 cup pure water

1 cup scrubbed potatoes (cut in
  chunks)
1 small onion

Whiz in blender until all are reduced to small chunks. Add
1 teaspoon of kelp and ½ teaspoon marjoram powder, 1 cup of
hot water. Simmer 5 minutes and serve. You can garnish the
bowls of soup with chopped parsley and brewer's yeast flakes.
Serves 3.

Mushroom-Vegetable Soup

In the blender (or food grinder) put the following:

2 cups meat and vegetable stock
2 cups mushrooms
2 medium potatoes, scrubbed
and cubed

1 small onion
1 teaspoon marjoram

Whiz or chop fine. Put 1 tablespoon cooking oil in a heavy saucepan, add the soup mixture, season with sea kelp and simmer about 5 minutes. Serves 2.

Noodles For Soup

Blend 3 eggs. Put in bowl:

1 cup corn, rice or soy flour   3 tablespoons plain dry gelatin

Mix well. Stir in the eggs and keep stirring. It will keep getting thicker as the gelatin softens. Use a rubber scraper to form it into a ball. This noodle ball can be put into the refrigerator and sliced very thin for quick noodles. It sets very hard and is easy to slice with a sharp knife.

For noodles right away, roll the ball in arrowroot flour. Divide it into 4 pieces. Roll out each piece on arrowroot flour or use the machine. Cut into strips. For noodle sacs, cut into squares or circles, fill with a little hamburger and fold the empty half over and seal. Brown in a little oil or cook in a broth or soup.

Nut Soup

A soup that's different and hardy.

½ cup chopped onion
2 tablespoons peanut oil
1 tablespoon rice flour
1½ teaspoons brewer's yeast

½ cup pure peanut butter
2 cups nut milk
2 cups tomato juice

Sauté onion in oil until tender but not browned. Add flour and seasoning. Blend in peanut butter. Add milk gradually, stirring to blend. Cook and stir until mixture comes to a boil and is thickened. Add tomato juice and bring just to a boil. Garnish with minced chives. Serves 4.

Oxtail Soup

½ cup natural (not pearled) barley
2 pounds oxtail rounds (cut one inch long)
1 large onion, minced
2 large celery stalks, sliced
2 medium carrots, diced
4 medium-sized ripe tomatoes, peeled
small amounts of cooked vegetables such as peas, limas, string beans, as desired

Put barley in large pot with two quarts cold water. Let soak one hour. Add oxtail, bring to boil, cover, simmer three hours. Remove oxtail, separate and reserve. Let broth chill and remove accumulated fat.

Add vegetables to broth and barley and cook until tender. Add meat from bones, omitting the fat, and put in any cooked vegetables to be used. Season to taste. If the broth has cooked down, and is too thick, add water, and correct seasoning.

A good way to prepare this soup is to cook oxtails and barley the night before, letting the broth chill in the refrigerator. Serves 6 to 8.

Peanut Soup

For each serving, use the following ingredients:

1 cup chicken broth
1 teaspoon each of arrowroot flour and rice polish
1 rounded tablespoon home-made peanut butter
¼ teaspoon minced onion (optional)

Bring the chicken broth to a boil and have the 2 flours stirred to a paste with cold water, add and stir until thick. Add the peanut butter and the onion if desired.

Cream of Peanut Butter

1 cup natural peanut butter	1 pint water
3 cups soy milk	1 grated raw potato
½ cup chopped celery	1 teaspoon sea salt

Mix peanut butter with 1 cup soy milk. Heat other 2 cups milk in double boiler. Cook celery in 1 pint water until tender. Add potato. Cook until thickened. Add peanut butter mixture, celery-and-potato mixture, and sea salt to hot milk. Reheat and beat before serving. Serves 6.

Pease Porridge

Wash 3 cups split peas and soak overnight. When ready to cook, add the following:

1 quart stock	2 stalks celery and leaves, diced
1 onion, chopped	2 sprigs summer savory
1 turnip, diced	2 sprigs marjoram
1 potato, diced	1 tablespoon sea kelp
3 carrots, diced	

Simmer until done. The herbs can be removed after cooking, if preferred. Serves 4.

Potato Carrot Soup

4 medium-sized potatoes	2 teaspoons sea salt
3 medium-sized carrots	1½ cups cooking water from
2 medium-sized onions	vegetables
3 cups boiling water	1⅔ cups soy milk

Peel and dice potatoes, carrots and onions. Add to boiling water, with sea salt until tender, about 15 minutes. Drain, saving the water, then rice or mash the vegetables thoroughly. There should be 1¼ cups of cooking water; if not, add fresh water. Combine with soy milk, scald and slowly stir into mashed vegetables. Add desired seasonings, reheat and serve. Serves 5.

Pumpkin Soup

3 tablespoons chopped onion
2 tablespoons chopped green
  pepper
2 tablespoons oil

2 cups soy milk
1 cup cooked pumpkin
¾ teaspoon chopped parsley

Simmer onions and pepper slightly and add remaining ingredients. Stir and heat slowly. Serves 4.

Red Beet Soup

7 small beets, unpeeled
2 teaspoons kelp
3 tablespoons apple cider
  vinegar

1 cucumber sliced
1 small onion, finely chopped
1½ quarts hot water

Add beets, vinegar, kelp, onion to hot water. Boil until tender. Drain, saving the cooking water. Peel and cut beets into strips. Return beets to cooking water. Cool. Add cucumber. Refrigerate. Serves 6.

Soybean Soup

2 cups tomatoes
1 medium chopped onion
½ cup chopped celery
½ cup diced carrots (about 1
  medium)

1¼ cup cooked soybeans,
  mashed or chopped
2 tablespoons soy flour

(Soybeans must be cooked in advance for at least an hour, or until soft. Try soaking beans overnight before cooking. A little oil added to the water before soaking helps to soften the beans.)

Cook celery, onion and carrots in 3 cups of water for about 10 minutes. Add tomatoes and mashed soybeans and heat through. Mix soy flour with a little cold water and stir into mixture, cooking over low heat until thickened. If desired, add your favorite seasoning. Serves 4.

Sunflower-Split Pea Soup

½ teaspoon kelp
2 tablespoons safflower oil
1 cup soy milk
2 diced pimientos

2 tablespoons chopped parsley
¼ teaspoon thyme
¼ cup sunflower-seed meal
2 cups split peas

Wash split peas thoroughly. Cook 2 cups split peas in 3 cups of water for 1 hour . . . then add all remaining ingredients. Simmer 15 minutes or until flavors blend. Serves 4.

Super Soup

Use any type of dry beans: split yellow, green pea, or lentils— 1 cup to 2 quarts of liquid.

2 medium or one large onion— quartered
2 stalks celery—diced or sliced (on an angle)
2 large carrots—sliced or shredded
1 medium potato—cubed or shredded
1 large turnip—sliced or shredded

cabbage—chopped small (other greens welcome) buckwheat, wheat, rice flour, barley, cooked rice, garlic, soy sauce, leafy sage, sea salt, parsley, basil, mint, leafy thyme, marjoram, ground all-spice, bay leaf, fennel and anise seed may be added. (This combination is especially refreshing.)

Wash beans thoroughly and soak for a few hours. Then cook over low heat lightly covered until very soft, about one hour. Add bay leaves and whole cloves and remove before adding vegetables.

Add the vegetables in order. If mostly shredded, simmer for 5 to 10 minutes. If mostly sliced—simmer about 10 to 15 minutes. Vegetables should remain crisp and retain their identity.

For extra thickening, mix a heaping tablespoon of flour (preferably buckwheat) to ½ cup of water and add to soup when vegetables are soft. Stir constantly for 1 minute and turn off heat. Add soy sauce, about ¼ teaspoon of each of the leafy herbs crushed, fennel and anise according to taste. Serves 6.

Swedish Rose Hips Soup

18 cooked prunes
3 cups fresh rose hips or 2 cups dried
1½ quarts boiling water

1 tablespoon potato starch (or 1½ tablespoons cornstarch)
⅓ cup honey (approx.)

Drop rose hips into vigorously boiling water. Cover and cook until tender, stirring occasionally, then strain through a fine sieve. If liquid does not measure 1½ quarts, add enough water to make that amount. Return to sauce pan and add starch and honey. Bring to boil, stirring constantly. Put into refrigerator when cool.

When ready to serve, place three cooked prunes into a soup bowl, pour over this about a cup of rose hip soup. This soup can be served hot, but is much better cold. Serves 6.

Tomato Soup

4 quarts tomatoes
3 medium-sized onions
tops and outer stalks from a bunch of celery
3 sweet peppers

6 fresh basil leaves or 1 table-spoon dried basil
2 hot peppers from mixed spices
4 bay leaves

Simmer these together till the vegetables are tender, then put through a sieve or wire strainer.

Work fast and get the hot mixture back on the fire. While it is reheating to the boiling point, make a thin pouring mixture of ½ cup honey, ½ cup arrowroot flour and 1 tablespoon sea kelp, adding as much cold water as is needed. Pour this thickening into the boiling mixture and stir and cook until the soup is fairly thick.

Have sterilized cans ready. Can up all the spare soup you have as soon as it is thickened and before the meal is ready. This saves re-heating and a possible scorching because of the thickening.

Green Cabbage, Apple and Tomato Soup

3 large fresh tomatoes, cut into quarters
½ cup cold water
3 cups shredded dark green cabbage
½ cup finely chopped onion

1½ cups peeled, diced apples
1 teaspoon honey
½ teaspoon sea salt
1 tablespoon caraway seeds
6 cups boiling water

In a large saucepan place the tomatoes and ½ cup cold water. Simmer for ten minutes, then press tomatoes through a sieve and return to saucepan. Add remaining ingredients and simmer gently for ½ hour. Serve piping hot. Serves 6.

Cream of Tomato Soup

3 cups fresh whole tomatoes	dash cloves
2 slices onion	2 tablespoons oil
1 bay leaf	2 tablespoons arrowroot
¼ teaspoon cinnamon	2 cups soy milk

Put tomatoes in the blender and whiz to cut the seeds. If using fresh tomatoes the skins will blend up. Put tomatoes into saucepan with the onion, bay leaf, cinnamon, cloves and salt. Simmer 10 minutes. Strain.

In the blender, make a white sauce of the oil, arrowroot and soy milk. Heat until thick, stirring constantly. Just before serving, slowly add hot tomato mixture to hot white sauce, while stirring. Serves 6.

Tomato-Pea Soup

1 medium chopped onion	2 tablespoons honey
1½ tablespoons oil	1 cup homemade tomato puree
6 cups boiling water	3 cloves of allspice
1 cup dry split peas	

Brown onion in oil. Add water, peas, and allspice. Boil gently about two hours, or until desired consistency. Add honey and tomato puree. Remove spice and serve. Serves 6.

Turkey Soup

Use bones and meat from leftover turkey.
Chop bones to fit a large vessel, cover with water. Add:

½ cup barley	1 small onion
1 tablespoon kelp	

Boil for a few minutes, turn to simmer for 2 hours. Take up all the bones, taking meat off, put back into broth. Add:

1 cup chopped celery 1 teaspoon kelp
1 tablespoon parsley

Cook for another 15 minutes or until celery gets to a point that you like. Serves 4.

Ukrainian Soup

2 cups cooked soybeans
1 large beet
1 carrot
1 potato
1 quart water
2 tablespoons oil
1 onion, chopped
⅓ green pepper

½ cup chopped celery
1 tablespoon soy flour (optional)
1 cup shredded cabbage
2 cups tomato juice
2 tablespoons chopped parsley
½ bay leaf (optional)
sea salt to taste

Mash beans lightly. Cube or shred beet, carrot and potato. Add vegetables and water to bean puree and cook slowly for 10 minutes. Add celery and cabbage. Cook for 5 minutes.

Sauté onion and pepper until browned lightly. Then add soy flour or cornstarch. Mix thoroughly and continue cooking 3 or 4 minutes. Add onion mixture to boiling soup. Add parsley, bay leaf and salt to taste. Turn off fire and let stand at least 2 hours before serving. Do not over-cook vegetables. Makes approximately 4 quarts.

Hearty Healthy Vegetable Soup

1 pound beef and a few 4-inch marrow bones
1 cup dried lima beans
3 quarts water
1 cup dried kidney beans
1 quart home-canned tomatoes
4 cups diced carrots
1 medium turnip (diced)

1 small head of cabbage (cut-up)
1 pint home-canned snap beans
2 cups cut-up celery and leaves
2 medium sized onions (sliced)
1 10-ounce package frozen peas
1 10-ounce package frozen corn

Put all ingredients (except the last three) into eight-quart pan. Cook until dried beans are well done, then add last three ingredients, season to taste with sea salt, add a half cup of cut-up fresh parsley. Cook slowly one more hour. Serves 6.

Vegetable Soup

Wash one cup navy beans. Soak overnight in three cups water. Simmer one hour. Brown ½ pound ground beef. Add to soup with ¾ cup each of diced cabbage, carrots and onions and ¼ cup brown rice. Season with two teaspoons sea salt, a bit of garlic, oregano or basil. Add two cups home-canned tomatoes, and more water if needed. Simmer until vegetables are tender. Serves 6.

Warming Winter Soup

Put in deep kettle the following:

2 quarts water	1¼ teaspoons sea salt
1 medium quartered onion	1¼ pounds of beef chuck

Boil the above for 10 minutes, then simmer for 2 hours. Remove beef, strain stock, and measure.

Add water to make 2½ quarts. Dice beef. Then heat the following in skillet:

3 tablespoons oil	1 garlic, sliced
1 medium onion, sliced	2 stalks celery, sliced

Cook ten minutes over medium heat, stirring frequently. Return diced meat to stock; add contents of skillet. Then add the following:

2 cups shredded cabbage	2 cups whole tomatoes
2 cups sliced carrots	

Cover, simmer until vegetables are tender. Add two cups cooked brown rice, ¼ teaspoon oregano. Mix well and serve with fresh parsley sprinkled over each serving. Serves 8.

This soup freezes well.

Zucchini Vegetable Stew

4 large or 8 small zucchini cubed into 1-inch pieces
2 large onions and 2 cloves garlic, diced
3 medium carrots, diced
¼ green pepper, diced
2 large stalks celery, diced
handful chopped parsley

2 tablespoons honey
1 8-ounce jar homemade tomato sauce, plus 8 ounces of water
pinch each: oregano, sweet basil
2 tablespoons olive oil

Put all ingredients in a large 6-quart sauce pot or dutch oven. Mix gently with a wooden spoon. Simmer in covered pot for half to three-quarters of an hour. Stir occasionally in the beginning until vegetables begin to simmer down to cook evenly. This tasty dish may also be cooked in a pressure cooker for 15 minutes at 15 pounds pressure. Turn heat off and let pressure reduce normally. This can also be made with meat, by browning a pound of ground round with the onions and garlic, before adding rest of ingredients. Serves 6.

Casseroles

Casseroles are the famous (or infamous) one-pot dishes whose mysterious combinations of creative cookery could contain a rich conglomeration of vitamins, minerals and protein if the original food had not been processed, devitalized and loaded with additives in the first place. Casseroles make an excellent disguise for soy powder, wheat germ, sea kelp, parsley, saffron and marjoram. Add some pumpkin, sesame or sunflower seeds to your favorite recipes and you know you'll be adding to your family's nutrition.

Casserole Recipes

Artichoke Beef Hash

Put the vegetables for this hash through the food grinder or in the blender with small amounts of water and grind or whiz them fine, adding more until the amounts are obtained.

1 cup raw carrot pulp
3 cups artichoke pulp
½ cup onion pulp
1 pound ground beef

½ teaspoon mace
½ teaspoon chili powder
1 tablespoon sea kelp

Blend ingredients and pack in an oiled 2-quart casserole dish. Bake about one hour at 350°. Serves 6.

Ground Steak Casserole

2 cups home-canned tomatoes
1 stalk celery, diced
½ green pepper cut into strips
2 small onions coarsely diced

6 potatoes peeled and sliced
1 teaspoon sea kelp
1½ pounds steak, ground

Place in blender tomatoes including juice, celery, green pepper, and onions. Cover and blend on high speed for 10 seconds. Oil a 1½ quart casserole. Place ⅓ of the potatoes in a layer at bottom and season with sea kelp. Add a layer of ground steak using about ⅓ of the meat, season with sea kelp. Pour ⅓ of the tomato mixture over the meat. Repeat to make 3 layers ending with tomato mixture. (Marjoram and thyme may be used.) Bake in a 350 degree oven for 2 hours. Serves 6.

All-in-One-Meal

1 pound ground beef
1 cup cooked brown rice
2 tablespoons finely chopped onion
½ teaspoon thyme
1 teaspoon kelp

1 egg
½ pound brussels sprouts
2 tablespoons cold-pressed oil
¼ cup water with 1 tablespoon dark honey (mixed)
½ cup tomato puree

Mix ground beef, rice, onion, kelp, thyme and egg. Shape a meatball around each brussels sprout. Brown meatballs on all sides in hot corn oil in skillet. Pour off any excess fat. Pour on tomato puree and water-honey mixture. Simmer in covered skillet for 15 minutes.

Serve with mixed green salad. Serves 4.

Applesauce Meat Loaf

1½ pounds ground lean beef
1 beaten egg
2 tablespoons chopped onion

1 teaspoon allspice
1 cup applesauce

Combine all ingredients. Pack into oiled loaf pan and bake one hour at 350 degrees. Serves 4-6.

Beef Chop Suey

1 pound beef, cut in cubes, cooked
½ cup onions, sliced
½ cup mushrooms
½ cup celery, chopped

1 cup Chinese vegetables
½ cup bamboo sprouts
2 tablespoons soy sauce
¼ cup oil
1 tablespoon cornstarch

Sauté meat in oil. Remove from pan. Add onions and celery, sauté until onions are clear. Add other vegetables, ½ cup of beef stock, and soy sauce. Simmer for five minutes. Add cornstarch to 2 tablespoons of stock or water and beef. Continue to cook for five minutes more. Serve with fluffy brown rice. Serves 6.

Baked Sweet and Sour Short Ribs

3 pounds beef short ribs, cut into serving pieces
2 tablespoons peanut oil
1 onion, chopped
½ cup diced celery
1 cup tomato sauce

¼ cup cider vinegar
2 tablespoons pure honey
½ cup cold water
3 tablespoons soy sauce
sea salt, to taste

Heat oil in a heavy skillet and brown meat and onions. Transfer to a baking pan. Combine remaining ingredients and pour over meat. Bake in a moderate oven for about 2 hours or until meat is tender. Serve hot. Serves 6.

Baked Rice and Meat

2 cups cold cooked meat
2 cups meat stock
1 cup tomatoes
    season to taste

½ cup brown rice
2 tablespoons safflower oil
2 medium size onions

Cook the meat, which has been cut in cubes, stock, tomatoes, one of the onions cut fine, and seasonings together for about ten minutes. Brown the onion and the uncooked rice lightly in safflower oil, and add to the other mixture. Turn into oiled casserole and bake 30 minutes. Serves 4.

Steak and Kidney Casserole

Two beef kidneys, cored and chopped into 1" pieces
1 pound chuck, cut in 1" pieces
1 large onion, chopped in small pieces
½ cup diced, fresh mushrooms
1 cup fresh green peas (cooked)

¼ cup chopped parsley
1 cup beef broth
1 tablespoon soy sauce
2 tablespoons cold-pressed oil
1 tablespoon potato starch dissolved in 2 tablespoons cold water
sea salt

1. In a large skillet, sauté pieces of chuck in oil until brown on all sides. Add onions and mushrooms and sauté until soft.

2. In a separate skillet, brown the kidneys quickly in two tablespoons oil. Add them to the meat mixture, along with beef broth, soy sauce and sea salt. Cook over low heat, covered, for 1 hour.

3. Add potato starch dissolved in water, turn the heat to high, and stir until sauce thickens. Stir in cooked peas and parsley.

4. Transfer mixture to casserole and bake, covered, in preheated 350°F. oven for ½ hour. Serves 4.

Buckwheat Groats Casserole

This is a hearty and highly nutritious casserole that, with a green salad, makes a complete meal.

Place 1 cup groats (Kasha) in a bowl and pour two cups rapidly boiling water over them. Let stand ten minutes. Meanwhile beat together:

2 eggs
3 tablespoons salad oil

½ teaspoon either sage or thyme
and sea salt to taste

Combine the soaked groats with:

1 cup diced celery
1 cup diced onion

1 cup of either diced carrots or
corn

Next pour over all the egg and seasoning mixture. Mix well, place in a baking dish, sprinkle generously with paprika and bake in a moderate oven for about 30 minutes. Serves 4-6.

Chicken and Apple Casserole

1 3-pound chicken, cut into
  serving pieces
1 teaspoon sea salt
  dash of paprika
½ cup safflower oil

2 large apples, peeled and
  sliced
2 teaspoons honey
¼ cup sweet apple cider

In a large skillet, heat the oil. Sprinkle chicken with seasonings and brown in the hot oil on all sides. Transfer to a baking casserole. Place apple slices between chicken pieces, drizzle with honey and pour cider over all. Cover casserole and bake in a 350 degree oven for about 50 minutes or until chicken is tender. Serve hot. Serves 6.

Chicken and Rice Casserole

2 cups brown rice

4 cups chicken broth

Cook the rice in the broth until it is done. To the hot mixture add these:

2 cups diced cooked chicken
½ cup chopped celery
1 small chopped onion

½ teaspoon rosemary
1 cup chopped mushrooms

Blend ingredients and put in a baking dish. Top with wheat germ flakes to which a tablespoon of brewer's yeast has been added. Put in the oven just long enough to lightly toast the wheat germ. Serve hot. Serves 4.

Hot Chicken Salad Casserole

2 cups cooked chicken, chopped   1 cup slivered almonds
2 cups celery, diced   home-made mayonnaise
1 teaspoon grated onion

Mix chicken, celery, onion and almonds together with desired amount of home-made mayonnaise salad dressing. Put into casserole, bake in a 375° oven until mixture is heated through and bubbling. Serves 4.

Pakistani Pellao

3 cups chicken broth   1 teaspoon saffron
1 cup brown rice

Simmer the rice in the chicken broth until nearly done, then add the saffron. This gives the rice a nice yellow color. Add the following vegetables and serve hot or cold:

½ cup chopped cucumbers   1 teaspoon fresh marjoram or
¼ cup chopped red bell pepper   thyme
¼ cup diced celery   sea kelp as desired
6 green onions cut fine

Serves 4.

Eggplant-Walnut Delight

1 medium sized eggplant   sea salt and oregano to taste
1 medium sized onion   ½ cup tomato sauce
½ cup walnut meats

Peel eggplant and cut into chunks. Put eggplant, onion and nut meats through a food grinder. Add seasonings and tomato sauce and mix thoroughly. Form into a loaf and bake in an oiled casserole for 20 minutes. Serve hot. Serves 4.

Fish Casserole

3 cups cooked salmon or other
fish
3 eggs
1 cup soya milk

1 cup mashed potato
¼ teaspoon marjoram
¼ teaspoon paprika

Mix, put in oiled casserole and bake at 350° for 30 minutes.
Serves 4.

Fish and Cabbage

8 scrubbed new potatoes
3 cups shredded new cabbage
8 fish fillets

1 tablespoon sea kelp
1 tablespoon caraway seeds

Put water over the new potatoes and cook about 10 minutes. Put
the shredded cabbage on top of the potatoes and add the 2 seasonings. Cover again and cook and steam gently until the cabbage and
potatoes are nearly tender. Now lay the fillets on the cabbage and
cover tightly and cook about 3 minutes. Arrange the cabbage on a
platter, with the fish and potatoes around it. Season with fresh herbs
if desired. Serves 8.

Salmon Spinach Casserole

1 pound salmon fillet
2 packages frozen chopped
spinach
2 eggs

1 cup soya milk
1 teaspoon marjoram
½ teaspoon thyme
½ cup stewed tomato

Mix, put in oiled casserole, and bake at 375° about 30 minutes.
Serves 6.

Yum-Yum Casserole

2 cups grated carrots
1½ cups cooked brown rice
1 cup tuna (or other fish)
¼ cup wheat germ
½ onion, minced

3 eggs slightly beaten
1¾ cups soy milk
1 teaspoon sea salt
parsley

Toss together carrots, rice, tuna, wheat germ and onion. Blend eggs, milk, sea salt. Pour over rice mixture and bake at 350° about 60 minutes or until inserted knife is clean. Garnish top with parsley. Serves 4.

Lamb Chops Deluxe

6 rib lamb chops or lamb riblets
1 medium carrot, sliced
1 medium onion, sliced
1 large potato, sliced
1 large stalk celery, cut into pieces

½ medium head of cabbage cut into chunks
1 teaspoon caraway seeds
1 teaspoon sea salt
1 tablespoon chopped parsley

Brown lamb chops on both sides in either an electric fry pan or a dutch oven. Remove from pan, trim off visible fat and pour grease from pan. Put vegetables into pan in layers in the order given in the recipe. When half is used, sprinkle with half the parsley, caraway seeds and sea salt. Finish with vegetables putting the cabbage on top. Lay browned lamb chops on top of cabbage and add the rest of the seasonings. Cover tightly and turn electric fry pan to 250°. Cook for about 40 minutes or until meat and vegetables are cooked the way you like them. If cooked in a dutch oven, put into a 300 degree oven for about the same length of time. Serves 2.

Lamb and Rice Casserole

1 medium onion chopped
1 tablespoon cooking oil
3 cups fresh tomato juice
2 cups cooked lamb, diced
½ cup rice

½ cup chopped pickles (home-canned)
2 tablespoons minced parsley
1 tablespoon sesame seeds

Sauté onion in cooking oil until tender. Combine remaining ingredients in 1½ quart casserole; add onion and mix well. Cover and bake (stirring occasionally) in moderate oven (350°F). Cook one hour or until rice is tender. Serves 4-6.

Quickie Rice Vegetable

3 cups brown rice, uncooked
2 carrots, diced small
1 bell pepper, diced small
2 tomatoes, diced

6 eggs, hard boiled
1 tomato, blended with juice
  from ½ lemon

Cook brown rice and hard boil eggs. When rice is almost cooked and some water still remains, add vegetables (carrots, pepper, diced tomato). Chop hard boiled eggs finely, add tomato juice with lemon, and heat. Pour over rice and vegetables in serving plate. Sprinkle with raw wheat germ. Serves 6.

Salads

Eat More Salad Greens!

Every recommendation for a balanced diet urges the use of green, leafy vegetables at least once a day. Many people have acquired the habit of eating a mixed salad with meals. Still there are those who think that a leaf of lettuce under a canned peach is the ideal salad.

Iceberg lettuce, which is what most of us think of when we think of salads, is one of the least nutritive varieties. Much has been sacrificed for crispness and appearance. It is almost white (which indicates relatively skimpy nutritional content) and seems bland in flavor compared with other greens.

Which are the most valuable green, leafy vegetables from the nutritional standpoint? A list of the most familiar ones—giving their vitamin content—appears on page 76.

Salad Recipes

Alfalfa Sprout Salad

2 cups fresh alfalfa sprouts	1 tablespoon minced onion
3 chopped hardboiled eggs	1 tablespoon chopped red and
½ cup diced celery	green bell peppers

Blend ingredients with Health Mayonnaise and garnish with rose hips powder and the left-over celery tops. Serves 4-6.

Vitamins and Minerals in About 1 Cup of Greens

Food	Calcium	Phosphorus	Iron	Sodium	Potassium	Vitamin A	Thiamin	Riboflavin	Niacin	Vitamin C
Beet greens	118 mg.	45 mg.	3.2 mg.	130 mg.	570 mg.	6,700 IU	.08 mg.	.18 mg.	.4 mg.	34 mg.
Brussels sprouts	34 mg.	78 mg.	1.3 mg.	11 mg.	450 mg.	400 IU	.08 mg.	.16 mg.	.7 mg.	94 mg.
Cabbage	46 mg.	31 mg.	1.3 mg.	9 mg.	300 mg.	80 IU	.06 mg.	.05 mg.	.3 mg.	50 mg.
Chard	105 mg.	36 mg.	2.5 mg.	84 mg.	380 mg.	8,720 IU	.06 mg.	.18 mg.	.4 mg.	38 mg.
Chicory (French endive)	18 mg.	21 mg.	.7 mg.	—	—	10,000 IU	.05 mg.	.20 mg.	—	15 mg.
Cress, water	195 mg.	46 mg.	2.0 mg.	—	—	4,720 IU	.08 mg.	.16 mg.	.8 mg.	77 mg.
Dandelion greens	187 mg.	70 mg.	3.1 mg.	76 mg.	430 mg.	15,170 IU	.13 mg.	.12 mg.	.7 mg.	16 mg.
Endive	79 mg.	56 mg.	1.7 mg.	18 mg.	400 mg.	3,000 IU	.07 mg.	.12 mg.	.4 mg.	11 mg.
Kale	225 mg.	62 mg.	2.2 mg.	110 mg.	410 mg.	7,540 IU	.10 mg.	.26 mg.	2.0 mg.	115 mg.
Lettuce, head	22 mg.	25 mg.	.5 mg.	12 mg.	140 mg.	540 IU	.04 mg.	.08 mg.	.2 mg.	8 mg.
Mustard greens	220 mg.	38 mg.	2.9 mg.	48 mg.	450 mg.	7,180 IU	.06 mg.	.18 mg.	.7 mg.	45 mg.
Parsley	193 mg.	84 mg.	4.3 mg.	28 mg.	880 mg.	8,230 IU	.11 mg.	.28 mg.	1.4 mg.	193 mg.
Spinach	81 mg.	55 mg.	3.0 mg.	82 mg.	780 mg.	9,420 IU	.11 mg.	.20 mg.	.6 mg.	59 mg.
Turnip greens	259 mg.	50 mg.	2.4 mg.	10 mg.	440 mg.	9,540 IU	.09 mg.	.46 mg.	.8 mg.	136 mg.

Apple Salad

3 apples, diced, unpeeled
1 cup celery and leaves,
  chopped fine

1 cup pitted chopped dates
1 cup soy granules

Blend with mayonnaise. This is like Waldorf salad, using the soy granules in place of nuts. Serves 4.

Artichoke Salad

1 peeled apple
3 globe artichoke hearts

1 strip of celery
1 small carrot

Dice all these foods into small chunks, and use 2 tablespoons of homemade mayonnaise to stir into mixture. Serves 3.

Asparagus Salad

2 cups thinly sliced, raw tender
  asparagus
2 tablespoons finely sliced green
  onions, including tender tops

¼ cup sliced radishes
  lettuce
⅓ cup homemade French dressing or mayonnaise

Lightly toss asparagus, onions, and radishes. Put mixture on lettuce leaves. Drizzle with dressing. Serve at once. Serves 4.

Avocado Salad

1 tablespoon pure gelatin dissolved in

¼ cup cold water. Melt in
½ cup boiling water.

Cool. Add to:

1 cup pineapple juice
1 cup chopped pineapple
1 peeled and pitted avocado
  (mashed)

½ cup homemade mayonnaise
½ cup chopped nut meats

Caution: Have the pineapple pulp and juice cooked as the raw pineapple destroys the gelatin.

Chill the salad and serve on lettuce. Serves 3 or 4.

Bean and Cabbage Salad

1½ cups cooked beans (soya,
    kidney or other)
¾ teaspoon kelp powder
⅓ cup mayonnaise, homemade
2 tablespoons cider vinegar

½ teaspoon paprika
2 cups shredded cabbage
½ cup chopped celery
¾ cup shredded carrots
2 tablespoons minced onion

Combine the beans, kelp, mayonnaise, vinegar and paprika. Mix in the cabbage, celery, carrots and onion. Chill. Serve on salad greens, garnish with tomato wedges and parsley. Serves 6.

Bean Sprout Salad

2 cups Mung bean sprouts
6 green onions

1 tablespoon of sweet red
    pepper slivers
¼ cup chopped celery

Blend with homemade mayonnaise and serve in lettuce cups. Garnish with rose hips powder or paprika. Serves 4.

Beanery Salad

1 cup kidney beans, cooked and
    drained
1 cup wax beans, cooked and
    drained

1 cup green beans, cooked and
    drained
6 chopped green onions
½ cup diced celery and tops
    fresh herbs

Dress with oil and pure cider vinegar to taste. Serves 6.

Beet Salad (Raw)

Shred 6 or 7 young *beets* on medium shredder. Dress with oil and cider vinegar. Add honey to taste—1 teaspoon to a tablespoon. Arrange in mounds on lettuce leaves. Top with slices or grated hard boiled eggs and chopped fresh dill or parsley. Serves 5.

Beet-Sardine Salad

4 large carrots, diced
1 medium finely chopped onion
1 cup diced sardines
3 cups, beets, diced
  dash cayenne

2 tablespoons vinegar
2 tablespoons vegetable oil
1 tablespoon grated parsley
  flakes
1 teaspoon honey

Combine carrots, onion, sardines and beets. Mix together well the cayenne, vinegar, oil, parsley and honey. Pour over vegetable and fish mixture. Chill for several hours. Mix and serve. Serves 4.

Broccoli Salad

½ cup apple juice
6 tablespoons cider vinegar
2 tablespoons sunflower seed
  oil
¼ cup water

½ teaspoon sea salt
½ teaspoon dried basil leaves
2 10-ounce packages frozen
  broccoli spears
2 hard-cooked eggs, chopped

In jar combine apple juice, vinegar, oil, water, sea salt, basil leaves; shake this dressing well; refrigerate. Cook broccoli; then cool. Now pour some of the dressing over broccoli; refrigerate, covered, tossing occasionally. Just before serving, arrange broccoli on individual salad plates; sprinkle each with some chopped egg. Serves 6.

Broccoli-Meat Salad

2 cups chopped chicory
2 cups chopped lettuce
2 cups cubed or sliced broccoli
  (cooked)
1 cup cubed beef (cooked)
¼ green pepper, chopped

1 celery stalk, chopped
1 tablespoon oil
1 tablespoon vinegar
  garlic
  seasoning

Place all ingredients in bowl and use dressing of your choice. Serves 6.

"C" Salad on Tomato Slices

Shred the following and combine with homemade mayonnaise:

1 large cucumber
1 tablespoon chopped onion
¼ head cabbage

2 carrots
2 tomatoes

Pile mounds of this mixture on tomato slices and garnish with parsley. Keep covered until serving time. You can add protein by putting a hardboiled egg slice on the top of each salad mound. Serves 4.

Cabbage Salad

Shred 2 cups cabbage very fine and add 2 cups unsprayed Thompson seedless grapes or Thompson seedless raisins which have been "plumped" in warm water in a covered dish for several hours. Blend in homemade mayonnaise and keep in a covered dish until serving. Serves 4.

Cabbage-Coconut Salad

2 cups shredded cabbage
2 cups diced cucumbers
½ cup chopped celery

½ cup shredded coconut
sea salt to taste

Mix with homemade mayonnaise dressing. Serve on crisp lettuce. Serves 4.

Cabbage and Fennel Salad

¼ head green cabbage, finely shredded
¼ head red cabbage, finely shredded
4 stalks fennel, cut into Julienne strips

¼ cup chopped black olives, pitted
3 shallots, chopped
1 teaspoon celery seed
sea salt to taste
½ cup olive oil
¼ cup cider vinegar

Combine all ingredients; add seasonings and oil and vinegar. Chill and serve in a large glass salad bowl, with a sprinkling of fresh minced parsley. Serves 4.

Cabbage Delight Salads

Cream Dressing:
This dressing will keep indefinitely in the refrigerator. It is very convenient to have on hand at all times. After you add it to your salad give the salad a few brisk stirs. This fluffs up the dressing.
In blender:

1 egg	1 teaspoon pure vanilla
½ cup honey	¼ teaspoon pure almond extract

Start blender, remove cover and add oil while it is running, until it's thick. The oil should be lying on top. Once you have it this way the longer it runs, the thicker it gets.

1. Slice cabbage and toss with sweet dressing.
2. Slice cabbage and toss with dressing and sliced bananas. Bananas and cabbage are a good flavor combination.
3. Sliced cabbage, banana, apple, raisins and nuts. Be sure to give these all a good brisk stir to cream the dressing.
4. Sliced cabbage, banana, apple slices (unpeeled, if organic, for red garnishing) with dressing. Allow ½ cup cabbage per serving.

Cabbage-Raisin Salad

1 small head of cabbage, finely shredded	2 teaspoons sea salt
½ cup seedless raisins	4 tablespoons homemade mayonnaise
2 tablespoons honey	1 tablespoon cider vinegar

Combine cabbage, raisins, honey, and sea salt in large covered bowl; let stand one hour to blend flavors. Drain off any liquid.

Mix homemade mayonnaise and vinegar in a cup; spoon into cabbage mixture; toss to mix well. Serves 4.

Cabbage Salad Supreme

2 cups raw green cabbage, chopped fine

1 cup purple cabbage, chopped fine

1 cup chopped fresh pineapple

4 oz. plain yogurt

⅛ teaspoon pure vanilla, if desired

Mix all ingredients and serve. Serves 6.

Cabbage, Walnut and Apple Slaw

6 cups finely shredded dark green cabbage

½ cup coarsely chopped walnuts

1 cup coarsely chopped tart apples

¾ teaspoon sea salt

¾ teaspoon ground ginger

½ cup homemade mayonnaise

1 tablespoon apple cider vinegar

1 tablespoon pure honey

Mix together cabbage, walnuts, apples, sea salt and ginger. Place in a large glass bowl. Combine mayonnaise with vinegar and honey and pour over the slaw. Toss lightly. Chill in refrigerator and serve cold. Garnish with parsley flakes, if desired. Serves 6.

Cardinal Salad

2 cups cooked red kidney beans

½ cup diced celery and leaves

1 small onion, minced

4 chopped hardboiled eggs

1 tablespoon rose hips as garnish

½ cup chopped nuts and sunflower seeds

Enough homemade mayonnaise to blend. Keep covered until serving time. Serves 4.

Carrot Salad

2 carrots

2 apples

½ cup raisins

½ cup yogurt or 2 tablespoons homemade mayonnaise for dressing

Grate carrots and apples together in a bowl. Add raisins and dressing and stir. Serves 4.

Celery Hearts Salad

Dice Pascal celery hearts, green onions and green peppers into a small glass dish. Dress with salad oil, honey and pure apple cider vinegar. Cover tightly until serving time.

Celery Root Salad

Steam one celery root until tender. When cold, peel and grate on medium grater enough for 2½ cups. If any remains, it can be saved for soup or stew or a different salad.

2½ cups grated celery root (medium grater)
½ cup grated fresh carrot (small grater)

¼ cup small pieces of green onion tops (cut with kitchen scissors)
2 chopped hard-cooked eggs
¾ cup homemade mayonnaise

Mix in order given. Serves 4.

Chicken Salad

Cook a 3 or 4 pound chicken, adding fresh herbs and parsley to the cooking water, and sea kelp the last 10 minutes of boiling time. Cool the chicken, then remove from the bones. Put the bones back in the broth and simmer a few minutes, then strain out the herbs and bones, and save this broth. When the chicken has become solid, cube it, putting all scraps in the broth for chicken soup or creamed chicken. Now is the time to make the chicken salad.

5 cups cubed chicken
2 cups diced celery and tops
1 medium minced onion
1 green bell pepper, slivered
1 red bell pepper, slivered

1 cup walnut halves
1 or 1½ cups homemade mayonnaise
1 tablespoon sharp cider vinegar

Blend the ingredients and put in a large casserole which can be covered. Garnish with salad greens or parsley and hardboiled egg slices, and sprinkle paprika over the top. Keep covered until eating time, and cover tightly any that is left.

Chicken and Rice Salad in Tomato Cups

2 tablespoons sunflower seed oil
2 tablespoons apple cider vinegar
1 teaspoon sea salt
1 teaspoon curry powder
1½ cups cooked brown rice

1½ cups cubed cooked chicken
1 cup chopped celery
2 tablespoons chopped green pepper
¾ cup homemade mayonnaise
6 fresh ripe tomatoes
lettuce

Combine oil, vinegar, onion, sea salt, and curry powder. Toss with rice, mixing well. Chill at least 1 hour. Meanwhile, peel tomatoes. Remove stem ends and starting at the top, cut tomatoes into fourths, cutting about ⅔ of the way down. Chill until ready to serve. Just before serving, add rest of ingredients to rice mixture. Blend well. Serve in tomato cups on lettuce. Serves 6.

Chinese Cabbage Salad

2 cups chopped Chinese cabbage
1 cup diced celery and leaves

½ cup cooked mushrooms
½ red bell pepper slivered

Blend with homemade mayonnaise, add supplements and put individual helpings in covered individual containers. Serves 6.

Christmas Bell Salad

3 cups grated raw beets
½ cup honey

¼ cup pure cider vinegar

Add a pinch of cloves, blend and let stand in a covered dish a half hour to season. Then dissolve a tablespoon of pure gelatin in

¼ cup cold water, then melt it in 1 cup of boiling water. Cool and add to the beet mixture. Pour it in an oiled round mold. When ready to serve, unmold on salad greens. Take a sharp knife and round out the 2 opposite sides until you have a shape like a bell. Serves 6.

Christmas Tree Salad

Shred salad greens, and the darker greens are prettiest, and dress with vinegar, oil and honey. Arrange them on a platter in the shape of a Christmas tree. "Trim" it with small pieces of red pepper and tomatoes. Then shred on fresh herbs if you have them, and chives and celery tops. This is a task the children will love to do.

Cole Slaw

3 cups finely shredded cabbage
1 cup grated carrots
½ cup drained crushed pine-
    apple (unsweetened)
½ cup chopped walnuts
1 tablespoon toasted sesame
    seeds

Combine above ingredients with dressing:

⅔ cup homemade mayon-
    naise
2 tablespoons apple cider
    vinegar
1 tablespoon honey

Serves 6.

Company Salad

2 cups fresh cooked peas,
    drained
4 good size stalks celery,
    diced
6 hard cooked eggs, sliced
½ cup or so of leftover white
    chicken or turkey meat, diced
⅓ cup homemade mayonnaise
    lettuce

Lightly toss peas, celery and eggs, and stir in the mayonnaise. Serve on lettuce leaves. Serves 6.

Cranberry Grape Salad

1 pound cranberries, ground   2 cups honey
½ pound tokay grapes, pitted

Grind cranberries and add honey. Let set for two hours and add pitted grapes and serve. Serves 6.

Cranberry Nut Salad

3 cups raw cranberries, chopped   1 banana
  fine   ¾ cup honey
1 cup whole English walnut
  meats

Chop or grind the cranberries, put in a covered dish and add the honey. Refrigerate until serving time when you add the nuts and banana. Serves 6.

Crazy Cranberry Mold

1 quart cranberries   1 cup chopped pecan meats
3½ cups boiling water   1 cup diced pineapple
1 pound organic, raw honey   1 cup white grapes
2 tablespoons gelatin, softened
  in ½ cup cold water

Cook cranberries in boiling water until berries burst. Add honey. Soften gelatin in cold water; add to hot mixture. Let stand until cold. Add the pecans, pineapple, and grapes.

Turn into molds, chill, and invert on crisp lettuce. Serve with homemade mayonnaise on top. Serves 6-8.

Crunchy Salad

1 cup unpeeled diced apples   ½ cup chopped pineapple
  (organically grown)   ½ cup raisins
1 cup diced bananas   ½ cup coarsely chopped pecans
1 tablespoon lemon juice   ⅓ cup homemade mayonnaise

Put apples, bananas and lemon juice in a large bowl and toss. Add pineapple, raisins, and pecans. Toss again lightly. Add mayonnaise and toss until mixed thoroughly. Serves 6.

Dandelion Salad

Young tender dandelion leaves make a wonderful salad, not only tasty but very high in vitamins and minerals.

Serve them "straight" with honey and pure vinegar.

Serve them with green onions, lettuce, bell peppers, tomatoes and French dressing.

Serve them with hardboiled eggs and homemade mayonnaise. Add herbs.

Easter Lily Salad

6 hardboiled eggs
2 cups shredded cabbage
1 chopped red pepper
1 cup cooked stringbeans

1 cup bean sprouts
6 green onions, cut fine
¼ cup celery leaves, chopped
1 cucumber, optional

Dribble 2 tablespoons pure cider vinegar over the vegetables, moisten with homemade mayonnaise and place individual servings on salad greens. Cut the tops off the hardboiled eggs, then cut narrow petals by slicing through the white only from the top nearly to the bottom. Spread the "petals" outward into a lily, leaving the yolk intact in the center. Use this lily on the top of each salad serving and garnish with chopped peanuts. Serves 6.

Easy Eating Combo

Blend together the following:

1 cucumber (skin too)
½ bell pepper
celery leaves or stalks

outer cabbage leaf
fresh herbs

Put a tomato slice on a salad plate, then cover it with the vegetable mush (drained) from the blender. Dress with a dab of your own mayonnaise, or a few sprinkles of homemade French dressing. Sprinkle on a few pignolia nuts for a garnish. Serves 3.

Egg Salad

5 hardboiled eggs
1 small onion
1 tablespoon celery leaves
2 tablespoons green pepper

1 teaspoon minced parsley
1 teaspoon honey
1 tablespoon sea kelp

Chop the above ingredients together until quite fine. (The onion, celery and pepper should be partly chopped before the other ingredients are added.) Then moisten with enough homemade mayonnaise to hold together and add a dash of cumin for zesty flavor. Chill in a covered dish. Serve in lettuce cups with matzos. The salad can be enhanced by dusting with paprika for color. Serves 4.

Egg and Mushroom Salad

6 hard-cooked eggs
¼ pound fresh mushrooms, sautéed in safflower oil
1 small diced onion, sautéed in safflower oil

1 tablespoon chopped fresh dill
6 ripe olives, pitted
sea salt, to taste

Put all ingredients in a chopping bowl, and chop to desired consistency. Add additional safflower oil, if necessary. Refrigerate and serve on crisp dark green lettuce leaves, surrounded by quartered fresh tomatoes. Serves 4.

Filled Avocado

2 medium avocados, cut in half, remove stones

1 cup fresh pineapple, cut to bite-size pieces
1 pint fresh strawberries

Minted French Dressing:

3 tablespoons salad oil
1 tablespoon apple vinegar
½ teaspoon sea salt
¼ teaspoon paprika

1 teaspoon honey
2 tablespoons minced fresh mint
leaves

Put salad dressing ingredients into jar with tightfitting lid. Shake vigorously to mix. Sprinkle one teaspoon dressing over each half of ripe avocado. Fill centers of ripe avocados with pineapple pieces and strawberries. Dress fruit with freshly shaken dressing and serve either as a salad course or combination dessert-salad. Serves 4.

Fruit Salad Mold

1 pound fresh cranberries, stemmed and washed
1 whole unsprayed orange
2 unsprayed apples, cored but not peeled
½ cup local nuts

½ cup sunflower seeds
1 tablespoon unflavored gelatin
½ cup honey
½ cup each boiling and cold water

Dissolve the gelatin in the cold water, then melt it in the half cup of boiling water. Set it aside to cool. Grind the cranberries, apples, orange (skin and all except seeds), nuts and seeds, catching all of the juice, which you cover immediately to preserve the elusive vitamin C. Add the honey to the ground ingredients, mix, cover and let stand until the gelatin is cool. Mix the gelatin into the juice, add it to the fruit and nuts, pour all into an oiled mold and chill. Unmold on salad greens. Serves 6.

Garbanzo Salad

2 cups chopped savoy cabbage
1 cup chick peas, drained
½ cup purple Italian onion chopped or sliced fine
¼ cup chopped pimiento

½ teaspoon sweet basil
sea salt to taste
½ cup pure cider vinegar
⅓ cup olive oil
1 tablespoon honey
1 tablespoon mayonnaise

Combine and serve. Serves 4-6.

Gala Garbanzo Salad

2 cups cooked garbanzos
4 sliced hard boiled eggs
1 cup diced celery and tops

6 chopped green onions
1 cup pignolias

Moisten with plenty of homemade mayonnaise and serve on salad greens. Garnish with homemade French dressing for added flavor and piquancy. Serves 4.

German Potato Salad

3 medium potatoes boiled in jackets
6 hard boiled eggs
1 medium onion minced fine
½ teaspoon sea salt

2 cups dandelions washed and cut
¼ cup soy oil
¼ cup cider vinegar
¼ cup water

Dice potatoes and hard boiled eggs, add minced onion, sea salt and dandelions. Then add vinegar and water to oil and bring to a boil. Pour over potato mixture and stir lightly. Nice served in a lettuce-lined bowl. Serves 5.

Green Bean Salad

Cook 2 pounds *green beans* in small amount of water. Slice two small *onions* very thin into a large bowl. Add 2 tablespoons *olive oil*, ¼ cup *cider vinegar* and one cup *water*. When the beans are done, put them into this mixture and turn several times to coat all of the beans. Prepare a day or two before serving, and stir occasionally. Drain well before serving. Serves 6.

Green Soy Salad

If you pick these young enough, you can use them raw, but otherwise they need to be steamed until tender, then cooled.

2 cups green soybeans
2 cups sliced cucumbers

1 cup chopped Chinese cabbage
1 minced garlic (optional)

Blend ingredients, add soy mayonnaise and serve in lettuce cups with shredded carrots for garnish. Serves 6.

Jellied Meat Salad

2 tablespoons pure gelatin
1¾ cups water, divided
1 cup beef broth (or chicken)
1½ tablespoons lemon juice
1 teaspoon grated onion

1 cup finely diced cooked meat
½ cup diced celery
½ cup cooked peas (organically grown)

Sprinkle gelatin on ½ cup of the water to soften. Add beef broth, place over low heat and stir until gelatin is dissolved. Remove from heat and add remaining water, lemon juice and onions. Chill to unbeaten egg white consistency, fold in meat, celery and peas. Turn into a 3-cup mold and chill until firm, cut into slices, and serve on crisp lettuce. Serves 4.

Jellied Vegetable Salad

3 medium sized beets—cooked with skins on, then peeled and sliced
1 small onion, sliced thinly

½ green pepper, diced
½ cucumber, sliced
3 stalks celery, diced

Arrange vegetables in layers in a dish.

1 package gelatin (dissolved in 1 pint of fluid)

1 heaping tablespoon unpasteurized honey dissolved in ¾ cup warm water
1¼ cups cider vinegar

Stir and pour over vegetables. Set in refrigerator.

Kidney Bean Salad

Drain cooked kidney beans, and for 2 cups, add:

4 hard boiled eggs, chopped
2 tablespoons minced onion

1 bell pepper, slivered
½ cup chopped celery and leaves

Homemade mayonnaise to moisten.
Store in a covered dish.

Minted Cucumber Salad

1 teaspoon dried mint
½ teaspoon garlic powder
1 cup unflavored yogurt

1 large cucumber, peeled and
sliced thin
dark green lettuce leaves
4 red radishes, chopped

Mix mint and garlic powder into yogurt. Distribute cucumber slices on crisp leaves of lettuce and pour yogurt on top. Garnish with chopped radishes. Serve cold. Serves 2-3.

Nasturtium Salad

Tear up the crisped salad greens and a few nasturtium leaves and stems cut very fine. Add slivers of young carrot, dress with oil, vinegar and honey, arrange in a salad bowl and garnish with nasturtium blossoms, which can be eaten along with the salad.

Lentil Salad

Soak one cup dry lentils in two cups water for several hours. Simmer until tender (most of the water will be absorbed by this time). While still hot, pour over French dressing made of:

3 tablespoons weak vinegar
3 tablespoons oil

½ teaspoon powdered dill
¼ teaspoon curry

Toss in lightly with a fork. Let stand to marinate for a few hours or overnight. Place in refrigerator when cool.

Toss in:

½ cup chopped celery
2 tablespoons chopped green
pepper
1 medium onion chopped

3 tablespoons ground sunflower
seeds
½ cup homemade mayonnaise

Pickled beets make a suitable garnish.
Serves 5-6.

Molded Green Salad

1 envelope unflavored gelatin congealed in ¼ cup of cold water. Add 1 cup of boiling water and stir until the gelatin is completely dissolved. Add 1 teaspoon dried thyme and let this stand for 30 minutes to release the herb flavor. Add 1 cup of cold water plus ¼ cup honey and ¼ cup vinegar. Stir until the honey is dissolved, then put the mixture in the refrigerator until it is chilled but not set.

Add:

1 cup shredded fresh lettuce	1 green pepper slivered
½ cup chopped celery and leaves	1 home-canned pimiento, slivered
6 green onions chopped fine	

Chill until firm in an oiled mold, then unmold on a bed of salad greens. This is a beautiful salad with the pimiento slivers in the green vegetables. Fresh herbs are even better, but they should be added with the vegetables and not steeped in the hot mixture. Any spring greens may be used for added vitamins. Serves 6.

Raw Vegetable Gelatin Salad

1 carrot, raw	1 handful celery greens (2½ celery stalks)
4 medium or 6 small fresh raw beets, cut	1 handful china peas (edible pod peas)
1 teaspoon undistilled apple cider vinegar (or lemon juice)	2 tablespoons soaked seedless raisins with juice
2 medium oranges	some parsley

Put all in a blender with some pineapple juice.

In a big bowl have ready the unflavored plain gelatin. (3 tablespoons to 2 cups of hot water.) Put all in bowl, refrigerate and eat the next day. Serves 4.

Salad Boats

Hollow out cucumbers. Heap the "boats" with a mixture of tuna, or chicken, chopped ripe olives, ripe green olives, chopped boiled eggs, diced celery, chopped pickles and mayonnaise. Sprinkle with sunflower seeds. Serve on lettuce leaves.

Sauerkraut Salad

2 cups sauerkraut, drained	1 cup chopped green pepper
2 cups bean sprouts, drained	1 cup honey
1 cup chopped onion	½ cup apple cider vinegar
1 cup chopped celery	¼ cup water

Mix sauerkraut, bean sprouts, celery, onions, and green pepper. Cook honey, vinegar and water for 5 minutes; cool, then pour over the kraut mixture. Cool in refrigerator for several hours before serving. Serves 6.

Red and Green Fruit Salad

In a fancy dish which can be covered, put thawed and drained red cherries, watermelon balls, and Thompson seedless grapes (light green). Add pineapple wedges from the freezer if desired. Dice fresh mint leaves over the salad and keep covered until serving time.

Red and Green Salad

Grate young beets (skins, too) in one side of a sectional dish and shred young green cabbage in the other side. Make Cucumber Dressing and mix with each vegetable. Keep covered until serving time. Garnish with carrot curls.

Salata (Mixed Salad From the Balkans)

1 bunch watercress, chopped fine	2 green peppers, cut fine
1 small head of lettuce, shredded	3 tomatoes, sliced
	10 black olives
6 green onions, chopped fine	½ cup olive oil
1 sliced cucumber	¼ cup sharp pure vinegar

Toss, and let stand in a covered dish in the refrigerator for 30 minutes before serving. Serves 4.

Sauerkraut and Apple Combo

2 cups sauerkraut
2 cups diced eating apples

1 cup seedless raisins
½ cup mayonnaise

Wash sauerkraut well by placing in a sieve and running cold water through it. Combine kraut, apples and raisins; chill well. Serve on lettuce. Garnish with mayonnaise. For added color, leave the peeling on the apples. Serves 6.

Nut Salad

1 cup chopped apples
1 cup English walnut halves

½ cup plumped raisins
½ cup chopped sunflower seeds

Blend, add dressing and serve on salad greens. Serves 4.

Pickled Egg Platter

Have some leftover beet pickle juice on hand. Cook eggs hard and shell, and drop them into the jar of juice about 24 hours ahead of time. They will turn a nice red color. Remove them, drain, slice and serve on a bed of salad greens, sprinkle with paprika and garnish any other way you like.

Pretty Sprout

1 pound bean sprouts
   liquid from pint of homemade
   pickled beets
2 tablespoons minced onion
2 tablespoons wheat germ

¼ cup sunflower seeds coarsely
   chopped or use sunflower
   meal
1 hard cooked egg, sieved or
   mashed with fork
   homemade mayonnaise

Marinate sprouts all day in beet liquid. Drain well. Add remaining ingredients except egg, which is to be used as garnish. The beet liquid makes the sprouts a pretty color and also gives them a good flavor. Serves 4.

Parsnip Salad

1 medium-sized parsnip, scraped and grated
½ cup celery, stalk and leaves finely cut
1 apple, grated
1 tablespoon minced onion
1 tablespoon sunflower seeds

Mix with your favorite salad dressing and serve on lettuce leaves. Serves 2.

Pineapple-Green Pepper Slaw

¾ cup mayonnaise
2 cups cabbage, shredded very fine
1 medium sized green pepper, minced
1 cup finely chopped fresh or frozen pineapple
12 slivered almonds or 2 tablespoons almond meal
12 sprigs parsley, minced
1 clove garlic, grated very fine
a sprinkling or two of sea salt

Pre-chill vegetables and fruit. Toss all ingredients in a large bowl except the almonds. Serve on individual salad plates. Garnish with almonds. Serves 4.

Protein Bean Salad

3 cups cooked cranberry or kidney beans
1 cup bean or alfalfa sprouts
3 chopped sweet pickles
1 tablespoon chopped chives or green onions
1 chopped green pepper
3 hardboiled eggs, sliced
1 teaspoon minced parsley

Blend ingredients and add enough homemade mayonnaise to moisten. Serve on salad greens and garnish with celery seeds and onion rings which have been marinated in pickle juice, preferably beet pickles. Serves 4-6.

Soybean Sprout Salad

2 cups sprouted soy or Mung beans
2 tablespoons chopped onion
4 chopped hardboiled eggs

slivers of red and green peppers
½ cup English walnuts

Blend all of the ingredients except the pepper slivers, add Soy Mayonnaise and pile the salad on salad greens. Garnish with the pepper slivers and paprika. Serves 4.

Springtime Salad

2 cups young tender dandelion leaves, washed clean
4 chopped hard boiled eggs

½ cup diced celery and leaves
3 young green onions, diced

Blend with oil, honey and vinegar or homemade mayonnaise and serve in individual salad dishes. Garnish with strips of home-canned pimientos or red bell peppers. Serves 6.

Sparkling Chicken Salad

2½ cups cold chicken, diced
1 cup white grapes
½ cup shredded almonds
2 tablespoons minced parsley
1 cup celery, chopped fine

1 teaspoon sea salt
1¼ tablespoons gelatin
4 tablespoons water
½ cup chicken stock
1 cup homemade mayonnaise

Mix chicken, celery, grapes, almonds, parsley, and season with sea salt. Soak gelatin in cold water 5 minutes; then dissolve over boiling water. Add gelatin and chicken stock to mayonnaise and stir until mixture begins to thicken. Fold in chicken mixture. Pack in molds. If desired, place sliced hardcooked eggs in the bottom of the molds. Unmold on a bed of greens. Serves 6.

Sprouted Lentil Salad

2 cups sprouted lentils, cooked, but still crispy (5 minutes or so).
Serve with warmed homemade soy mayonnaise made as follows:

In a blender place:

1 cup water   ½ teaspoon sea salt
½ cup soy flour

As it blends add cold-pressed oil until the mixture thickens (hole almost fills). Add juice of one fresh lemon just before you stop machine. Serves 4.

Steamed Vegetable Mold

1 cup onions, sliced and sautéed
1 cup tomatoes, chopped fine
3 eggs, beaten
¼ cup almonds, ground
¼ cup walnuts, ground
½ cup wheat germ
3 tablespoons soy flour
¼ cup soy grits, soaked in
¼ cup water or stock
1 tablespoon parsley, minced
½ teaspoon rosemary
½ teaspoon sea salt
3 tablespoons brewer's yeast

Mix all ingredients in blender. Place in oiled mold. Cover tightly. Steam for 1½ hours. Let stand 5 minutes. Unmold carefully. Chill. When cold, can be sliced and served on lettuce. Serves 6.

Stuffed Cucumber Salad

3 cucumbers
2 tomatoes
½ cup celery
1 tablespoon onion, chopped
sea salt
homemade mayonnaise

Peel chilled cucumbers. Cut in halves, lengthwise. Remove center pulp. Peel and chop tomatoes. Mix cucumber pulp with chopped onion, celery, sea salt and mayonnaise. Mix well and fill cucumber halves. Arrange on lettuce leaves and garnish with parsley. Serves 6.

"Sunday Salad"

Cut 1 head of lettuce into bite-sized chunks.

Peel 2 unsprayed, organically-grown oranges. Seed the segments, then cut each one in thirds.

Peel and slice 2 bananas. They should be ripe enough so that they are spotted with brown.

Blend above ingredients, and use just enough homemade mayonnaise to coat them nicely.

Serve in a deep salad bowl and garnish with rose hips powder. Serves 6.

String Bean-Cauliflower Salad

1 pound fresh string beans, cut
into 1-inch pieces
6 cauliflower flowerets
1 large red onion, minced
6 ripe olives, pitted and chopped

¼ cup cider vinegar
⅓ cup olive oil
3 ripe tomatoes, cut into
quarters

Cook string beans and cauliflower until barely tender. Drain off liquid. Mix together onion, oil, olives and vinegar and pour over the beans and cauliflower. Arrange on a platter of crisp dark green lettuce leaves and garnish with tomato quarters. Chill in refrigerator and serve. Serves 4-6.

Stuffed Prune Salad

1 pound large pitted prunes
1 cup shredded apple
¾ cup homemade mayonnaise

1 cup chopped nuts
Romaine lettuce leaves

Mix the apples, nuts and mayonnaise well. Stuff the large prunes with this mixture.

Serve on bed of large Romaine lettuce leaves. Serves 4-6.

Sweetbreads-Chicken Salad

4 sweetbreads
2 cups cooked, cubed chicken
2 tablespoons finely chopped
  green pepper
¼ cup chopped pitted black
  olives

¾ cup homemade mayonnaise
1 tablespoon fresh lemon juice
¼ teaspoon pure honey
½ teaspoon onion juice
½ teaspoon sea salt

Drop sweetbreads in boiling water to cover; lower heat and simmer for about 25 minutes or until tender. Chill in refrigerator and break apart into small pieces. Combine sweetbreads with cubed chicken; add remaining ingredients and mix until completely blended. Serve in a large glass bowl lined with crisp, dark green lettuce leaves. Serves 4.

Sweet Potato Salad

2 cups cubed cooked sweet
  potatoes
1 cup diced celery
1 cup chopped apple

⅓ cup chopped nuts
2 teaspoons honey
½ teaspoon kelp
¼ cup homemade mayonnaise

Combine potatoes, celery, apple and nuts in bowl. Add honey and kelp to mayonnaise, mix well and pour over potato mixture. Toss lightly with fork. Serves 4.

Turkey Salad Bowl

1 cup diced white meat of
  cooked turkey
1 cup diced celery
½ cup chopped raw cauliflower
1 medium sized chopped carrot

¼ cup diced green pepper
2 chopped hard cooked eggs
1 bunch lettuce
8 sprigs parsley
4 green olives

Dressing of mixed cold-pressed oils:

3 tablespoons soy oil
3 tablespoons safflower oil
1 tablespoon lemon juice
4 tablespoons wild red cherry
  juice

1 clove of garlic grated very
  fine
3 tablespoons sesame oil
3 tablespoons corn oil
¼ teaspoon sea salt

Combine oils, lemon juice, cherry juice, garlic and sea salt in large bowl. Mix thoroughly.

Add all other ingredients except olives. Toss salad lightly but thoroughly.

Divide into 4 salad bowls and top each salad with olive. Serves 4.

Sweet Corn Salad

2 cups raw tender sweet corn	2 green onions, chopped
½ red bell pepper or pimiento, chopped fine	homemade peanut butter
	4 tomatoes or green peppers

Blend the first three ingredients, then add enough peanut butter to make a thick mixture. Leaving the stem on a tomato or green pepper for a handle, slice off the top, hollow it out, and fill with the Corn Salad. Put the lid back on and wrap tightly. Serves 4.

Tomato Aspic

2 cups homecanned tomato juice	1 rounded tablespoon gelatin dissolved in ¼ cup cold water

Heat the tomato juice very hot, add the gelatin and stir until it is melted. Cool and add the following:

1 teaspoon grated onion	1 tablespoon chopped green pepper
1 teaspoon dried basil	
1 stalk of celery and leaves (chopped)	1 teaspoon each of vinegar and honey
	1 teaspoon kelp

Pour in an oiled ring mold. When set, unmold on a bed of salad greens and fill the center with sprouts which have been mixed with nuts, sunflower seeds and homemade mayonnaise. Garnish the sprouts with slivers of red pepper and powdered rose hips. Serves 4.

Tuna Salad

2 cups flaked tuna, chilled	1 cup diced avocado
1 cup of celery, chopped fine	

Homemade mayonnaise to blend the ingredients together. Serve on salad greens and garnish with hardboiled egg slices sprinkled with rose hips. Serves 6.

Turkey-Stuffed Apple Salad

6 large apples
2 cups cooked, diced turkey
½ teaspoon sage
¼ cup oil

½ teaspoon sea salt
1 tablespoon chopped pimiento
2 tablespoons chopped ripe olives

Peel apples one third down. Remove core and hollow out the center well. Combine turkey, sage, oil, sea salt, pimiento and olives thoroughly. Stuff apples, arrange in baking dish with enough water to cover the bottom. Bake at 350°F. for about 45 minutes, basting often. Serves 6.

Two-Tone Cole Slaw

Use green cabbage and red cabbage for this gorgeous salad. It is served in a transparent bowl, so that the colors show up. For the bottom portion, shave red cabbage and add diced cucumbers, and blend with the dressing. The top portion is made of green cabbage and red kidney beans (cooked and drained) and the dressing. Blend them separately, of course. The dressing is made of homemade mayonnaise thinned down with a tablespoon each of oil, honey and vinegar. Herbed vinegar adds to the flavor greatly.

Yam Salad

⅓ cup homemade mayonnaise (tart and seasoned with dill)
2 tablespoons chopped green pepper
1 tablespoon chopped onion
½ cup chopped celery

¼ cup chopped walnuts or pecans
2½ cups cooked yams cut into small pieces
1 cup apple in small thin pieces

Mix the ingredients in the order given. Serves 4.

Salad Dressings and Dips

Salad dressings increase the nutritional value of your greens. Vegetable oils are the richest food sources of the unsaturated fatty acids, which help your body to use cholesterol properly. What kind of salad oil is best? Sunflower seed oil, corn oil, cottonseed oil, peanut oil, olive oil—all contain about the same amount of unsaturated fatty acids.

There are hints in medical literature that olive oil might be more than just tasty. The free use of it might help to explain the mysterious fact that, while the Latins are highly emotional, hard-working people who, as a rule, eat highly seasoned foods, the incidence of peptic ulcers and hardening of the arteries is lower in Latin countries than in Britain and the United States.

We suspect that other vegetable oils have much the same effect as olive oil has on the intestines, coating the mucous membranes and acting to prevent, perhaps even cure ulcers. We do know that other oils have a definite capacity for actually reducing the cholesterol level of the blood. Safflower oil heads the list in this department.

The evidence favoring the use of all unsaturated fats in the diet is abundant. So, while olive oil has a special flavor that makes it appealing to many, use corn oil, safflower oil, peanut oil, or one of the others, if you prefer.

Recipes for Dressings and Dips

Basic Salad Dressing

1 egg	3 tablespoons honey
⅓ cup cider vinegar	1 cup cold-pressed oil—sun-
1 tablespoon paprika	flower seed and corn combined
1 teaspoon kelp	or any good bland oil
1 clove garlic	

Blend egg in blender at low speed for about one minute. Stop and add other ingredients except oil. Blend these for about one minute, then while blender is still running, remove cover and add oil. Blend for a few seconds.

Almond-Banana Dressing

Tender green peas are delicious eaten right from the pod or mixed with almond-banana dressing.

Mash a ripe banana with a fork until creamy and smooth; add same amount of almond butter and thin with half as much cool water. When well beaten, add two tablespoonsful mayonnaise and a teaspoonful honey and beat again. As a variation, try peanut butter or tahini which is sesame butter.

Cucumber Dressing

½ cup grated cucumber
½ cup yogurt
1 tablespoon sharp cider vinegar
1 tablespoon honey

1 teaspoon sea kelp
1 mashed hardboiled egg
1 teaspoon minced onion
1 teaspoon shredded fresh marjoram

Mix ingredients and keep in a covered jar.

Emerald Dressing

1 cup soy oil
⅓ cup salad vinegar
¼ cup chopped onion
¼ cup minced parsley

2 tablespoons finely chopped green peppers
2 teaspoons honey
1 teaspoon sea salt
½ teaspoon paprika

Combine all ingredients in jar or blender. Cover and set aside for an hour. Shake 5 minutes or blend thoroughly before serving. Makes about 1½ cups of dressing. Nice with seafood or tossed green salads.

French Dressing

1 cup oil
1 cup tomato juice or two or three fresh tomatoes
½ cup honey

½ cup pure apple vinegar
½ tablespoon sea salt
½ tablespoon paprika
1 small onion cut up

Put all in blender and when blended pour over fresh greens, for a fresh and delicious salad.

Herbed Oil

Keep a bottle of sunflower seed, safflower or peanut oil to which you have added pinches of the following dry herbs: basil, sage, marjoram, oregano, cumin, fennel, tarragon and crushed bay leaves.

Add minced onion or garlic if you like either flavor. You can strain out the herbs after a few days and have the oil ready for instant use.

Low Cal Dressing

½ cup homemade tomato soup
¼ cup pure cider vinegar
1 teaspoon celery seeds

honey to taste
1 teaspoon kelp

Mix thoroughly.

Marrow Dressing

Ask for shank beef bones at your meat counter, and have them cut in short lengths. Keep very cold until used. Scrape out all of the marrow from both ends of each bone and mix it with your own mayonnaise. It gives a lovely pink color and actually adds to the flavor, too. You can melt it over hot water and use it for the oil in French dressing too, but it isn't very practical as it should be served warm, and tends to wilt the salad. Much better to use it cold in mayonnaise type dressing. It can also be used in soups.

Three Oils Salad Dressing

⅔ cup safflower oil
3 tablespoons pure olive oil
1 tablespoon peanut oil
¼ cup apple cider vinegar
1 heaping teaspoon parsley flakes

½ teaspoon sea salt
1 teaspoon honey
dash of garlic powder
dash of paprika

Put all ingredients in a glass jar with a screw top and keep in the refrigerator until used up. Shake thoroughly before each use.

Mayonnaise

Beat together with electric beater (high speed):

4 egg yolks
1 teaspoon mustard
¼ cup honey

⅛ teaspoon paprika
¼ cup cider vinegar

Continue beating while adding 4 cups salad oil, at first drop by drop, gradually increasing amount as mixture thickens.

Slowly add another ¼ cup cider vinegar. Beat well. Keep refrigerated.

Chives-Lemon Mayonnaise

1 large egg
¾ teaspoon sea salt
¾ teaspoon dried chives or
2 tablespoons chopped fresh chives

¼ teaspoon paprika
2 tablespoons fresh lemon juice
2 teaspoons apple cider vinegar
1 cup oil (cold-pressed)

Break the egg into the bowl of an electric blender. Add remaining ingredients except the oil and blend over low speed until smooth. Continue blending and add oil in a fine stream until oil is completely absorbed into the remaining ingredients and mixture is thick and smooth. Transfer to a screw-top jar and keep in refrigerator.

Potato Mayonnaise

3 egg yolks
¾ cup pure olive oil (cold-pressed)

juice of 1 lemon
sea salt, to taste
1 small boiled potato, mashed

Beat egg yolks until thick. Add oil by drops, beating constantly. Gradually add lemon juice. Add sea salt and mashed potato and beat until mixture is very smooth. Place in a glass screw-top jar and refrigerate until ready to use. Keep jar in refrigerator until contents are used up. This mayonnaise is delicious on fish or cooked vegetables.

Soy Mayonnaise

¾ cup water
¾ cup soya bean powder
1 tablespoon honey
½ teaspoon sea salt

¼ cup lemon juice or cider
    vinegar
½ cup vegetable oil
1 teaspoon lecithin (liquid)

Stir soya bean powder into oil. Add other ingredients slowly, stirring continuously. Can be heated for a hot dressing.

Dip Base

In blender:

2 hard cooked eggs
1 cup water
1 cup cooked brown rice

1 tablespoon each of cider
    vinegar and honey
2 teaspoons kelp

Blend until very smooth. Ingredients can be hot or cold. When smooth add 1 cup oil and blend in.
Pour into bowl and flavor to your taste.

Easy Mayonnaise Dip

In blender:

1 egg or 2 egg yolks
½ cup cider vinegar

½ cup honey
2 teaspoons kelp or sea salt

Start blender and remove cover. While blender is running, pour corn oil in a steady stream down the middle until the ingredients start to thicken and the oil lies on the top. Blend until thick and heavy. Now add color to it with bits of red and green pepper, parsley, celery, pickles, etc. Put this in a bowl in the center of the platter, or for a novelty, hollow out a pepper or vegetable and fill that with the dip.

Meats

Meat in Your Diet

Why is meat such an important food? Perhaps the outstanding reason is that it is a complete protein, which means that meat contains all the amino acids which we human beings need, but cannot manufacture inside our bodies. These "essential amino acids" must be present in our food since that is our only source for them.

All vegetables contain some of the essential amino acids, and for those skilled enough in nutrition, it is possible to plan meals that consist entirely of vegetables, yet include all the essential amino acids. But this requires considerable knowledge, patience and care in planning each meal. You cannot make up at lunchtime the essential amino acids that were lacking at breakfast. All must be eaten at the same time to achieve the proper effect, nutritionally speaking.

Basically, our bodies are made of protein. To be healthy we must eat enough of the right protein to repair and replace the cells that are constantly breaking down and wearing out.

Vitamins in Meat

Another valuable food element in meat is its vitamin content. All meats, but especially the organ meats, are high in B vitamins. Different kinds of meat vary in their B content but, as you can see in the accompanying chart, all rank high. The B vitamins that have been removed from starches such as white flour and white sugar during their processing must be supplied somewhere in the diet, for they are necessary for the proper digestion of the carbohydrates. In America, where refined carbohydrates make up so much of the diet, meat becomes doubly important.

Glance at the tables below, which show the vitamin and mineral content of the various meats. The organ meats contain more nutrients than other cuts. Make certain that you serve some organ meat at least once a week—oftener if possible. Get accustomed to using the less popular ones—kidneys, brains, sweetbreads, heart. There are many appetizing ways in which these can be served.

B Vitamins in Poultry and Meat

Milligrams per 100 grams
(In general 100 grams equals an average serving)

	Thiamin	Riboflavin	Niacin	Pyridoxine	Panto-thenic acid	Biotin
Chicken	.90 - .150	.070-.260	8.6	.100	.550	.005-.009
Goose	.150		3	?	?	?
Turkey	.120- .150	.190-.240	7.9	?	?	?
Duck	.360	.230	3	?	?	?
Beef	.100- .220	.120-.270	4.5	.077	.490	.002
Lamb	.80 - .210	.230-.266	5.9	.081	.600	.002
Pork	.90 -1.040	.040-.240	.9-4.4	.086-.270	?	?
Veal	.170- .180	.140-.280	3.1-6.5	.056-.130	.110-.260	.001

Mineral Content of Organ Meats

Milligrams per 100 grams

	Calcium	Phosphorus	Iron	Copper
Brains	8	380	2.3	0
Heart	10	236	6.2	0
Kidney	14	262	15.0	.11
Liver, beef	8	373	12.1	2.15
Liver, calf	11	205	5.4	4.41
Sweetbreads	14	596	1.6	0
Tongue	31	229	3.0	0

Vitamin Content of Organ Meats

Milligrams per 100 grams

	Vit. A	Thia-min	Ribo-flavin	Niacin	Inosi-tol	Pyri-doxine	Panto-thenic acid
Brains	0	.25	.26	6.0	200	?	1.8-3.6
Heart	0	.54	.90	6.8	260	.120	2.0
Kidney (I.U.)	750	.45	1.95	7.4	0	4.0	37.0
Liver (I.U.)	19,200-53,000	.27	2.80	16.1	55	.170-.730	4.4-7.6
Pancreas	0	.320	.590	.584	?	?	?
Sweetbreads	0	.150	.550	3.3			10.6
Tongue	0	.15	.23	4.0		1.25	
Tripe	0	.006	.12	.003			

	Biotin	Folic acid	Choline	Vit. C	Vit. D
Brains	.0074	.052	?	14	0
Heart	.0049	.130	?	14	0
Kidney (I.U.)	.92				
Liver (I.U.)	.096-.112	.325-.380	.380	31	15-45
Pancreas					
Sweetbreads				20	
Tongue	.003				

Beef Recipes

Green Bean-Pepper Steak

1½ pounds round steak
2 tablespoons soya sauce
¼ cup wheat germ or soya flour
4 tablespoons corn oil
1 cup fresh green beans (cut up)
1 cup chopped green peppers

Cut steak into small even portions. Dip in soya sauce, then in wheat germ until well coated. Brown steak in corn oil in skillet over medium heat. Add string beans and green peppers, and any remaining soya sauce. Pour in skillet, cover and let simmer until steak is tender. Serve with mashed potatoes. Serves 6.

Russian Steak

Heat a large heavy iron skillet and put in 2 tablespoons of cooking oil. Add 2 pounds of round steak, spreading it evenly. Cover and simmer gently for 30 minutes. Turn the steak and simmer gently for another 30 minutes. Add the following:

2 chopped green peppers
1 sliced onion
1 potato per person
½ cup diced celery and leaves
2 cups fresh mushrooms
3 cups home-canned tomatoes
1 tablespoon sea kelp
1 teaspoon paprika
1 teaspoon each of fresh or dried basil and marjoram

Cover the skillet, place in a 350 degree oven and bake until the meat is tender, probably 30 minutes. Pour the broth into a saucepan and thicken with rice flour, then pour it back over the meat and vegetables. Serve in one dish. Serves 6.

Saucy "Steak" Strips

4 tablespoons vegetable oil
1 tablespoon soy flour
2 cups meat broth
1 bay leaf
3 whole cloves
3 whole allspice

1¼ pounds steak
1 large green pepper
½ pound mushrooms
4 ounces pimiento
sea salt to taste

Heat 2 tablespoons of oil in a skillet; blend in flour. Add broth, bay leaf, cloves and allspice. Stir and simmer for 2 minutes; remove spices. Cut steaks, green pepper, mushrooms and pimiento into long strips about ¼ × 2 inches long. Brown steaks in a skillet using remaining oil; add green pepper and cook until tender. Add broth mixture to steaks, mushrooms and pimiento; heat to boiling. Add sea salt, if desired. Serve over brown rice. Serves 5.

London Broil

⅓ cup safflower oil
½ clove garlic
2 tablespoons cider vinegar
½ teaspoon sea salt
⅛ teaspoon paprika

1 tablespoon soy sauce
1 medium onion (sliced)
1 small bay leaf
1 beef flank steak (about 2 pounds)

Combine safflower oil with garlic, vinegar, seasonings and onion slices. Place flank steak in flat pan and pour oil mixture over steak. Marinate in refrigerator several hours, longer if possible. When ready to cook, remove bay leaf and garlic. Preheat broiler and broil meat 3 inches from source of heat 4 to 5 minutes on each side, basting with marinade. Carve in thin slices diagonally. Serve with juice from broiler. Serves 6-8.

Oven-Baked Swiss Steak

In a casserole dish which has a tight cover, place a 2 pound chuck or round steak cut about 1 inch thick. Over it, put the following ingredients:

1 cup chopped onions
½ bell pepper, chopped
1 shredded basil leaf

1 cup hot tomato juice
sea kelp to taste

Put in a pre-heated 400 degree oven, then bake at about 375 degrees until done, about 1½ hours. When the meat is almost done, add 2 cups of halved mushrooms around the edge of the steak. Serve in the casserole dish. Serves 6-8.

Bell Pepper Loaf

2 pounds ground beef
3 green bell peppers, chopped
3 red bell peppers, chopped
1 medium onion, chopped
2 cups tomato juice (home-canned)

1 tablespoon sea kelp
1 teaspoon marjoram
1 teaspoon chili powder
2 eggs

Blend all ingredients together, pack in an oiled bread tin and bake about an hour at 350°. Serve either hot or cold. Serves 8-10.

Blender Meat Loaf

1 pound ground beef
¼ cup soaked soybeans
¼ cup cooked brown rice
¼ cup oatmeal
¼ cup wheat germ
¼ cup tomato juice

¼ teaspoon sea salt
¼ teaspoon sage
¼ cup coarsely chopped celery
¼ cup coarsely chopped onions
¾ cup soy milk
1 egg

Place onion, celery, rice, oatmeal, wheat germ, soaked soybeans, sage, salt, egg, tomato juice, and soy milk in blender. Blend until well mixed. Pour blended ingredients into large bowl with ground meat. Mix well. Place mixture in oiled pan. Bake at 350 degrees for 45 minutes or until done. Serves 4.

Chuckwagon Meat Loaf

1 pound lean ground beef
1 egg
¼ cup wheat germ
1 teaspoon Italian seasoning
½ teaspoon sage
½ teaspoon sea salt

1 cup plus 2 tablespoons
   tomato sauce or juice
dash of pepper
2 tablespoons onion, minced
⅓ cup raw grated carrot
2 tablespoons parsley
¼ cup diced green pepper

Mix ingredients together well. Place in a baking dish and shape into loaf. Cover bottom of baking dish with water to a depth of ¼ inch to prevent any scorching. Bake at 350 degrees for one hour. Pour hot tomato sauce over meat loaf before serving. Garnish with parsley. Serves 4.

Meat Loaf with Herbs

2 pounds ground beef
3 eggs, slightly beaten
½ cup chopped onion
¼ cup chopped green pepper
1 clove garlic, minced
   (optional)
1 teaspoon sea salt

2 tablespoons fresh or dried
   parsley
2 tablespoons brewer's yeast
   flakes
2 tablespoons yellow corn meal
¼ teaspoon oregano
1 medium raw potato, grated

Mix all ingredients together, form into loaf, and bake in oven for 1 hour at 350 degrees. Serves 8.

Meat Loaf Marvelous

1½ pounds ground beef
¾ cup oatmeal uncooked
3 teaspoons brewer's yeast
3 tablespoons wheat germ

1 egg beaten
¼ cup chopped onion
1½ teaspoons sea salt or kelp
1½ cups tomato juice

Combine all ingredients, pack firmly in an ungreased 8½ × 4½ × 2½ pan. Bake in a preheated oven at 350° for 1 hour and 15 minutes. Let stand 5 minutes before slicing. Serves 8.

Peanut Meat Loaf

1 cup finely chopped peanuts
1 pound ground beef
2 tablespoons finely minced
onion
1 teaspoon powdered kelp

¾ cup mashed potato
2 eggs
½ cup soy milk or nut milk
¼ teaspoon marjoram
¼ teaspoon rosemary

Mix, bake in an oiled pan at 350° for approximately one hour. Serves 6.

Hamburger Puff

1 pound ground beef
2 eggs
1½ cups cooked barley

1 small onion (grated fine)
1 teaspoon sea salt

Mix, put in pan and bake at 350° about 40 minutes or until done. Serves 4-6.

German Beef Burger

1 cup chopped raw carrots
1 cup unpeeled chopped raw
potatoes
2 tablespoons chopped onion
2 tablespoons chopped parsley
1 pound ground lean beef

½ cup chopped celery
1 beaten egg
¼ cup water
¼ cup wheat germ
2 teaspoons vegetable salt

Mix all together, then form into patties and place on lightly oiled shallow pan. Bake in hot oven (400°) for 20 minutes. Serves 4.

Patioburgers

1 pound of round steak, ground
3 tablespoons of wheat germ
flakes

1 tablespoon of sunflower seeds,
ground
2 whole eggs

Mix all ingredients together and put on broiler. Serves 4.

Polynesian Beef Roast

1   3 to 4 pound beef chuck
    roast
1   large onion, sliced
1   cup pineapple juice
¼   cup soy sauce
1½ teaspoons ground ginger
1   cup diagonally sliced celery

4   carrots, cut in 3 to 4 inch
    strips
½   pound garden spinach,
    cleaned and stems removed
1   pint fresh mushrooms, sliced
2   tablespoons cornstarch

In a shallow baking dish, cover meat with onion rings. Combine pineapple juice, soy sauce, ginger, and ¼ teaspoon sea salt. Pour over meat. Let stand in pineapple mixture 1 hour at room temperature, turning meat once. Place meat and onions in Dutch oven, or any heavy pan.

Pour pineapple juice over; cover and simmer 2½ hours, or till meat is tender. Add celery and carrots. Sprinkle with sea salt; bring to boiling, then simmer 20 minutes, arranging spinach and mushrooms on top of meat. Simmer 10 minutes or till spinach is wilted and other vegetables are crisp and tender. Remove meat and vegetables to heated platter; keep hot. Skim fat from meat juices. Blend together ¼ cup cold water and cornstarch. Stir into juices, cook and stir till thickened and bubbly. Serves 8.

Fruited Pot Roast

1   4-5 pound rump of beef
2   medium onions, peeled, sliced
¼   teaspoon ground cloves
2   teaspoons sea salt

2   tablespoons honey
2   cups apple cider
1½ cups sun-dried apricots
1½ cups sun-dried prunes

In Dutch oven, brown roast well on all sides. Then add onions, cloves, sea salt, honey and 1 cup cider. Bring to boil; then simmer, covered, 2 hours. Meanwhile soak apricots and prunes in water to cover. After roast has cooked 2 hours, add drained fruits and 1 cup cider to it. Then simmer, covered, 30 minutes, or until roast is fork-tender and apricots and prunes are cooked. Serves 6.

Herbed Pot Roast

3 pounds beef roast with fat trimmed off
½ teaspoon each of dried marjoram, thyme and mace

1 garlic clove cooked with meat, then removed

Simmer the meat and herbs until the meat is nearly tender. Add enough potatoes, carrots and onions for your family, season them with sea kelp and simmer until the vegetables are done. Serves 6 or 8.

Pot Roast with Prunes

4 pound rump of beef
2 tablespoons soy flour
1 teaspoon sea salt
2 tablespoons olive oil
1½ cups prune juice

4 cloves
1 bay leaf
½ teaspoon thyme
12 whole prunes, pitted

Rub flour and sea salt into meat. Heat oil in a large, heavy pot and brown meat on all sides. Add remaining ingredients, cover pot and cook over low flame from 3 to 4 hours, turning meat occasionally, until meat is tender. Serves 8.

Zesty Pot Roast

2 pounds round steak
1 tablespoon oil (cold-pressed)
1 onion, chopped
2 cups hot water
1 cup home-canned tomatoes

1 teaspoon allspice
½ teaspoon basil
1 tablespoon pure honey
1 slice lemon

In a large pot, heat the oil and brown the meat. Add onions and hot water and stir. Add remaining ingredients. Simmer slowly for about 3 hours or until meat is fork tender. Serve hot accompanied by a crisp green salad. Serves 6.

Savory Rice Meat Balls

1 cup cooked brown rice	2 teaspoons grated onion
1 egg, slightly beaten	1/8 teaspoon marjoram
1 pound ground beef	1/2 teaspoon kelp

Mix together. Gently shape mixture into balls. Blend together 2 1/2 cups homemade tomato juice and 1/2 teaspoon honey.

Place meat balls in oiled pan. Pour tomato juice over. Bring just to a boil. Cover, simmer 15 minutes, basting occasionally, till done. Sprinkle with chopped parsley. Serves 4-6.

Meat Balls and Mushroom Gravy over Millet

It has an appetizing aroma that perks up even a finicky appetite.

1 pound ground beef	2 cups water
1 tablespoon vegetable oil	1 pint mushrooms
1 medium onion	sea salt to taste

Chop onion fine and mix 1/2 into the meat and form into 1-inch meat balls.

Brown in oil, then add the water and rest of the onion and mushrooms. Simmer 1/2 an hour.

Cook 1 cup of millet in 5 cups of boiling water for 20 minutes on medium heat. Turn off heat, cover, and let stand until all the water is absorbed.

For the gravy add 2 tablespoons arrowroot flour to 1 cup cold water. Stir until all is dissolved in the water. Then pour at once into the meat balls and mushrooms in the pan, stirring until it thickens. Serve the meat balls and mushroom gravy over the millet. Serves 4.

Meat Balls in Cranberry-Tomato Sauce

1 pound fresh cranberries, cooked and sweetened with honey	2 teaspoons finely minced onion
1 cup tomato sauce	1/2 cup cold water
1 pound ground lean beef	1/2 teaspoon sea salt
	1/8 teaspoon oregano

In a saucepan over low heat, cook the cranberry and tomato sauce until heated. In a bowl combine the remaining ingredients and form into balls. Add the meat balls to the sauce and cover and cook over low heat until the meat balls are tender. Serve hot with a freshly tossed vegetable salad. Serves 6.

Cabbage Rolls

8 cabbage leaves
1 pound lean ground beef
1 cup cooked brown rice
2 tablespoons bone meal powder

¼ cup chopped onions
1 egg
½ cup wheat germ
2 cups home-canned tomatoes
1 cup water

Blanch cabbage leaves. Combine and mix all ingredients except tomatoes. Roll mixture in cabbage leaves. Pour tomatoes on top of cabbage. Place in greased casserole, bake at 325 degrees for 1 hour. Serves 4.

Champion Chop Suey

In a large pot:

Sauté lightly in 3 tablespoons corn oil for 5 minutes:

3 medium onions, chopped
4 large stalks celery, sliced thin

¾ pound sandwich steaks cut in 1 inch wide strips

Then:

Add 1 pound fresh mung bean sprouts
Cover with water to 1½ inches over all ingredients. (Water will provide gravy so put at level you desire.) Simmer 1 hour, covered.

Mix:

2 tablespoons blackstrap molasses
⅓ cup soy sauce

3 tablespoons corn starch (level) mixed with enough cold water to make a smooth paste

Add to pot mixture, stir well. Simmer 20 more minutes. If too thin, add additional corn starch and cold water.
Serve over brown rice. Add soy sauce to taste.

If desired, add last:

½ cup sliced mushrooms and   ½ cup water chestnuts

Serves 4.

Chinese Casserole

1½ to 2 pounds braising beef   arrowroot flour
  3 cups (approximately)   kelp
    vegetable water   paprika
  1-1½ cups brown rice   parsley
  1 bell pepper, diced   rosemary and/or marjoram
  1-2 tablespoons soy sauce

Cut meat into rather small strips and coat lightly with flour, kelp and paprika.

Steam in small amount of oil in 1½ quart casserole, turning until nicely browned on all sides.

Add approximately ½ cup water and simmer approximately one hour.

Add rice, rest of water (twice as much water as rice), parsley, rosemary and marjoram to taste (¼ teaspoon or more crumbled between fingers).

Simmer tightly covered, approximately 45 minutes or until rice is virtually done.

Add soy sauce and pepper. Cover and steam until pepper is soft (not more than 5 minutes).

Add bean sprouts at same time as pepper, if desired. Serves 6.

Sukiyaki

1 pound sirloin flank roast   ½ pound mushrooms
  (sliced paper thin)   1 celery cabbage
1 bunch scallions   1 tablespoon blackstrap
3 medium onions, cut in rings   molasses
2 pounds spinach   soy sauce

Ask your butcher to quick-freeze the meat and slice it thin for you. Cut all the vegetables in bite-size pieces and arrange with meat, on a platter. Heat skillet and add oil; put in small amounts of all vegetables—start with onions, add scallions and spinach, mushrooms and celery cabbage. Add meat last. Sprinkle a tablespoon of blackstrap molasses over the mixture. Add enough soy sauce to cover the bottom of the pan to prevent burning. Serves 4.

Broiled Ribs

Take beef ribs and pre-cook to save broiling time. Boil them until tender in water which is seasoned with herbs, sea kelp, onions, bay leaves and a teaspoon of vinegar. Remove from the cooking water and drain before placing in the broiler. Brush often with the following sauce.

Mix:

1 crushed clove garlic (optional)	½ cup pure cider vinegar
2 teaspoons shredded thyme	½ cup cooking oil
2 teaspoons shredded marjoram	1 teaspoon paprika
2 tablespoons sea kelp	

Brush this sauce almost constantly on the ribs until they are browned on both sides, then serve. Allow ½ pound per serving.

Tenderized Beef and Gravy

Take a 2-pound chunk of boiling beef and cut slits every inch or so, across the flat side. Put a clove garlic in 1 slit, a slice of onion in the next, and keep this up until you have the slits all filled. Pour a half cup of pure cider vinegar into the slits and cover and refrigerate for 24 hours. Heat a Dutch oven type steel or iron utensil and add cooking oil. Sear the beef on all sides to hold in the juices, add boiling water and boil until done, seasoning as you like it. Thicken the gravy with arrowroot and serve with mashed potatoes. Serves 6.

Mexican Chili Con Carne

First heat the heavy utensil very hot and put about 1 tablespoon of cooking oil in the bottom. Add the following ingredients which are already prepared, cover tightly and turn to simmer, opening to stir as little as possible:

1 large onion, sliced
1 bell pepper, cut fine

1 pound ground beef or
  hamburger meat
1 teaspoon sea kelp

Simmer until the onion is soft and the meat loses its red color. Then add the following ingredients:

2 cups cooked kidney beans
  (hot)

1 cup home-canned tomatoes
  (hot)
1 teaspoon chili powder

Simmer together about 30 minutes and serve with hot brown rice. Serves 6.

Soybean Chili

1½ pounds ground beef
  ¼ cup chopped onion
  3 cups tomato puree

1½ cups water (beans
  cooked in)
4 cups soybeans

Cook meat and onions together, drain off any fat that comes from meat. Then add tomato puree and water, slowly simmer for 30 to 45 minutes. Add the cooked soybeans and heat thoroughly. Freeze any leftovers for quick meal at later date. Serves 6.

Beef Goulash

2 pounds round steak—cut into
  one-inch cubes

1 pound lean veal—cut into
  one-inch cubes
¼ cup cooking oil

Brown the meat on both sides in the hot oil.

Add and sauté: 1½ cups chopped onion. Then add:

1 cup boiling stock or fresh
  tomato juice

1 teaspoon sea salt
½ teaspoon paprika

Use just enough stock to keep the meat from scorching and add more gradually during the cooking, as necessary. Cover the pot tightly and simmer the meat for 1½ hours. Remove the meat from the pot and thicken the stock for gravy with soy flour. Serves 6-8.

Hungarian Goulash

2½ pounds boneless chuck (all
    fat removed)
2 medium onions
2 medium ripe fresh tomatoes

2 tablespoons imported paprika
4 tablespoons vegetable oil
12 small potatoes
    sea salt, garlic, paprika

Chop onions fine and place in a 3-quart pot with oil and simmer until brown. Dice tomatoes, add to onions when brown. Cut chuck into 1-inch cubes and add to onions and tomatoes.

Season with paprika, sea salt, and a little garlic. Cover and allow to simmer until meat is almost done.

Dice potatoes and add to pot 15 minutes before meat is done. Serves 6.

Country Garden Hash

2 cups cold roast beef or other
    cooked meat
2 medium potatoes (raw)
2 medium onions

2 carrots
½ green pepper
1 cup chopped raw cabbage
    seasoning as desired

Put all ingredients through coarse food chopper. Place in greased heavy iron skillet on low heat. After it starts to steam add ½ cup water and cover tightly. Cook slowly, turning with spatula to brown well. More water may be added as needed. Serves 4.

Muffin-Pan Hash

1 cup cold roast beef, chopped
4 cups boiled potatoes, chopped
2 small onions, chopped
    sea salt to taste

1 green pepper, chopped
1 egg, well beaten
1 cup tomatoes

Mix together the chopped potatoes, onions and green pepper. Add the meat and tomatoes. Season with sea salt. Add the egg. Drop by spoonfuls into muffin pans. Bake in a hot oven (400° F.) 20 to 25 minutes. Serve with tomato sauce:

Tomato Sauce:

1 tablespoon oil
1 minced onion
2 cloves garlic
½ teaspoon sea salt

½ teaspoon thyme
2 cups fat-free meat stock
1 cup tomato puree

Brown the onion and garlic in the oil. Blend in all the other ingredients and simmer until slightly thickened. Serves 4.

Shepherds Pie

1 medium onion, chopped
1 tablespoon soy oil
1 pound freshly ground round steak
1 teaspoon basil

½ pound steamed green beans
1 cup home-canned tomatoes
2 medium potatoes cooked in jackets
1 beaten egg

Sauté onion in soy oil until golden—add meat and basil—brown. Add beans and tomatoes. Pour into 1½ quart casserole dish. Mash potatoes, after removing skins, with ½ cup water and beaten egg. Spoon over meat mixture. Bake at 350° for 15 minutes. Serves 4.

Carbonada Criolla (Meat and Fruit Stew)

1½ pounds boneless sirloin beef
1 tablespoon sunflower seed oil
1 cup chopped onion
1 tablespoon tomato paste
1 bay leaf
½ teaspoon sea salt
¼ teaspoon ground thyme
2½ cups water

2 medium potatoes, pared, cut into large cubes
½ medium acorn squash, seeded, pared, cut into large cubes
1 medium sweet potato, pared, cut into large cubes
1 pear, pared, cubed
1 medium apple, pared, cubed
2 tablespoons sun-dried raisins
1 tablespoon snipped parsley

Trim away as much fat as possible from meat. Cut meat into 1-inch cubes. In oil, in a large skillet with a tight-fitting cover, sauté beef until well browned on both sides. Add onion, tomato paste, bay leaf, sea salt, thyme, and water, cover; simmer gently 1 hour and 15 minutes or until meat is almost tender. Add potatoes, squash and sweet potato; cover; cook 20 minutes longer. Add pear, apple and raisins; cover, cook 10 minutes more. Serve in soup bowls; sprinkle with parsley. Serves 6.

Beef and Potato Sticks

1 pound lean ground beef
1 tablespoon corn oil
1 cup coarsely chopped onion

1 tablespoon rice flour
½ cup water
1 potato, sliced french-fry style

Lightly brown beef in hot corn oil. Add onion, cook until tender. Blend in flour and desired seasonings. Add water. Cover. Simmer 15 minutes to blend flavor. Sauté potato slices in hot oil. Serve atop beef mixture with raw garden salad. Serves 4.

Beef Curry

3½ pounds lean beef
2 pounds onions
2 kernels garlic

soy sauce (about 3 teaspoons)
2 teaspoons curry powder
small piece fresh ginger

Put in large skillet about 6 tablespoons cooking oil, slice and brown onions and garlic. While onions are browning, slice meat into one inch cubes. Brown meat in big pot, add onions. Add 6-7 tablets kelp, soy sauce and ginger sliced very thin. Simmer on low heat. Add homemade apple sauce (about 1½ cups) and ½ cup white raisins. Add curry—cook 5 minutes more and serve with brown rice. Serves 4.

Beef Fingers

¾ pound top round of beef
1½ tablespoons vegetable oil
  (cold-pressed)

1 tablespoon minced fresh dill
½ teaspoon sea salt
4 tablespoons unflavored yogurt

Cut beef into very thin, finger-like strips. Heat oil in skillet and brown beef strips on all sides. Add dill and sea salt to yogurt and beat until smooth. Add to skillet and let simmer until beef is fork tender. Serves 2.

Beef Pinwheels

1 pound lean ground beef
1 egg
2 tablespoons safflower oil
6 tablespoons wheat germ

2 tablespoons cold water
1½ cups cooked mashed carrots
1½ cups seasoned mashed
   potatoes

Mix together beef, egg, oil, wheat germ and water. Place mixture between sheets of wax paper and roll into a rectangle ½ inch thick. Remove top sheet of wax paper and spread meat surface with the mashed potatoes and carrots. Roll meat firmly (as for a jelly roll). Place rolled meat on a baking sheet and bake for 45 minutes at 350°. Slice and serve hot and with fresh tomato and/or mushroom sauce. Serves 4.

Beef and Eggplant Main Dish

1¼ cups cubed lean beef
3 tablespoons oil
3 large onions, chopped
8 stalks celery, diced
1 large eggplant, peeled and
   diced
2 pounds bean sprouts

1 teaspoon sea salt
1 cup hot water
2 tablespoons blackstrap
   molasses
2 tablespoons cornstarch
⅔ cup warm water

Brown meat in oil and cook till tender (a little water may be necessary). Add onions, celery, eggplant, and bean sprouts. Add molasses and water (1 cup). Cook 15 minutes. Mix remaining water and cornstarch and add. Heat to boiling point and serve on natural brown rice. Serves 4.

Stuffed Eggplant

1 large eggplant
2 or 3 stalks celery
1 medium onion

1 pound ground chuck
1 quart tomatoes
1 teaspoon kelp

Wash and cut eggplant in half. Using sharp knife cut around eggplant taking out inside, leaving about ¾ inch shell. Cut these pieces into small chunks and with cut-up celery and onion cook in small amount of oil for about 5 minutes. Add ground meat to this mixture along with your seasonings and brown meat. Put the two halves of eggplant in deep dish and fill with vegetable and meat mixture. What doesn't fit can be put around sides. Pour tomatoes over top and bake covered at 325° for one hour. Serves 4.

Beefy Squash

1½ pounds beef
½ dozen organically grown
squash
2 tablespoons safflower oil

1 medium onion
few sprigs parsley
sea salt

Cut beef in small pieces, sprinkle with sea salt and brown in oil in heavy dutch oven. Peel and cut squash in small pieces. Add to browned meat. Then add chopped onion and parsley. Cover tightly with lid. Cook over low heat until tender, stirring occasionally. Serves 6.

Karnutzel

1 pound of ground meat
2 medium sized carrots (grated)
1 onion
1 tablespoon brewer's yeast
1 egg

pinch of thyme, marjoram and
oregano (optional)
1 tablespoon wheat germ
1 teaspoon kelp
(sesame seeds and soy flour
for coating)

Combine all ingredients, except coating. Roll into portions about the size and shape of frankfurters. Roll these in a mixture of sesame seeds and soy flour. Broil. Serve with hot tomato sauce. Makes 8.

Sweet Potato Pizza

5 or 6 large sweet potatoes
or yams
1 pound ground beef
1 medium onion, minced

2 teaspoons oregano
2 teaspoons sea salt
1 or 2 ripe tomatoes

Boil sweet potatoes until tender. Drain and peel. Mash thoroughly, adding 1 teaspoon sea salt. Spread mashed sweet potatoes into oiled 9″ by 10″ baking dish, patting mixture firmly.

Sauté onion and ground beef until lightly brown, adding 1 teaspoon sea salt and oregano. Mix thoroughly, remove from heat and spread evenly on top of sweet potatoes.

Immerse tomatoes in boiling water just until the skins can be slipped off easily. Now slice very thin or chop fine, and spread over mixture in baking pan.

Bake in 375 degree oven for 30 minutes or until mixture is cooked and bubbly. Serves 6 to 8.

Lamb Recipes

Baked Lamb Chops

Take 1 lamb chop per person, choose a baking dish large enough to accommodate them. Cover the bottom of the dish with fresh thyme (or use the dried thyme) then a layer of chops topped by sea kelp. Do this until you have enough layers of thyme and chops. Cover tightly and bake 1 hour at 375 degrees.

At serving time, remove the chops to a platter, pour off all fat, add water or soup stock and make gravy in the bottom of the baking dish. Scrape off most of the herbs and put the chops back in the gravy if so desired.

Baked Lamb Chops with Vegetables

4 boned lamb chops
1 green pepper, sliced
1 small onion, diced

2 large tomatoes, sliced
1 teaspoon sea salt

Heat oven to 375 degrees. Wipe the chops with a clean damp cloth. Sear them quickly on both sides in a large frying pan. Place chops in a baking dish or leave them in the skillet. Arrange green pepper, onion and tomatoes over the lamb chops, sprinkling them with the salt. Cover and bake about 40 minutes; remove cover and cook 10 minutes longer. Serves 4.

Yugoslavian Djuvece (Lamb and Vegetables)

1 lamb chop per serving

Place the lamb chops in the bottom of a Dutch oven type of utensil. Next a layer of sliced potatoes, then a layer of sliced carrots, then a layer of sliced onions, then several green pepper halves. Season with caraway seeds, sea kelp and paprika. Have enough hot soup stock to cover. Pour it over, cover the dish and bake until the chops and vegetables are done, probably an hour. Pour off the liquid and thicken it, and add a teaspoon of soy sauce to give it a good brown color. Return it to the mixture and garnish with slices of sweet red pepper and parsley. Serve in the Dutch oven.

Broiled Lamb Chops and Oven Fried Potatoes

Prepare the chops the night before and keep refrigerated in a covered dish. If you leave any fat on, cut it every half inch to prevent curling. Brush each chop with cooking oil, then sprinkle with either dried mint leaves or dried herbs and sea kelp. Our favorite is marjoram. Stack the chops so that they are seasoned from both top and bottom through the night. In the morning, place them on the broiler rack at room temperature while you prepare the potatoes.

Scrub the potatoes and cut in thin slices. Arrange them on the broiler rack around the lamb chops, then brush with cooking oil and sprinkle with sea kelp.

Broil the chops and potatoes slowly, turning the chops when browned on one side. Just before turning out the broiler, sprinkle the potato slices with sesame seeds and let them toast slightly. Serve chops and potatoes very hot. Allow one medium-sized potato and two chops per person.

Herbed Lamb Chops

4 lamb crops	1 teaspoon basil
2 tablespoons soy oil	1 teaspoon parsley (chopped)
1 teaspoon thyme	1 teaspoon kelp

Brush lamb chops with oil. Preheat broiling oven for 5 minutes. Place chops on oiled broiling rack 2 inches below heat. Broil 10-12 minutes, turning occasionally. When chops are done, sprinkle a little kelp on each chop. Then sprinkle the herbs which have been mixed with a little soy oil over each chop. Serves 2.

Lamb Chops in Spanish Sauce

8 lamb chops
½ cup minced onions
½ cup finely chopped green peppers

¼ cup soybean oil
1 cup carrot juice
1 teaspoon sea salt

Brown lamb chops in oil. Add onions and peppers and cook until tender. Add carrot juice and sea salt. Cover. Simmer 1 hour or until tender. Serves 4.

Endive and Lamb Chops Cantonese

4 endives, coarsely chopped
¾ cup chopped celery
¼ cup chopped green pepper
4 tablespoons corn oil

4 lean lamb chops
¼ teaspoon nutmeg
sea salt to taste

Braise chops on one side only in skillet, seasoning with sea salt and nutmeg. Arrange, browned side up in shallow, oiled casserole; brush with oil. Steam celery and green pepper until delicately brown and tender. Add endives and stir gently. Carefully spread vegetables over chops in casserole, browned side down. Top with small amount of oil. Bake at 350° F. for 30-40 minutes until nicely browned, basting frequently with oil. Serve with mounds of cooked brown rice. Serves 4.

Herbed Leg of Lamb

Buy a leg of lamb and have it boned, and have the bones cracked up to release their juices. Simmer the bones for gravy stock. About

3 hours before the meal, set the oven to 350 degrees and prepare the lamb by rubbing inside and out with the split sides of 1 clove of garlic. Make a cheesecloth bag about 4 × 8 inches and stuff it with 1 cup of frozen basil and 1 cup of frozen marjoram. Tie the end and wrap the lamb around this herb stuffing and tie with clean stout thread, wrapping the thread every 2 inches or so the length of the roast. Tie. Roast the lamb uncovered for 1 hour, then season well and roast covered for the next 2 hours or until well done.

Remove to a heated platter and keep very hot. All mutton fat should be removed and the quickest way is to throw a handful of small ice cubes into the hot broth, then remove ice cubes and congealed fat with a slotted spoon. Add the bone stock and thicken the gravy with arrowroot flour. If it is too light colored, add soy sauce until you have a rich gravy.

Serve with baked potatoes which have been slit across the top, seasoned with sea kelp, yogurt and chives or green onions.

You can arrange steamed asparagus tips on the platter with the lamb if desired. Season to the family's taste. Serves 10.

Roast Leg of Lamb

Place 5 pound leg of lamb on a roaster rack with the fat side up. Rub it heavily with sea kelp. If you like mint with lamb, then cut through the fat at intervals and pack mint leaves in the cuts. If you prefer other herbs, use them instead of the mint. Bake at 325 degrees for about 3 hours, or 35 minutes per pound. To slice, cut 2 or 3 slices from the knuckle side, turn and slice from shank end down to leg bone, then start at shank end again and cut around the bone. Serves 8.

Apricot-Glazed Lamb

leg of lamb (6 or 7 pounds)
2 cloves garlic, slivered
1 teaspoon vegetable salt
½ pound dried apricots
1 onion, thinly sliced
1 cup water
2 tablespoons oil

Remove skin and fat from lamb. Insert slivers of garlic in gashes made in leg of lamb with a sharp paring knife. Preheat oven to 275 degrees. Sprinkle lamb with sea salt and place on rack in uncovered shallow pan. Spoon the oil over the lamb. Put water and sliced onion in bottom of pan. Bake about 2 hours.

While lamb is baking, steam apricots in enough water to cover. Pass through sieve or chopper. Set aside.

After 2 hours, remove lamb from oven and pour off gravy and remove fat. Mix remaining gravy with the apricot puree and pour over lamb. Return to oven and cook for one more hour, basting frequently with apricot gravy. When lamb is nicely glazed and golden brown, slice thin and serve on platter with the gravy. Serves 8-10.

Honey of a Lamb

5-6 pound lamb-shoulder (broiled to half done!)

Basting:

1 cup pure honey	½ teaspoon powdered kelp
1 small clove garlic or onion, very finely chopped	½ teaspoon powdered cayenne pepper

Wash and dry lamb-shoulder. Broil or put into oven to bake. When half done, baste with the honey dressing. Baste on coat after coat about 10 minutes. When meat is done, serve it with the leftover basting. This sauce is delicious too over baked potatoes, cooked along with the roast. Serves 8 to 10.

Oven "Boiled" Lamb Dinner

5 small white turnips cut in quarters

3 small boiling potatoes in their jackets

2 or 3 carrots cut in diagonal thick slices

1 cup mushroom caps (small, whole)

1 medium onion, chopped, or 6 to 8 tiny whole ones, peeled. Some bones sawed into short pieces (your butcher will cut them up free, beef or veal without visible fat)

1 pound lean lamb shoulder cut in 1″ chunks

2 cloves garlic, put through a garlic press

1 tablespoon oil
sea salt, pepper, rosemary, thyme

3 cups beef broth

1 lemon
coarsely chopped parsley

You will need a large casserole or pot that has a lid and that can go into your oven, a large frying pan, a large wooden spoon.

Put the first three ingredients in the casserole.

Rub the meat with the garlic. Brown the meat and bones quickly and lightly in the 1 tablespoon oil. Add them to the casserole, retaining the oil in the frying pan.

Sauté the onions and mushrooms a few minutes in the remaining oil. Add to the casserole.

Boil one cup of the broth in the frying pan, stirring to get up all the brownings. Add this and enough of the remaining broth to not quite cover the contents of the casserole. Sprinkle with sea salt, pepper and the herbs. Add a slice of lemon peel and a squeeze of lemon juice. Cover. Bring to a simmer slowly on top of the stove.

Place in a 225-degree oven and cook slowly until all is tender— this may take 2 to 3 hours because of the low temperature. Cool, chill. Remove all fat. Reheat gently and serve garnished with lots of parsley.

Add separately-cooked artichoke hearts; crisp-cooked green beans; barely cooked tiny peas, eggplant, or crisp-cooked celery chunks for variations. Serves 4 to 6.

Lamb Ragout

Take a 3 pound lamb shoulder and cut it in serving-sized chunks. Simmer it gently until nearly done with a cheesecloth bag of the following herbs:

2 bay leaves	1 clove garlic (optional)
1 teaspoon thyme	1 teaspoon rosemary

Remove the bag of herbs and add the following vegetables:

6 potatoes	2 green pepper halves
4 turnips	2 tablespoons sea kelp
6 carrots cut in 2″ lengths	2 cups home-canned tomatoes
1 large onion, quartered	1 teaspoon honey
2 stalks celery and leaves, cut in 1″ lengths	

Simmer gently until the vegetables are done, then thicken the broth with arrowroot flour. Serves 6.

Broiled Lamburgers

3 pounds ground spring lamb
1 tablespoon sea kelp

1 teaspoon dried marjoram
½ teaspoon curry powder

Mix the seasoning into the lamb, shape into patties and broil until browned on both sides. Pour off all fat and make gravy of the drippings, adding 1 teaspoon of soy sauce for flavor and a lovely rich brown color. Serves 8.

Lamb on Brown Rice

1 tablespoon corn oil
2 pounds ground lamb
1 cup chopped onion
3 cups chopped celery and
  leaves

2 cups sliced mushrooms
1 green pepper, finely chopped
3 cups soup stock, hot
1 tablespoon kelp
1 teaspoon dried marjoram

Place all ingredients in heavy Dutch oven or chicken fryer. Have utensil hot. When celery is done, in about 20 minutes, thicken the mixture with rice polishings and add 1 teaspoon soy sauce. Serve over steamed brown rice. Garnish with parsley and slivers of red pepper. Serves 8.

Shanghai Lamb on Brown Rice

Using the heavy Dutch oven or chicken fryer type utensil which generates much steam in which to cook the ingredients, have the utensil hot, add 1 tablespoon cooking oil, then add the ingredients in their order, just as fast as you get them washed and chopped, and stir as you add, covering tightly between additions:

2 pounds ground lamb
1 cup chopped onions
3 cups chopped celery and tops
2 cups sliced mushrooms

1 green pepper, slivered
3 cups soup stock (boiling hot)
1 tablespoon sea kelp
1 teaspoon dried marjoram

When the celery is done, thicken the mixture with arrowroot flour or rice polishings and add 1 teaspoon soy sauce for color and flavor. Serve over steamed brown rice, garnished with parsley and slivers of red pepper. Serves 8.

Lambikin Pie

2 pounds ground lamb
1 cup fresh or home-canned tomatoes
½ cup chopped onion
1 teaspoon kelp
1 teaspoon basil

½ cup chopped celery
3 cups mashed sweet potatoes
¼ cup honey
1 teaspoon cinnamon
¼ teaspoon sea salt

Brown ground lamb with onion, add tomatoes and herbs. Heat thoroughly. Put mixture in oiled casserole. Add rest of the ingredients over the meat. Spread evenly, over all, the mashed potatoes to which the cinnamon and sea salt have been added. Cover mixture and bake 1 hour at 350°. Eight servings.

Highland Fling

Cook 2 pounds stewing lamb until it is just tender, seasoning as you like it. Have the split peas and barley soaking in cold water the last half hour or so of the meat cooking time. Add the following, season with sea kelp and dried parsley and cook until the vegetables are tender.

½ cup split peas
1 cup barley
1 teaspoon marjoram

¾ cup chopped carrots
¾ cup diced potatoes
1 chopped onion

The last thing before serving, add chopped parsley and a sprinkle of paprika. Serves 6 to 8.

Liver Recipes

Liver-Veal Loaf

½ pound beef liver
1 pint boiling water
1 medium onion, diced
1½ pounds boneless veal, ground

2 eggs, slightly beaten
1 cup tomato sauce
½ cup wheat germ (or more)
⅛ teaspoon sage
sea salt to taste

In a bowl, pour the boiling water over the liver and let stand for 10 minutes. Drain off the water and cut the liver coarsely. Grind liver with the onion, using a medium blade. Combine with the ground veal. Add tomato sauce, seasonings, eggs and wheat germ. Mix thoroughly and pack into an oiled loaf pan. Bake in a moderate oven for 1½ hours. Serve hot, accompanied by a mixed green salad. Serves 6.

Liver Loaf

1 pound beef liver, cut in
  ½-inch slices
3 tablespoons oil
½ cup onion, minced
¼ cup diced celery
4 tablespoons finely chopped
  green pepper

1 pound ground beef
1½ cups chopped carrots
2 tablespoons parsley, minced
1 tablespoon wheat germ
1 teaspoon vegetable salt
½ teaspoon paprika
2 eggs slightly beaten

Sauté beef liver in oil for a few minutes. Put through food chopper using fine blade. Add onion, celery and green pepper to hot skillet adding more oil if necessary, and sauté for 3 minutes or until onion is golden brown. Add this to liver, then ground beef, carrots, parsley, wheat germ, salt, paprika, and eggs. Mix thoroughly. Place in a well oiled pan or casserole. Cover and bake 30 minutes in 375° oven. Uncover and bake 15 or 20 minutes longer. Serves 8.

Liver-Heart Loaf

¾ pound beef liver, cubed
1 thick slice beef heart, cubed
1 tablespoon cold-pressed oil
1 teaspoon sea salt
⅓ cup tomato juice

1 tablespoon lemon juice
1 cup seasoned mashed
  potatoes
1 beaten egg

Lightly sauté liver and heart in oil, and put through a grinder or chop in a wooden bowl. Add remaining ingredients and mix well. Form into a loaf and place in an oiled loaf pan. Bake in a 350° oven for 1 hour. Serve hot accompanied by a mixed vegetable salad. Serves 4.

Liver Patties

1 pound beef or steer liver   ½ medium green pepper
1 medium onion   small clove of garlic

Put above through meat grinder or chop fine in wooden bowl. Add a little sea salt.

¼ cup wheat germ   1 egg

Mix well and drop by teaspoonful into pan in which 1 tablespoon of corn oil has been heated. Brown well on both sides. Serves 4.

Chopped Beef Liver

Take a pound of beef liver which has been sliced thin. Score any places where it will thicken, then broil on both sides. Season and run it through the food grinder along with a small onion. Now chop 4 hardboiled eggs, keeping out 1 yolk for a garnish. Add the eggs to the liver and add enough beef broth or stock to moisten the mixture to a consistency which can be lifted from the platter to the plate without breaking. Mound on a platter, crumb the egg yolk over for a garnish and sprinkle the yolk with paprika. Add parsley sprigs and serve. Slices of hardboiled eggs can be arranged around the platter if desired. Serves 4.

Stewed Liver

1 pound liver   4 medium size potatoes,
½ cup liquid (soup stock, apple   quartered
   cider, or plain water)   ¼ teaspoon kelp
1 cup chopped onions   ½ teaspoon thyme
1 bunch carrots cut into   1 teaspoon rosemary
   ½-inch pieces

Slice liver into thick slices or chunks and place in iron kettle with liquid. Over this, spread chopped onion, next the carrots and then the potatoes. Sprinkle with spices. After about 15 minutes of cooking with tight cover over medium heat, turn contents over to mix and add more moisture if needed. Cook until vegetables are done. Serves 4.

Liver and Apples

3 tablespoons sunflower oil
   (or olive oil)
1 pound liver, sliced
2 tablespoons wheat germ

1 teaspoon powdered thyme
1 apple, cut in slices
½ teaspoon sea salt

Combine thyme, sea salt and wheat germ. Dredge liver slices. Brown in oil, on both sides. Cover with fruit. Cover skillet and cook over low heat about 15 minutes. Serves 4.

Liver with Avocado

1 pound calves' (or baby beef)
   liver, thinly sliced
1 large ripe avocado, sliced
   sea salt

pinch of cayenne pepper
3 tablespoons cold-pressed oil
2 tablespoons lemon juice
⅓ cup water

Sauté slices of liver in oil, slowly, over medium heat until browned. Remove from pan and place in covered serving dish. Sauté avocado slices in same pan until slightly browned, then arrange them over the liver. Add a little water, sea salt and cayenne pepper to the leavings in the pan and bring to boil, stirring, until reduced to a glaze. Pour this over the liver and avocado, then sprinkle with a bit of lemon juice and serve accompanied by brown rice and a green salad. Serves 4.

Liver Cabbage Rolls

12 large cabbage leaves,
   parboiled
 1 cup lightly broiled ground
   liver
 1 cup cooked brown rice
 1 egg, beaten

1 grated onion
1 teaspoon sea salt
2 tablespoons minced parsley
2 tablespoons safflower oil mixed
   into 1 cup tomato juice

Mix all ingredients together thoroughly with the exception of the oil and tomato juice. Put a tablespoon of the liver mixture in the center of each cabbage leaf and roll, tucking in the ends. Secure with toothpicks. Place cabbage rolls in a baking pan, pour oil and tomato juice mixture over them and bake at 375 degrees for 45 minutes. Serve hot. Serves 6.

Liver Canape

4 pieces of cooked baby liver (beef)
½ cup onion
⅛ cup soy oil
⅛ cup olive oil

⅛ portion of garlic clove
¼ teaspoon caraway seeds
½ teaspoon chives
dash savory

Blend above ingredients in blender. Delicious as an appetizer on a bed of lettuce or stuffed in celery. Serves 4.

Liver Delight

2 cups cubed liver (beef, calf or chicken)
2 tablespoons cooking oil
3 tablespoons soya flour

2 cups fine-chopped cabbage
1 cup fine-chopped onions
1 cup chopped fresh tomatoes
heavy skillet

Cut liver in one-fourth inch cubes and toss with soya flour till coated. Place skillet on lowest heat. Add liver and oil. Simmer till liver is tender. Use a tight fitting lid. When the liver is no longer red, add the vegetables and a dash of kelp and garlic. Let simmer till vegetables are tender but not overcooked. Serves 4.

Liver Dumplings and Dill Sauce

Put 2 *cups of liver* through the food grinder. Add the following ingredients:

2 heaping tablespoons corn flour
2 eggs, beaten
1 teaspoon minced onion

1 teaspoon fresh or dried marjoram
2 teaspoons sea kelp

This will make a stiff dumpling dough. In a large kettle, put 3 cups of meat and vegetable stock and put it on medium heat.

When it boils, dip a large tablespoon in the broth, then dip up a heaping tablespoon of the dumpling batter, shaping it into a round ball with the tablespoon. Drop it in the boiling broth, dip the spoon in the broth again and repeat until you have 8 or 9 round liver dumplings distributed evenly in the boiling broth. Cover tightly and cook gently for 15 minutes.

Lift the dumplings out with a slotted spoon and place them in a rather deep serving dish. Keep warm. Put 2 tablespoons of green dill seeds (from the freezer if they aren't available in the garden as yet) in the broth. Thicken it with 1 rounded tablespoon of arrow-root flour moistened in cold water. Pour this dill gravy over the liver dumplings and serve very hot. Serves 4.

Liver Ribbons

1 pound calves' liver	3 tablespoons oil
1 large onion, sliced	½ teaspoon sea salt
2 tablespoons wheat germ	

Cut calves' liver in thin ribbon-like strips. Put the oil in heavy skillet, and in it sauté the sliced onion and wheat germ. When onion and wheat germ turn golden brown, add strips of liver and sauté for 3 minutes. Sprinkle with sea salt. Cover skillet for 1 minute before removing from fire. Serves 4.

Veal Recipes

Roast Stuffed Veal

Buy a 3 or 4 pound veal shoulder and have the butcher bone it, then make a pocket to hold the stuffing. Preheat oven to 325 degrees. Mix sea kelp, thyme and marjoram together for seasoning. First rub the shoulder with either cut garlic or onion, then rub the dry seasoning in it all over. Then fill the pocket with Corn Bread Stuffing and skewer it together. Tie if needed. Place on a rack in the roaster and bake slowly for 2½ or 3 hours at 325°. Remove fat and thicken drippings with cornstarch paste (one tablespoon starch to one cup liquid) if gravy is desired. Serves 6.

Jellied Veal or Tongue Loaf

About 2 pounds of veal or
1 beef tongue
1 large onion
celery leaves or an outer stalk

a bunch of fresh marjoram
leaves
a small semi-hot pepper, or
pinch of dried hot peppers
sea kelp to taste

Boil the above ingredients until the meat is done. Lift out the meat and strain the broth, and measure out 2 cups of it, or add hot water to make 2 cups. Put this amount back on the fire while you dissolve 1 tablespoon of gelatin in ¼ cup of cold water. When the broth is very hot, stir in the congealed gelatin and stir until it is dissolved and clear. Remove from the fire.

Remove the bones if you have veal. Peel it, if you have tongue. Then either grind the meat through the food grinder, or whiz it up in the blender. Put the meat back in the broth, mix well and pour into an oiled mold. Refrigerate until it is set. Unmold on salad greens and garnish with scored cucumbers. Serves 8.

Savory Jellied Veal Loaf

2 breasts of veal
1 bunch carrots
1 cup diced celery
1 teaspoon sea salt

1 medium onion
1 teaspoon powdered kelp
½ teaspoon summer savory

Cover veal with water, add the celery, onion, sea salt, powdered kelp and summer savory. Cook until the meat comes easily from the bones. Strain stock and cook down to one cup. Oil mold, line with the steamed sliced carrots, then a layer of veal, etc. until all are used. Pour over the cup of stock and press down. Chill until set. Serve unmolded on platter garnished with some of the choice celery leaves. Serves 6.

Veal and Mushroom Bake

4 rib veal chops
2 tablespoons safflower oil
sea salt to taste
½ pound fresh mushrooms,
sliced

1 tablespoon soya flour mixed
into:
⅓ cup cold water
parsley flakes

Heat oil in a heavy skillet and brown the chops on both sides. Place in an oiled baking pan. Cover chops with mushrooms and pour flour and water mixture over all. Sprinkle liberally with parsley flakes. Bake in a slow oven from ¾ to 1 hour, until chops are fork tender. Serve hot. Serves 4.

Broiled Veal Cutlets

Have 1 pound cutlets cut less than ½ inch thick. Pound with a cleaver or plate edge on both sides, then dip each side in cooking oil which has had dried herbs added the night before. Sprinkle with sea kelp, then broil until tender in a heavy skillet. Remove cutlets to a warm platter. Serves 4.

Veal Patties

4 veal patties
1 egg, slightly beaten
½ cup wheat germ
1 tablespoon brewer's yeast
⅛ teaspoon each marjoram, thyme, basil, oregano
¼ teaspoon paprika

Combine wheat germ with other dry ingredients. Dip patties in beaten egg, then in wheat germ mixture. Sauté lightly in oil until tender and golden brown. Or place in a 350° oven on an oiled cookie sheet for about 20 minutes. Good with tomato sauce. Serves 4.

Rognons au Vin

4 veal kidneys or 8 lamb kidneys, cored
1 large onion, finely chopped
½ cup chopped mushrooms
1 cup chopped fresh celery
½ cup dry red or white wine
1 tablespoon cold-pressed oil
1 tablespoon potato starch, dissolved in 2 tablespoons cold water
sea salt to taste

1. Sauté the cored, whole kidneys in oil over medium high heat for about ten minutes, or until they are browned nicely on the outside and pinkish inside. Set them aside in a warmed bowl.

2. In the oil and juices left over from the kidneys, sauté the chopped mushrooms, onion, and celery until soft.

3. Cut the kidneys into small pieces and return them (and their juices) to the skillet. Season with sea salt and freshly ground black pepper. Pour the wine over and simmer over medium heat for about five minutes.

4. Add a teaspoon of the potato starch mixture, and continue to simmer, stirring constantly. If the sauce does not become as thick as desired, add more potato starch dissolved in cold water. Serve immediately over brown rice. Serves 4.

Veal and Eggplant Casserole

18 veal scallops (1½ pounds)	2 cups cubed tomatoes
3 tablespoons corn oil	1 cup diced green peppers
1 eggplant, peeled and sliced thin	1½ teaspoons sea salt
	½ teaspoon paprika
1 cup thinly sliced onions	½ teaspoon oregano

Trim any visible fat from the meat. Heat 1 tablespoon oil in a skillet; brown the meat in it on both sides. Oil a casserole with 1 teaspoon oil; arrange successive layers of the eggplant, veal, onions, tomatoes and green peppers, seasoning each layer with a mixture of the salt, paprika and oregano. Sprinkle with the remaining oil. Cover and bake in a 350 degree oven 1 hour and 15 minutes, removing the cover for the last 15 minutes. Serves 6.

Curried Veal on Brown Rice

1 pound veal steak cut in cubes	1 chopped onion
	1 tablespoon cooking oil

Use a chicken fryer or Dutch oven type utensil with a rounded cover so that you can cook the veal and onion in its own steam. Keep the cover on tight except when stirring or adding ingredients. Put the oil in the utensil, heat medium hot, add the veal and onion and simmer gently for about 20 minutes. Then add the following:

¼ teaspoon ginger

½ teaspoon curry powder

1 teaspoon sea kelp

1 cup chopped mushrooms

1 cup pineapple chunks

Simmer with the cover on tight for another 10 minutes and serve on hot fluffy brown rice.

In India, they would use more curry powder and omit the pineapple. In the tropical islands, they would use more pineapple and less curry powder. Serves 4.

Veal Supreme

1 pound veal, cubed

2 tablespoons safflower oil

1 teaspoon paprika

2 onions, sliced thin

sea salt

wheat germ

1 cup unflavored yogurt

In a heavy skillet heat oil mixed with paprika and sauté onion lightly. Season the veal cubes and roll in wheat germ. Place in skillet and sauté until veal is nicely browned. Whip yogurt until creamy and pour slowly over meat. Cover skillet and cook over low heat for another 20 minutes. Serves 4.

Soysprout Sukiyaki

Take a chicken fryer or Dutch oven type heavy utensil and heat. Put 2 tablespoons of oil in it and add the following:

2 cups diced lean veal (or lamb)

1 large chopped onion

1 cup chopped celery and leaves

1 chopped green pepper

2 cups chopped Chinese cabbage

1 tablespoon fennel seeds

Simmer gently for about 10 minutes then add the rest of the ingredients:

1 cup mushrooms

1 cup diced Tofu

2 tablespoons soy sauce

Cook until the meat and vegetables are done and serve over brown rice or bean sprouts. Serves 6.

Veal Chop Suey

Place a heavy Dutch oven on low heat and add 2 tablespoons of cooking oil. Then add these ingredients:

1 medium onion, sliced
1 cup celery, diced

2 cups lean veal, diced

Simmer about 15 minutes with the cover on tight except for frequent stirrings. Then add the following:

1½ cups fresh-made sprouts (either alfalfa or Mung bean)

1 green pepper, slivered
1 cup fresh mushrooms, chopped
1 tablespoon soy sauce

Simmer for another 5 minutes. Keep the cover on tight until serving over hot brown rice. Garnish with rose hips powder. Serves 4.

Sicilian Piccadillo

2 pounds ground veal
4 medium-sized onions
2 green peppers, diced
1 clove garlic, mashed
1 cup sliced olives
½ cup raisins

½ cup blanched sliced almonds
1 tablespoon chopped fresh basil
1 teaspoon honey
3 ripe tomatoes, quartered

Sauté the ground veal in a heavy skillet with just enough vegetable oil to coat bottom. Cook until all the red disappears. Put veal into large pot. Sauté the onions, pepper, garlic adding a small amount of oil until soft and golden, but not brown. Add vegetables to veal in pot. Add olives, raisins, almonds, basil and honey. Combine well and season with sea salt to taste.

Cover and simmer until all ingredients are blended. Remove from flame and hold until serving time. Just before serving add quartered tomatoes and reheat. Serve with fluffy rice. Serves 8.

Brains Barbizon

1¼ cups cooked pearl barley	1 egg
1½ pounds beef brains	1 tablespoon soy flour
10 cabbage leaves	1 tablespoon cooking oil
clove garlic	

Poach brains in enough water to cover. Simmer 15 minutes then blanch in cold water before removing membrane and blood vessels. (Refrigerate until ready to use.)

Mince the garlic or squeeze for juice and mix with the barley and brains. Add the slightly beaten egg and soy flour. Blanch the cabbage leaves in boiling water. Roll about 2 tablespoons of the barley mixture in a cabbage leaf and place in casserole. Dribble the oil over all the cabbage rolls and bake in oven for 25 minutes at 350°. Serves 6 to 8.

Sautéed Brain Slices

Cut boiled, cooled brains into thick slices. Roll in wheat germ, seasoned egg and then wheat germ again. Sauté in oil. Remove slices and season oil in pan with lemon juice. Pour over the slices. Garnish with parsley. One pound serves 4.

Stuffed Beef Heart

1 beef heart	½ teaspoon sea salt
½ cup beef stock (this can be made from soup bone or beef)	¼ teaspoon sage
	¼ teaspoon sweet basil
	⅓ teaspoon marjoram
1 cup wheat germ	½ teaspoon summer savory
1 chopped onion	mushrooms if desired

Steam heart 5 to 6 hours or until tender. Cut off fat and connective strips. Cut strips in side heart to put dressing without cutting heart through. Mix stuffing and fill heart. Bake in oven 300 degrees for about 3 or 4 hours. Remove from oven and slice crossways. Serve hot. Serves 6.

Heart Stew

1 beef heart, about 1½ pounds	1 cup cold water
2 tablespoons safflower oil	2 onions, sliced
½ pound fresh mushrooms, sliced	½ teaspoon basil
½ cup tomato juice	1 cup fresh peas

Remove membranes from heart and slice thin. Season with sea salt and brown lightly in hot oil. Add mushrooms and sauté lightly. Add onions, tomato juice, water and basil. Cover skillet and simmer for ½ hour. Add peas and continue simmering until peas are tender. Sprinkle with parsley flakes and serve hot. Serves 6.

Kidneys en Brochette

4 veal or 8 lamb kidneys, cored and cut into 1″ pieces	cherry tomatoes
½ cup cold-pressed oil	whole mushrooms
2 cloves garlic	green pepper, cut into 1″ pieces
1 teaspoon oregano	onion, cut into 1″ pieces
juice of ½ lemon	sea salt to taste

1. Make marinade of oil, crushed garlic, oregano and lemon juice.

2. Place kidney pieces in marinade, making sure they are thoroughly coated. Cover bowl and put in refrigerator for an hour or two, stirring occasionally.

3. Thread marinated kidney pieces, tomatoes, pepper, mushrooms and onion, alternately, on skewers. Broil for about 15 minutes or until vegetables are soft and kidneys are browned and juicy.

4. Pour juices obtained from kidneys over brown rice. Place skewers of meat and vegetables over rice and serve immediately. Cucumber and yogurt salad makes a fine accompaniment.

Serves 4.

Kidney Stew with Scallions

1 pound lamb kidneys
3 carrots, sliced
4 potatoes, cubed
2 stalks celery, chopped

4 small onions
seasoning, to taste
5 scallions, chopped

Wash and soak kidneys in vinegar for an hour. Remove veins, and cut into cubes. Brown in oil along with onions, scallions, celery, and carrots. Add cubed potatoes, seasoning and enough water to cover kidneys and vegetables. When done add 1 tablespoon arrowroot flour to thicken stew. Serves 4.

Soya-Creamed Kidneys

1 pound kidneys
1 cup beef broth
½ cup sliced mushrooms
    clove garlic, chopped

small onion, chopped
sea salt
paprika
½ cup soy milk

Prepare kidneys by covering with cold water in saucepan and bringing to boil. Throw off first water. Slice kidneys in half lengthwise.

Sauté onions and garlic in ¼ cup safflower oil. Add to the prepared kidneys, mushrooms and beef broth. Simmer gently 30 minutes. Add ½ cup water to ½ cup soy milk and add to the kidneys and mix until creamy. Season to taste. Serves 4.

Sweet and Sour Tongue

1 4-5 pound tongue (water to
    cover)

3 bay leaves
3 cloves

Simmer for 4 hours.

Vinegar Sauce:

½ cup cider vinegar
½ cup honey
¼ teaspoon allspice

¼ teaspoon cinnamon
¼ teaspoon cloves
½ cup raisins

Skin tongue. Simmer 45 minutes in vinegar sauce. Serves 8.

Cold Beef Tongue

Boil the tongue in water to which the following have been added: ½ bell pepper, celery tops, fresh or dried herbs, 1 small onion and sea kelp. Cool and peel the tongue. Wrap in a clean cloth, cutting off as needed. This makes a delicious Sunday night dish, so quick to serve. Serves 6 to 8.

Poultry Recipes

(Chicken and other Fowl)

Roast Chicken

Take a 6 or 7 pound roasting chicken. Wash thoroughly, pat dry. Rub with cooking oil, then rub the outside with sea kelp and poultry seasoning. Rub the inside with the same. Tie the wings and neck to the body with clean white thread. Bake 30 minutes at 350 degrees, remove and stuff, sewing the cavity together. Roast in an open pan until done, turning occasionally. Allow 40 minutes per pound and roast at 325 degrees. Baste often with the fat which cooks out. Serves 4 to 6.

Chicken Breasts Alexis

1½ cups chopped dates
¼ cup chopped onion
½ cup wheat germ oil
1 cup finely shredded carrots

2 cups brown rice cooked (¾ cup uncooked + 2½ to 3 cups water)
½ teaspoon crushed rosemary
½ cup diced almonds
6 large boned chicken breasts

Precook rice—¾ cup brown rice—3 cups water—dash kelp. Bring to boil. Simmer about 40 minutes.

Chop dates. Sauté onion in oil until transparent. Combine dates, onion mixture, carrots, rice, rosemary and almonds; toss gently. Spoon equal amounts of date mixture onto breasts—overlap edges and skewer. Place seamside down in shallow baking pan. Brush with oil. Bake 350°—1½ hours. Serves 6.

Chicken Breast with Carrots

4 halves chicken breast	1 teaspoon paprika
2 cups sliced carrots	1 tablespoon chopped parsley
¼ cup wheat germ	2 tablespoons corn oil

Place carrots in baking dish or pan. Dip chicken breast in corn oil and roll in wheat germ which has been mixed with paprika and parsley. Arrange chicken on top of carrots. Cover and bake at 275 degrees for about three hours. Sprinkle with sea salt. Serves 4.

Mushroom and Chicken Liver Blend

3 tablespoons oil	1 teaspoon sea salt
3 onions, chopped	1 teaspoon soy flour
1 pound chicken livers, chopped	3 tablespoons brewer's yeast
	1 teaspoon basil
½ cup mushrooms, sliced	⅛ teaspoon nutmeg, ground
3 stalks celery and tops, chopped	2 cups brown rice, cooked in stock

Heat oil. Sauté onions, livers, mushrooms and celery. Remove from oil and set aside. Stir into oil the salt, flour, yeast, basil and nutmeg. Blend thoroughly. Blend with rice and sautéed mixture. Heat thoroughly. Serve garnished with soy grits. Serves 6.

Chicken Livers and Mushrooms

Simmer 6 chicken livers about 5 minutes, or until they are nearly done. Then add ½ box of mushrooms which have been washed and chopped and simmer about 3 mcre minutes. There should be not over a cup of water on them, which you thicken with 2 level tablespoons of arrowroot flour and 1 teaspoon sea kelp. Cook and stir until the broth is moderately thick. Add 1 teaspoon minced onion and serve over the mashed potatoes or steamed brown rice. Serves 4.

Chopped Chicken Liver

Broil one pound of chicken livers, sauté one chopped onion in oil or chicken fat. Hardboil two eggs. Reserve one egg yolk for garnish.

Chop all ingredients together in a wooden bowl with two or three lettuce leaves and a little parsley. If you like a finer texture, you may put all ingredients into the blender. Garnish with egg yolk strained through a sieve. Serves 4.

Chicken Liver Cutlets

12 chicken livers
1 egg, well beaten
1 cup soya flour
¼ chopped onion

¼ chopped green bell pepper
¼ cup vegetable oil
1¾ cups mushrooms (halved)
1¼ cups water

Cut chicken livers in half. Beat egg, dip livers into egg. Roll livers in the soya flour, coating them well. Pour the vegetable oil into your skillet. Heat the livers and onions and pepper until golden brown.

Heat mushrooms and water to a good boiling point. Add this to the other mixture, then stir well and serve. Serves 4.

Chicken Liver Kabobs

1 pound chicken livers
2 onions
1 green pepper

8 fresh mushroom caps
3 tablespoons safflower oil
seasoning to taste

Cut livers in half. Cut onions and green peppers into thick wedges. Alternate livers and vegetables on skewer. Add seasonings to oil and mix well. Brush livers and vegetables with seasoned oil. Broil, turning skewer once or twice, until livers are golden brown. Serve at once. Serves 4.

Chicken Liver Pate

Boil one pound chicken livers in water to which a handful of celery leaves, fresh marjoram and sea kelp have been added. Strain the broth and keep it for use as the liquid in a molded or pressed meat dish later. Chop livers fine and add your own mayonnaise. Place in a mold and chill. Serve garnished with a sprinkling of chopped egg and onion rings. One pound serves 6.

Chicken-on-Eggplant

1 frying chicken, cut up	¼ cup raisins
1 medium sized onion, minced	½ cup almonds, slivered
½ cup chopped celery	sea salt to taste
2 cups home-canned tomatoes	pinch of cinnamon
1 cup sliced mushrooms	curry powder to taste

Bone chicken. Place pieces of chicken in greased baking dish with all ingredients except almonds. Bake at 300° F. until the chicken is very tender, about 80 minutes.

When mixture is almost ready, slice 1 eggplant to desired thickness. Broil slices until they are well done, but not too brown. Add almonds to hot chicken mixture and serve immediately on broiled eggplant slices. Serves 4.

Broiled Chicken Halves

Take young fryers which have been split in halves. Dust with sea kelp and powdered poultry seasoning and place on the broiler rack in the bottom of the oven. Broil 30 minutes, turn and season the other sides as you did the first ones. Broil another 30 minutes and serve piping hot. This slow broiling preserves valuable nutrients and juices, and makes a marvelously-flavored protein dish. One half small chicken per person.

Oven Fried Chicken

3 pound frying chicken, cut up	large, shallow glass baking pan, well oiled

A dipping mixture made as follows:

1 cup yellow cornmeal	1 teaspoon cumin
1 tablespoon minced onion	1 tablespoon chopped parsley
1 tablespoon sea kelp	

First dip the chicken chunks in corn oil, then in the cornmeal mixture, and lay them, not touching, in the oiled baking dish. Sprinkle any remaining mixture over the larger chunks of chicken. Bake in a 400 degree oven about 20 minutes, then turn each piece of chicken and bake another 20 minutes, or until tender. Serves 4.

Chicken and Leek Dinner

1 tablespoon oil
2½-3 pound chicken, cut up
   as for frying
4 to 6 leeks

1 cup chicken broth
¼ cup white wine (when wine
   is heated, the alcohol evapo-.
   rates, but the flavor remains)

Cut leeks lengthwise (shoestring). Sauté in oil till clear. Lay giblets, then chicken on top of leeks. Add liquids and cook slowly, steaming chicken till done, ¾ hour or more. Season with sea salt. Add more chicken broth or water, if needed during cooking. Thicken slightly. Serve with brown rice. Serves 4.

Crunchy Baked Chicken

½ cup safflower oil
1 teaspoon sea salt
1 clove garlic, crushed
½ teaspoon paprika

2 broilers—about 3 pounds
   each, cut into serving pieces
½ cup wheat germ

In a bowl, combine oil, sea salt, garlic and paprika. Brush chicken pieces with this mixture. Roll each piece in wheat germ. Place skin side down in a shallow baking pan and brush each piece again with the oil mixture. Bake in a 350° oven until brown, turn each piece and bake until brown and tender. Serve accompanied by a mixed green salad. Serves 4 to 6.

Chicken and Walnuts

1 broiler chicken stewed and
   removed from bone
1 cup olive oil
3 walnut halves

1 cup chicken broth
3 teaspoons soy flour
1 tablespoon vegetable salt

Heat oil in large skillet. Sauté walnuts slightly. Drain on paper towel. Sauté slivered chicken in oil until no longer pink (about five minutes). Add chicken broth and cook over medium heat five minutes. In a small bowl mix soy flour and 3 tablespoons water. Add to chicken in skillet. When thickened add walnuts. Serve chicken and sauce with stewed brown rice. Serves 3.

Chicken Pie with Corn Topping

Stew a 3 pound chicken, seasoning it with sea kelp, herbs, celery tops and onion tied in a cloth. Cool the chicken and remove from the bones. Thicken the broth with arrowroot flour moistened with cold water. Arrange the chicken pieces in a large baking dish and pour the gravy over it.

Preheat the oven to 375 degrees and make the Corn Topping. Bring 2 cups of water to the boil and sift in 1 cup of yellow corn-meal, stirring all the time. Cook and stir until the mixture is very thick, then add 2 egg yolks which have been beaten until thick and lemon colored. Beat the egg whites until stiff, fold in the corn mixture and pour it over the hot chicken. Bake at 375 degrees about 35 minutes. Garnish with parsley and serve immediately. Serves 6.

Chicken Chop Suey

Heat a Dutch oven type stainless steel or enameled iron utensil and add a tablespoon of cooking oil, 1 cup chopped celery and 1 large onion cut fine. Cover and simmer the vegetables in the steam and oil until the celery is tender. Add the following and serve on brown rice:

2 cups diced chicken	sea kelp to taste
1 cup fresh sprouts	chicken broth to make it moist
1 teaspoon curry powder	

Serves 4.

Pakistani Chicken

2- or 3-pound chicken cut up. Dry the pieces, then dredge them in the following:

1 cup corn meal	½ teaspoon each of paprika and
1 minced onion	ground ginger
1 teaspoon crushed coriander seeds	¼ teaspoon turmeric, sea salt to taste

Pour 2 tablespoons sunflower oil in the bottom of a baking dish, lay the pieces of chicken in, cover and bake at 350° until browned, turn and add more sunflower oil if needed and bake until done. Remove cover if it doesn't brown nicely. Serves 3 or 4.

Chicken Milanese

Cut up a 2 or 3 pound chicken. Dry the pieces, then dredge them in:

1 minced onion
2 tablespoons cornmeal
2 tablespoons arrowroot flour
2 teaspoons tapioca
1 teaspoon paprika

1 teaspoon Italian seasoning
¼ teaspoon sea salt
1 teaspoon parsley (flaked or fresh)
⅛ teaspoon garlic powder

Pour ¼ cup of sunflower or corn oil in the bottom of a baking dish. Dip chicken skin side down into oil, then place skin side up. Cover and bake in a moderate oven (375°) about one hour or until done. Remove cover last fifteen minutes. Serves 4.

Coq au Doux

2 plump chickens, cut up
  dip each piece of chicken into
  a dish of raw honey

dredge honey-coated chicken in a dish of wheat germ mixture

Wheat-Germ Mixture:

1½ cups wheat germ
1 tablespoon snipped parsley

½ teaspoon thyme
½ teaspoon basil

Braise chicken in ½ to ¾ inches of soy oil at low medium heat. Keep temperatures at medium heat all during cooking of chicken as wheat germ mixture has a tendency to brown too quickly. Cook until tender to fork touch. Serves 6-8.

Chicken Rice Skillet Meal

½ cup chopped onion
½ cup oil
3 cups diced, cooked chicken
⅛ teaspoon sea salt
  garlic to taste
½ teaspoon thyme

1 cup brown rice, cooked
2½ cups chicken broth
½ cup drained home-canned tomatoes
½ cup chopped walnuts

Sauté onion in oil over low flame until golden. Stir in chicken, sea salt, garlic, thyme, rice, broth and tomatoes. Cover and simmer over low flame about 25 minutes, stirring occasionally. Stir in nuts. Garnish with tomato wedges and parsley. Serves 6.

Chicken with Brown Rice

4 cups brown rice, cooked
3 tablespoons soy oil
¼ cup rice flour
½ teaspoon paprika
½ teaspoon celery powder

2 cups nut milk
1 cup chicken broth
3 cups chopped cooked chicken
1 cup mushrooms
¼ cup pimiento strips

Add 1 tablespoon oil to cooked rice; set aside. In a 3-quart saucepan place rest of oil, heat and stir in flour, paprika and celery powder. Remove from heat and gradually stir in milk and chicken broth. Cook over medium heat, stirring constantly until thickened. Add chicken, mushrooms, pimiento and rice; heat thoroughly. Place in shallow casserole and garnish with parsley. Serves 6 or 8.

Chinese Chicken and Rice

3 cups cooked brown rice, chilled
2 tablespoons corn oil
¾ cup sliced scallions
1 teaspoon sea salt

1½ cups cooked julienne cut chicken
1 egg, beaten
3 tablespoons minced parsley
1 tablespoon soy sauce

Heat oil in skillet, stir in rice until browned. Mix in scallions, sea salt, and chicken. Make a well in center of rice and pour the egg into it, stirring until barely set, then stir into the rice mixture. Add parsley and soy sauce and stir, cook only 1 minute. Serves 6.

Pressed Chicken

Cook hen until tender in 2½ cups water, adding sea kelp, celery tops, a small diced onion and a handful of fresh herbs tied in cheesecloth the last half hour of cooking time. Cool and remove all of the meat from the bones.

Skim off the fat from the chicken. Then add the flaked chicken to the following ingredients:

½ cup diced celery
1 onion, minced

sea kelp to taste
½ cup relish (optional)

Pour this mixture into an oiled glass loaf pan and allow to thoroughly congeal. Slice off cold and serve on a platter, garnished with cucumber slices and parsley. Serves 4 to 6.

Molded Chicken Loaf

Simmer a small chicken, along with a handful of celery tops, 1 onion, a pinch of sage, and 1 teaspoon of rosemary, until the chicken is very tender. Cool. Remove from bones. Chop.

Put ½ cup of the broth on the fire while you dissolve 1 tablespoon of gelatin in ¼ cup of cold water, then melt it in the hot broth. Add it to 1½ cups more of the broth. If you don't have this amount, add vegetable stock or water.

Blend the chopped chicken with ½ cup diced celery, 1 tablespoon minced onion, ½ red bell pepper minced. Add the gelatined broth and pour into an oiled Pyrex-type bread tin. Chill until set. Serve by cutting off thick slabs of the jellied meat and garnishing with parsley and chives. Serves 6.

Boiled Chicken with Herbs

Select a young chicken which has a small amount of fat, and boil it with a big handful of celery tops and a small handful of marjoram leaves, plus sea kelp. Use a small amount of water, cook it gently, letting the water cook nearly up. Serve hot. It is a most delightful meat when fixed this way. One 3-pound chicken serves 2-4.

Christmas Roast Goose with Dressing

Roast goose for Christmas originally came from Germany but is now traditional with many nations. After the bird (a 10-pound goose serves 6) is prepared, washed and dried, rub it inside and out with a mixture made of the following ingredients: 1 onion minced very fine, 4 tablespoons sea kelp, 2 tablespoons poultry seasoning, 1 teaspoon thyme. This is for a moderately sized goose.

Place the bird on a rack in a large roaster and start in a moderate oven at about 300 degrees, uncovered. Bake for 1 hour, at which time the bird is pricked all over to release the fat. This is done at intervals all during the baking time and a sharp-tined fork is jabbed just through the skin about every half inch all over the fat parts of the bird. When the roaster becomes full of fat, dip some of it out. It shouldn't cover the rack at any time.

The goose should be stuffed and skewered after an hour or so of baking. You may add more seasoning when you stuff it if the bird is large.

Keep the pricking process going every half hour or so, removing excess fat from the roaster. Bake the goose until it is very browned and tender, about 20 minutes to each pound of bird at least, and more if needed.

Holiday Dressing

The giblets should be cooked the day before, and in plenty of water which is needed for preparing this dressing.

2 cups brown rice, cooked in giblet broth until half done
1 cup cornmeal, cooked in 3 cups giblet broth until thick
1 large onion, minced
1 teaspoon sage
1 teaspoon thyme
2 teaspoons poultry seasoning
4 eggs
1 cup celery, diced
1 cup wheat germ
1 cup sunflower seed meal (simply whiz the seeds fine) all of the chopped giblets
1 cup nut meats (optional)
2 cups mushrooms
4 tablespoons cooking oil
4 tablespoons sea kelp
2 tablespoons parsley, chopped

Blend all ingredients and add more giblet broth if needed for the proper consistency. Heat in the oven before stuffing the goose so that baking time is not interfered with.

After the fat is all poured off the drippings, the remainder of the giblet broth is poured on them and thickened with arrowroot flour for gravy.

Roast Duck with Mushroom Dressing

With stout white thread, tie the duck's legs, neck and wings down tight to the body. Take a tablespoon of sea kelp and a teaspoon of poultry seasoning and rub it all in the inside of the duck. Put the duck in the roaster, leaving the cover off, and put it in a preheated 375 degree oven for 30 minutes.

Remove the duck from the oven and prick just through the skin with a sharp fork, going all over the duck. This is to let the fat out. Stuff the duck with the Mushroom Dressing and sew the opening shut. Return the duck to the oven for another 20 minutes, when you again prick it all over, and turn the heat down to about 300 degrees. Prick the duck every 20 minutes or so, and when it is nearly done, season on the outside with more sea kelp and poultry seasoning.

When done, remove from roaster, pour off the fat. Serve with Mushroom Dressing. One duck serves 4 or 5.

Mushroom Dressing

2 cups chopped mushrooms	1 teaspoon each of sea kelp
1 cup oatmeal	and sage
½ cup wheat germ	chopped giblets (cooked)
1 egg	1 small minced onion
	1 tablespoon cooking oil

Moisten with the giblet broth and put in the oven to heat very hot while the duck is roasting. Stuff with the hot dressing.

1 stalk celery   ½ bell pepper

Add ½ cup each of raw honey and pure cider vinegar and keep refrigerated in a tightly covered dish.

Holiday Roast Turkey

For the holiday turkey, we recommend slow oven baking. To hold in the moisture and juices, we recommend an oil covering and low heat, which holds in the juices without detriment to the nutritional value of the meat. When the turkey is washed, inside and out, it is patted dry. The inside is rubbed with the following seasoning mixture: 1 teaspoon each of poultry seasoning or sage, teaspoon thyme, 1 teaspoon marjoram and 1 tablespoon of sea kelp—this to each 5 pounds of turkey. Stuff with Plymouth Dressing.

Place the turkey in a roaster which is big enough so that the cover fits tightly. Tear a piece of clean white cloth large enough to cover the top of the turkey. Saturate the cloth with cooking oil and cover the turkey. Place it in a preheated 300 degree oven, leaving the pan uncovered. After an hour, remove the cloth and season the outside by rubbing on another seasoning mixture like the first one. Repeat cloth operation. When almost done remove the cloth, add a cup of boiling water to the roaster and bake until done with the roaster covered. Bake approximately 20 minutes to each pound of bird, or until very tender and gently browned.

Remove the turkey, pour off all fat from the drippings, add stock, heat and thicken the gravy with arrowroot flour. Allow one pound of turkey per person.

Plymouth Dressing

Cook the giblets the day before and use the cooking water as a moistener for the following dressing:

1 cup rolled oats	2 tablespoons cooking oil
1 cup chestnuts (chopped)	1 teaspoon sage
2 stalks diced celery and leaves	1 tablespoon sea kelp
1 small onion, minced fine	½ teaspoon each of thyme,
2 beaten eggs	marjoram, and parsley
giblets, chopped fine	

Soak the wheat germ and rolled oats in the giblet broth until they are soft, then add the other ingredients and enough more broth to make the dressing moist.

Turkey Roll

Skin turkey, starting at back, with help of sharp knife. Take off breast meat, best parts of wings and thighs. Boil giblets, cool, put through food chopper. Add:

¼ cup carrots, chopped	½ teaspoon thyme
¼ cup celery, chopped	1 teaspoon food yeast
1 teaspoon onion flakes	4 tablespoons soya flour
1 teaspoon parsley flakes	2 eggs (mix well)
5 stuffed olives, chopped	1 teaspoon sea salt or kelp

Pour into double boiler, steam till it holds shape. Shape into roll—wrap meat around it—then wrap skin around this and tie with string. Drench in olive oil. Dust with kelp salt and paprika. Bake in moderate oven for one hour. About 8 servings.

Stuffings, Sauces and Gravies

Making your own sauces and gravies has a distinct advantage: you know exactly what's *not* in them—additives. Save every bit of the water you use in cooking vegetables and use it in gravies. Store remaining water in the refrigerator, tightly covered, until you're ready to use it. Vitamins B and C dissolve in water, as does vitamin P.

Use soy flour or whole wheat flour, instead of bleached white flour, to thicken your gravies and sauces. These flours are rich in riboflavin, which helps to convert carbohydrates to energy, aids vision, protects hair, nerves, skin, lips, tongue.

Recipes for Stuffings, Sauces and Gravies

Brown Rice-Nut Stuffing

1 cup uncooked brown rice	1 cup chopped celery
2½ cups chicken broth	1 garlic clove, minced
½ teaspoon kelp	1½ tablespoons oil
1 teaspoon sea salt	1 cup chopped pecans
1 cup chopped onions	

Combine rice, broth and seasonings; heat to boil; stir once. Reduce heat and simmer, covered until done, about 35 minutes. Cook onions, celery and garlic in oil until tender; add to rice along with pecans. This may be used as a stuffing or as a side dish.

Millet Stuffing

1 cup whole hulled millet	3 cups water

Cook in double boiler one hour.

2 cups diced cooked celery	2 beaten eggs
2 cups shredded raw apple (peeled)	

Mix millet, celery, apple and eggs.
Herbs and raisins may be added, also wheat germ or sesame seeds.

Corn Bread Stuffing

1 cup crumbled corn bread	1 small chopped onion
½ cup soya granules	½ slivered green pepper
½ teaspoon each of sea kelp, thyme and sage	2 tablespoons cooking oil
1 cup chopped mushrooms	1 egg

Use just enough broth or soup stock to dampen the dressing. It should be quite moist.

Matzo Meal Stuffing

4 cups crumbled matzos	4 tablespoons schmaltz (fat) or oil
1 cup cold water	
1 small onion, chopped	1 cup fresh chopped mushrooms
1 stalk celery and leaves, chopped	2 beaten eggs
	season with sage and sea kelp

Soak the matzo crumbs in the water, add the other ingredients and more crumbs or more water if too wet or too dry. Put the dish of stuffing in the oven so that it is hot when you stuff the chicken. You save ½ hour of baking time this way.

Squash Stuffing

2 cups mashed squash or pumpkin	1 tablespoon chopped parsley
1 egg	1 green pepper chopped
1 large onion finely chopped	2 tablespoons meat drippings
1 cup celery finely chopped	2 leaves of sage, chopped
	1 sprig of thyme

Mix together, stuff into bird and roast.

Potato Stuffing

Grate potatoes very fine, grate a medium sized onion, add ½ teaspoon sage, one teaspoon marjoram, one teaspoon sea kelp. Mix and stuff chicken, or other fowl with it, and bake until fowl and stuffing are done.

Vegetable Stuffing

2 cups cooked buckwheat groats
1 egg slightly beaten
¼ teaspoon kelp
  pinch of sage or herbs to taste
2 cups coarsely cut raw spinach
4 tablespoons cut parsley
½ cup ground carrot
1 small green pepper
1 medium onion
2 cups ground celery
4 tablespoons oil

Put vegetables through food chopper using medium cutter.

Cook vegetables in oil about 10 minutes. Add to buckwheat and other ingredients, warm water to moisten. Pack lightly into cavity of fowl. This will be enough for a 4-pound chicken. Increase ingredients for turkey.

Mint Sauce for Lamb

Gather young spearmint, and strip off the leaves, discarding the stems. Shred the leaves into a glass jar. To each cupful, add 2 tablespoons honey. Mix, cover tightly and keep in the sun for several hours, then add 6 tablespoons pure cider vinegar. Keep refrigerated. Use both leaves and sauce on the lamb for best flavor.

Herb Sauce

Good for broiled steak, chops, burgers, and broiled fish.

2 tablespoons chopped scallions
2 tablespoons oil
2 tablespoons chopped chives
2 tablespoons chopped fresh tarragon leaves
3 tablespoons chopped fresh parsley
3 tablespoons oil
½ pound mushrooms, sliced
  sea salt, to taste
½ cup fresh chicken broth
1 tablespoon honey

Sauté scallions in oil until soft. Remove pan from fire, add chives, tarragon, parsley. Sauté mushrooms in 3 tablespoons oil, quickly season, add herbs, chicken broth, simmer for 5 minutes, stir in honey, simmer 2 minutes more.

Barbecue Sauce

1 cup tomato purée
1 large tomato
2 tablespoons cold-pressed oil
¼ cup apple cider vinegar

⅛ teaspoon cayenne
3 tablespoons honey
1 medium onion (sliced)
½ green pepper (sliced)

Mix in blender until smooth. Serve on meats, etc. Use as a basting sauce on broiled or roasted meats, or chicken. Keep refrigerated.

Hollandaise Sauce

(Serve hot on cauliflower, asparagus or fish.)

yolks of 2 eggs
2 tablespoons safflower oil
½ tablespoon vinegar

½ cup boiling water
1 teaspoon sea salt

Add egg yolks one at a time to the safflower oil. Beat well; add vinegar and seasoning. About five minutes before serving, add boiling water slowly and stir rapidly—over water in a double boiler until it thickens.

Mock Hollandaise Sauce

Combine:

½ cup potatoes
¼ cup carrots

¾ cup water

Cook until tender, about 20 minutes. Place this mixture in blender and liquefy. Add:

1 tablespoon vegetable oil
½ teaspoon sea salt

1 tablespoon cider vinegar

Liquefy till smooth.

Mushroom Sauce

Take either a heavy Dutch oven type of utensil, or the chicken fryer type, with a rounded top which collects enough steam to cook the food. Barely cover the bottom with water and heat medium hot. Add these ingredients:

2 cups sliced mushrooms
½ cup chopped onion
1 green pepper, chopped
1 sprig each of thyme and marjoram
1 teaspoon sea kelp

Cover tightly and keep it on except when stirring the vegetables. Simmer very gently and the steam will cook the ingredients in about 10 minutes. Stir very little. Add 2 cups of hot beef broth and turn off the fire.

When the hamburgers are done, put them in a casserole-type serving dish and keep warm in the oven. Pour the fat off the drippings and using their pan, add the mushroom sauce, heat to boiling and thicken with arrowroot flour. Pour this sauce over the hamburgers and serve immediately.

Nutty Gravy

3 tablespoons of any nut butter   3 cups hot water

Blend these ingredients and then heat to the boiling point while you stir up enough arrowroot flour to thicken to the desired consistency. Then season with tomato pulp, onion, garlic, sage, herbs, sea kelp, pepper slivers, or any desired flavoring.

Non-meat Main Dishes

Eat More Fish!

Fish is complete protein, as good as meat. By this we mean that it supplies all the different protein elements that are needed for health. Some protein foods contain all the ingredients known to be needed for building and repairing tissues, while other protein foods lack some of these "amino acids." About 10 of these are absolutely essential for health—*required* in the diet of man. When compared for amino acid content, fish is as good as, or better than, chicken and beef.

Fish also contains relatively large amounts of calcium, copper, iron, magnesium, phosphorus, potassium, sodium and strontium. It is the high phosphorus content of fish that has made it famous as a "brain food," for phosphorus is one of the important constituents of brain matter.

Vitamins and Minerals in Fish

Here is how fish stacks up in the vital matter of minerals and vitamins. These figures must be approximate, for the content of fish varies, depending on when and where they were caught. We have chosen to give the food values in halibut, a popular and typical fish.

	Amount in 1 serving (about ¼ pound) of halibut
Calcium	20 milligrams
Phosphorus	200 milligrams
Iron	1 milligram
Copper	.23 milligrams
Magnesium	.01 milligrams

*Amount in 1 serving
(about ¼ pound)
of halibut*

Iodine	250	parts per billion
Vitamin B		
Thiamin	90-120	micrograms
Riboflavin	222	micrograms
Niacin	6	milligrams
Pyridoxine	100	micrograms
Pantothenic acid	150	micrograms
Biotin	8	micrograms
Calories	121	

Fish Recipes

Holiday Baccala (Codfish)

1 pound of dried-boned baccala (codfish)

Soak baccala in cold water for 3 days, changing water twice each day. After soaking period, break fish into serving pieces. Put aside and make sauce.

1 quart of home-canned tomatoes
1 cup tomato paste
¼ cup olive oil
1 medium onion, diced
10 oil-cured black olives
1 tablespoon dry seedless raisins
10 Pignoli nuts
few sprigs of celery leaves, chopped
sea salt to taste
basil, parsley

Heat olive oil and sauté onion, add tomatoes and paste. Cook for 15 minutes. Add olives, raisins, nuts, celery leaves; basil, and parsley. Cook ½ hour. Add soaked, cut up baccala and cook until tender. Serves 4.

Onion-Apple Stuffed Cod

1 pound fresh cod fillets
1 tablespoon cold-pressed oil
¼ cup finely chopped onion
2 tablespoons finely chopped celery
¾ cup chopped apple
3 tablespoons finely chopped fresh parsley
⅛ teaspoon sea salt
1/16 teaspoon thyme
1 tablespoon lemon juice
paprika

Heat oil in skillet and sauté onion and celery until soft. Stir in apple, parsley, sea salt, thyme and lemon juice. Mix until well blended. In a shallow baking dish (lightly oiled) lay one half of the fish fillets. Spoon stuffing mixture over the entire surface. Lay remaining fillet over stuffing. Drizzle top with oil and sprinkle with paprika. Bake in a 400 degree oven for about 20 minutes or until fish flakes easily with the tines of a fork. Serve hot, accompanied by broiled tomatoes. Serves 4.

Cold Flounder Salad

1 pound fillet of flounder, cooked, flaked and cold
1 medium red onion, finely minced
⅓ cup homemade mayonnaise
⅓ cup unflavored yogurt

2 tablespoons chopped fresh parsley
6 hard cooked eggs, quartered
3 ripe tomatoes, quartered
12 ripe pitted olives

In a bowl, combine the flaked fish, onion, mayonnaise, yogurt and parsley. Toss until blended. Transfer to a large platter lined with dark green lettuce leaves (crisply cold). Surround platter with alternate quartered eggs, tomatoes and pitted olives. Serves 4.

Baked Flounder Roll-Ups

4 flounder fillets
½ cup cooked kale, chopped
1 egg

4 tablespoons wheat germ
4 slices tomato
1 clove garlic, finely chopped

Mix the kale well with the egg, wheat germ and garlic. Spread mixture on fillets and roll up (as for a jelly roll). Fasten with toothpicks. Oil a baking dish and place the fillets in the dish. Place a slice of tomato on top of each fillet, moisten with a little safflower oil and bake in a moderate oven for ½ hour. Serves 4.

Fish with Fresh Mushrooms

1 tablespoon sunflower seed oil
1 medium onion, thinly sliced
¾ pound mushrooms, thinly sliced

1 pound flounder fillets, cut crosswise into 1 inch slices
1 tablespoon soy sauce
1 large stalk green celery cut into thin crosswise slices

In oil, in a large skillet with a tight-fitting cover, sauté onion one minute. Add mushrooms and sauté, stirring constantly, 2 minutes or until mushrooms are wilted. Spread fillet slices on mushrooms. Season to taste. Add soy sauce and celery, cover, simmer 10 minutes. Serves 4.

Easy Fish Chowder

½ cup thinly diced celery
2 tablespoons oil
¼ teaspoon sea salt
4 boiled potatoes

½ cup diced cooked carrots
½ cup soy milk
½ cup water
1 cup flaked cooked haddock

Cook celery in oil until tender. Add sea salt and remaining ingredients. Heat, cooking until bubbly.

Serve with sprinkling of chopped parsley and paprika. Serves 2.

Baked Halibut

4 medium potatoes, boiled
2 pounds fresh halibut
  (1 inch thick)
2 tablespoons cold-pressed oil
½ cup finely chopped onions
2 cloves fresh garlic, puréed

¼ cup chopped green peppers
2 fresh tomatoes, diced
2 teaspoons lemon juice
1 teaspoon sea salt
2 tablespoons finely chopped
  parsley

Cut the cooked potatoes into ¼ inch slices, and arrange them in an oiled 2½ quart shallow baking pan. Cut halibut into serving pieces and place on top of potatoes. In a heavy skillet, heat the oil and sauté onion, garlic and green pepper until onion is soft. Stir in tomatoes, lemon juice, seasoning and parsley and cook for 5 minutes. Spoon over the halibut and bake in a 400° oven for about 20 minutes or until halibut flakes easily with the tines of a fork. Lift fish and vegetables with a wide spatula onto platters and serve immediately with a tossed green salad. Serves 6.

Poached Halibut

2 pounds halibut (in one piece)   1 stalk celery
1 carrot, scraped   1 bay leaf
1 medium onion, peeled   sea salt to taste

Place fish in a dutch oven with just enough boiling water to cover. Add remaining ingredients. Cook over low heat for 20 minutes or until fish flakes easily with the tines of a fork. Remove to a serving platter and serve with either homemade mayonnaise or unflavored yogurt. Fish may be garnished with freshly minced parsley or watercress. Serves 8.

Halibut Pilaf

½ tablespoon safflower oil   ½ cup cold water
¼ cup chopped green pepper   2 cups tomatoes
¼ cup chopped celery   sea salt and dash of paprika
½ cup brown rice   to taste
2 tablespoons minced onion   2 cups cooked halibut, cut into chunks

Heat the oil in a large, heavy skillet. Add pepper, celery, rice and onion, stirring constantly for fifteen minutes. Add water, tomatoes and seasonings and stir until well blended. Add halibut chunks and stir for five minutes. Transfer to an oiled casserole. Cover tightly and bake in a slow oven until rice is tender. Serve hot. Serves 6.

Baked Salmon

For 4 pieces of salmon steak, about 1 pound, prepare ½ cup of mixed fresh herbs, preferably thyme, savory and marjoram. Pour enough cooking oil in a shallow baking dish to cover the bottom, lay the steaks in place and oil the tops. Season with sea kelp and light shakes of paprika. Then sprinkle the herbs over the fish and bake about 15 minutes at 400 degrees, then turn the steaks and bake another 15 minutes, or until browned nicely. Lift onto a warm platter. Pour 1 cup soup stock in the baking dish, thicken with 1 tablespoon arrowroot flour, and pour this over the steaks. Garnish with parsley. Serves 4.

Salmon and Vegetable Omelet

10 eggs
 1 cup bean sprouts
½ teaspoon sea salt
 2 tablespoons soy sauce

½ cup corn meal
¾ cup wheat germ
½ cup salmon (or 1 cup chicken
   or turkey)

Beat the eggs and add the rest of the ingredients. Drop enough into a moderately hot griddle to make an omelet about 4 inches across and sauté slowly, being careful not to overheat and toughen the protein in the eggs. Serves 4-6.

Snapper (Ocean Perch) Creole

1 pound snapper
1 medium sized onion (minced)
1 large bell pepper (minced)
2 large ripe (or home-canned)
   tomatoes

4 tablespoons safflower oil
1 garlic clove (minced)
1 teaspoon sea salt
⅛ teaspoon paprika

Place the safflower oil, onion, pepper and garlic in a saucepan and simmer about 10 minutes, or until tender. Then add tomato and seasoning; boil for 5 minutes. The clear meat of the snapper cut into strips of not over ⅝ of an inch thick may be boiled in the sauce for about 10 minutes and served over brown rice. Serves 4.

Tuna-Stuffed Cabbage

2 cups tuna fish
½ cup brown rice, raw
2 tablespoons oil
6 large cabbage leaves,
   blanched
½ cup diced green pepper

¼ cup walnuts, chopped
¼ cup diced onions
⅓ cup diced celery
1½ cups water
⅓ cup lecithin granules
   seasoning

Combine and mix ingredients. Put mixture in cabbage leaves. Bake at 350 degrees for 40 minutes. Serves 3.

Baked Stuffed Whitefish

Select firm whitefish. Clean fish thoroughly. Wash in cold water. Sprinkle with sea salt and let stand while preparing stuffing.

Stuffing

Toss together:

1 chopped onion
2 apples

1 cup celery
1 tablespoon chopped parsley

Add:

½ teaspoon celery seed
¼ teaspoon fresh powdered sage

⅛ teaspoon coriander seed
1 tablespoon safflower oil

Rinse fish. Fill with stuffing. Stitch or pin together the opening in the fish.

Brush lightly with safflower oil.

Bake in open pan, either turning or oiling occasionally, at 375 degrees, about one hour, depending on size of fish. Serve with tomato wedges. Garnish with parsley, and eat the garnish! Allow one fish per person.

Jellied Fish

2 cups cooked diced fish (pike, pickerel, ocean perch, haddock, salmon, tuna, whitefish, bass, trout, halibut or herring)
½ cup chopped homemade dill pickle
1 cup shredded cabbage

½ cup chopped celery and leaves
½ pimiento or red pepper, slivered
1 rounded tablespoon pure gelatin
¼ cup cold water
1½ cups meat or vegetable stock, hot

Dissolve the gelatin in the cold water then disperse it in the hot stock. Cool. Then add the other ingredients and pour in a fish mold. Chill until set, then serve on a bed of salad greens. Serve homemade mayonnaise or corn relish with it. Serves 4.

Fillet Fish Amandine

This is suitable for several types of fish fillet: fresh or frozen had-dock, perch, flounder, rock, or other mild white fish. Use ¼ cup vegetable oil in 8-inch square glass baking dish. Dip fish fillets in oil, coating both sides, then arrange skin side down in dish. Sprinkle liberally with paprika and ¼ cup slivered almonds. Insert meat thermometer in thickest fillet and bake in a hot oven until tempera-ture reaches 140 degrees, about 15 minutes. Sprinkle with parsley and serve. One pound serves 4.

Gefillte Fish

Put the following ingredients through the food grinder:

2 pounds of filleted ocean fish	1 carrot
1 small onion	1 stalk celery

Blend together along with 1 teaspoon sea kelp, 2 eggs and enough matzo meal to make into loaf consistency. Bake about 45 minutes at 350 degrees in an oiled loaf pan.

The traditional Gefillte fish is usually made into little balls and simmered on the fish head and bones, and the cooking water poured over it. Serves 6-8.

Baked Fish Fillets

Several hours before baking time, take a small bowl half full of cooking oil and add fresh green dill seeds, fresh marjoram leaves and fresh basil leaves. Dried herbs and dill can also be used, but in this case, soak the dried herbs in the oil overnight.

Strain out the herbs, whether fresh or dried. Take the fillets and brush with oil, then dip them on each side in yellow corn meal.

Place the fillets in a shallow baking dish which has been well-oiled so that the fish won't stick.

Bake at 375 degrees about 25 minutes, or until well-browned, then turn and bake until brown on the other side. One pound fillet serves 4.

Broiled Fish Fillets

Combine in a bowl:

½ cup cornmeal   1 pound fish fillets
1 teaspoon each sea kelp and
  fennel seeds

Dip the fillets in the cornmeal mixture on both sides and arrange in an oiled shallow baking pan or on the broiler rack. Put them at least 6 inches from the broiler so that they brown slowly, and give them at least 10 minutes on each side. Serve in the baking pan, or in the center of a platter, surrounded by broiled potato slices and garnish with finely cut parsley and bunches of young green onions. Serves 4.

Eggs Foo Yung (With Fish)

8 eggs   1 teaspoon pure honey
2 cups cooked fillet of fish,   2 teaspoons soy sauce
  flaked   sea salt, to taste
½ cup chopped green onions 3 tablespoons safflower oil

Beat eggs slightly and add remaining ingredients except the oil. Mix until blended. Heat oil in a large skillet and drop mixture by tablespoonfuls in the hot oil. Brown on each side and serve hot with homemade applesauce or with unflavored yogurt. Serves 4.

Fish Banana Bake

fish slice (at least one inch thick) wheat germ or sesame seeds
nut milk or soy milk (thick)   bananas sliced lengthwise

Dip fish in milk, then in sesame seeds or wheat germ (both sides). Place on oiled cookie sheet; put bananas on top. Sprinkle lemon juice over fish and bananas. Bake at 450° for about 15 to 20 minutes, depending on thickness of fish. This dish needs no other seasoning. One pound of fish serves 3 or 4.

Fish Chowder

In a heavy saucepan, put 1 tablespoon cooking oil and the following vegetables and simmer for 10 minutes:

2 large chopped tomatoes
1 cup chopped celery and
   leaves
½ cup chopped onion

½ green pepper
1 potato, diced
2 teaspoons sea kelp
2 basil leaves, diced

Now add 1 cup diced leftover fish and 1 chopped parsley leaf and simmer until the celery is done. Serves 2.

Fish-Cornmeal Balls

1 cup fish, cooked, flaked
2 cups cornmeal mush, cooked
1 egg
1 tablespoon oil
1 tablespoon soy flour
1 tablespoon dulse, minced

2 tablespoons brewer's yeast
½ teaspoon celery seeds,
   ground
3 tablespoons chives, minced
   wheat germ
1 teaspoon sea salt

Combine all ingredients and mold into balls. Roll in wheat germ. Drop into simmering fish stock or soup. Cover. Simmer for 10 minutes. Serves 6.

Meatless Dishes

While we are wary of the nutritional problems presented by a steady vegetarian diet, occasional meatless main dishes provide variety and economy in everyday menu-planning. We recommend all kinds of nuts and seeds in nut loaves and patties, salads and desserts, either whole or chopped. Mushrooms are a fine protein and can be used as the basis for the main course, or raw in salads. Buy the commercial variety for safety, unless you are sure of the right ones to pick from the lawn or woodlands.

Brown rice contains precious B vitamins that you don't get in pasta, so we suggest that you use brown rice, in place of macaroni and spaghetti. Eggs are a good, nutritious standby and can always be added to any dish to fill out the protein. Use plenty of fruits in any part of a meal and remember bananas are particularly "filling."

Dried beans, peas, lentils and soybeans are valuable and inexpensive elements in side dishes, loaves, patties, soups, stews, and salads. Use plenty of vegetables, both raw and cooked. The starchy ones can be used as satisfying replacements for noodles and the like.

The Versatile Soybean

The soybean can be used throughout the day's menu in every kind of recipe, from "soup to nuts." The following list of soybean products will help acquaint you with the many forms the soybean can take.

Tofu: Soybean milk curd or cheese. Used in countless dishes in the Orient to add valuable protein, inexpensively.

Dried Soybeans: The best of many varieties is the Bansei which tastes like our Navy bean, is not fat or greasy and is quick to cook.

Green Soybeans: Pick them and use them as you would limas; put very young ones in raw salads, or steam them with herbs.

Soy Milk: It is made from the dried beans and is often preferable to cow's milk.

Instant Soy Milk: A commercial soy milk powder is the basic product; directions are on the can.

Soybean Oils: Try to get the cold-pressed oil for salads and fall back on the processed kind for cooking and baking.

Soybean Flour: This is the 46 per cent protein flour, that can be mixed with potato starch flour, rice flour, wheat germ and other flours as a substitute for wheat.

Soybean Lo Fat Flour: Probably the highest protein flour—over 52 per cent protein, and *no* starch—this product can also be used to make a drink by adding water. These flours can be added in small amounts to almost every dish, cooked or raw, that you serve to improve the amino acid. They are especially valuable for fat-free diets.

Soybean Granules: Add these to cereals, salads, dressings, soups, stews; they are 52 per cent protein. In baking they can provide crunchiness, when desired.

Soybean Grits and Flakes: These high protein breakfast cereals are good for breading, extending ground meats, meat substitute dishes for vegetarians. Some are quick cooking but read directions carefully as some require more preparation time.

Soy Sauce: Is commonly used in Chinese dishes. When you are faced with a pale colored gravy, use a tablespoon of soy sauce to enhance the appearance, the flavor and the protein content.

Lecithin: This supplement that works to control cholesterol build-up, is made from soya.

Infant Milk: Milk made from soybeans is often recommended by doctors for feeding infants with milk allergies or other physiological problems.

Low Fat Soy Products: These are available for dieters and low-fat diets.

Nuts Are Good for You

What do you think of a food that has this kind of nutritive value, grows wild and free for the picking, needs little care while it is growing, is harvested by picking it up from the ground, needs no processing and no cooking and keeps well with no refrigeration or preservatives? Doesn't it sound like the absolutely ideal food that we have been waiting for all these years?

Speaking generally, most nuts are high in protein and low in carbohydrate.

One pound of nuts can equal the calories in 2.3 pounds of bread, 3.7 pounds of steak, 12.3 pounds of potatoes or 15 pounds of oranges. One pound of oil-rich nuts supplies all the calories needed for the day plus 40 per cent of the protein, 60 per cent of the phosphorus, 30 per cent of the calcium and iron and 4 times the daily requirement of fat.

This high fat content indicates that nuts are an excellent food for anyone trying to gain weight. They make a delicious snack between meals. They are high in protein which means that they do a good job of helping to regulate blood sugar, so important to good health.

Most nuts contain a good supply of vitamin A and thiamin, one of the B vitamins. Some of them contain vitamin E. Immature English walnuts have been found to contain large amounts of vitamin C, which disappears as the nuts ripen.

Nuts are not complete protein, even though their protein content is high. We mean by this that they do not contain all of the amino acids, or kinds of protein essential for human health. But, even so, nuts are a most important food if you want to increase your protein intake, and most of us should.

Nuts in their shells keep well. Shelled they become rancid in 3 or 4 months, especially in the summer. They can be kept at refrigerator temperatures for a year. They are an excellent and unusual dessert.

For those housewives who no longer serve cakes, pies, puddings or cookies for dessert, why not offer a big bowl of the family's favorite nuts, a couple of nutcrackers and picks and bring them to the table after each meal along with fresh fruit? We often forget about nuts if we keep them in a bag in the kitchen cupboard. So try to keep a bowl of them handy for everyone to dip into for snacks—on a table in the family room or living room.

Here is the composition of a number of kinds of nuts. Note, please, that some of them have a relatively high starch content; some are high in protein. Remember that, although the protein of nuts is excellent protein, it does not contain all of the essential amino acids that are present in foods of animal origin.

	Carbohydrate	Percentage of Protein	Fat	Calories per pound
Acorn	57.10	6.65	5	1909
Almond	4.3	20.5	16	3030
Beechnut	13.2	21.9	57.4	2846
Brazil nut	4.1	13.8	61.5	3013
Butternut	3.5	27.9	61.2	3165
Cashew	29.4	21.6	39	2866
Chestnut	36.6	2.3	2.7	1806
Coconut	27.9	5.7	50.6	2760
Filbert	9.3	14.9	65.6	3288
Hickory nuts	11.4	15.4	67.4	3342
Lychee	78	2.9	.80	1539
Macadamia nuts	8.2	8.6	73.0	3507
Peanuts	8.6	28.1	49	2645
Pecans	3.9	9.4	73	3539
Pine nuts	6.9	33.9	49.4	3174
Pistachio	16.3	22.3	54.0	2996
Walnut, black	10.20	27.6	56.3	3180
Walnut, English	5.0	12.5	51.5	3326

The percentage of the mineral content of nuts is given in the following chart:

	Phosphorus	Potassium	Calcium	Magnesium	Sodium	Chlorine	Iron	Sulfur	Zinc	Manganese	Copper
Almond	.475	.759	.254	.252	.026	.020	.0044	.150	.0019	.0008	.0015
Brazil	.602	.601	.124	.225	.020	.081	.0028	.198	....	....	.0014
Butternut	....	....	....	....	....	....	.0068	....	....	....	.0012
Cashew	.480	....	.048	....	....	....	....	....	....	....	....
Chestnut	.093	.560	.034	.051	.065	.006	.0070	.068	.0004	.0031	.0078
Coconut	.191	.693	.043	.077	.053	.225	.0036	.076	.0010	....	....
Hazelnut	.354	.618	.287	.140	.019	.067	.0041	.198	.0010	....	.0012
Hickory nut	.370	....	....	.160	....	....	.0029	....	....	....	.0014
Macadamia	.240	....	.053	....	....	....	.0020	....	....	....	....
Peanut	.392	.614	.080	.167	.039	.041	.0019	.226	.0016	.0020	.0009
Pecan	.335	.332	.089	.152	....	.050	.0026	.113	....	.0043	.0010
Pistachio	....	....	....	....	....	....	.0079	....	....	.0007	.0012
Walnut, black	.091	.675	.071	.098	....	....	.0060	....	....	.0033	.0032
Walnut, English	.038	.332	.089	.134	.023	.036	.0021	.146	.0020	.0018	.0011

Although they are not as rich in vitamins as some other foods, nuts provide some of the vitamins that exist in all natural food products that have not been refined. The B vitamins are scarce in modern American diets, for we have removed them from foods during the processing. So nuts, even in the small quantities in which we eat them, compared to other foods, are an excellent source of the B vitamins. Here is the vitamin content of some of the common nuts:

	Vitamin A	Thiamin	Riboflavin	Niacin
Almonds (¾ cup)	0	.25 mg.	.67 mg.	4.6 mg.
Brazil nuts (¾ cup)	trace	.86	....	....
Cashews (¾ cup)	....	.63	.19	2.1
Chestnuts (40)	0	.108	.24	1.0
Coconut (2 cups)	....	.30 .60	1.0	....
Peanuts (¾ cup)	0	.30	.13	16.2
Peanut butter (6 tbs.)	....	.12	.13	16.2
Pecans (1 cup)	50 I.U.	.72	.11	.9
Walnuts, Eng. (1 cup)	30 I.U.	.48	.13	1.2

In addition, peanuts are rich in pyridoxine, pantothenic acid and biotin, 3 other important members of the vitamin B family.

Peanut butter is made of peanuts that have been roasted and halved. Then their skins are removed and they are ground. Usually oils are added to keep them in a smooth, buttery condition. If you have access to it, buy raw peanut butter or make your own from raw peanuts.

Nuts, like other natural products, should be eaten in as nearly the natural state as possible. But we civilized folks tend to process nuts until we finally almost destroy their food value. Cooking the nuts in oil causes considerable loss of vitamin contents. Modern commercial methods of processing nuts bring about destruction of perhaps 70 to 80 per cent of the thiamin.

What can you do to secure nuts whose food value has not been ruined before you get them? First of all, never buy nuts that have been shelled or roasted. If you have ever tasted an almond right out of the shell, you will know that there is no excuse for roasting them.

Recipes for Meatless Meals

Beanburgers

2 cups cooked dried beans
½ cup chopped celery and leaves
1 small onion minced
¼ teaspoon sage or poultry seasoning

1 teaspoon sea kelp
½ teaspoon dried or fresh marjoram
½ teaspoon minced parsley
¼ cup grated carrot
2 eggs

Mash the beans, add the other ingredients and add peanut flour if necessary to make patties which will hold their shape. Roll the patties in sesame seeds, place in a hot oiled iron-type skillet and bake under the broiler, turning once, until done. Serves 4.

Raw Carrot Burgers

1 cup grated raw carrot
1 cup ground walnuts
1 cup ground sunflower seeds

1 tablespoon fresh herbs, coarsely chopped
2 raw egg yolks

Blend ingredients together, shape into patties and roll in raw peanut flour. Keep in a tightly covered dish until served. Serves 6.

Carrot Loaf

1½ cups grated, raw carrots
1 cup cooked brown rice
¾ cup coarsely chopped, raw peanuts
2 tablespoons green pepper, chopped fine

4 tablespoons parsley, chopped fine
4 tablespoons soy powder
1 tablespoon minced onion
2 beaten eggs
2 tablespoons oil
sea salt to taste

Mix ingredients in order given. Bake in oiled loaf pan at 350° F. for one hour. Serve with tomato sauce. Serves 4 to 6.

Carrot-Nut Patties

Mix:

1 cup grated carrot
½ cup ground peanuts or cashews

2 tablespoons olive oil
1 egg, well beaten

Sauté in 2 teaspoons of olive oil:

2 small green onions, chopped
1 stalk diced celery

½ green pepper
1 teaspoon sea salt

Add to carrot mixture. Shape in loose patties and bake at 350° for 25 minutes. Serves 2.

Potato-Carrot Souffle

4 medium potatoes, grated
2 medium carrots, grated
1 small onion, grated
3 eggs, separated

½ cup soy flour
1½ teaspoons kelp
½ cup safflower oil

Drain liquid from potatoes, add carrots, onion, egg yolks, flour and season. Mix well, add oil and stir until well blended. Fold in stiffly beaten egg whites. Pour into an oiled souffle dish and bake one hour in a 375° oven. Remove from oven and serve immediately. Serves 4 to 6.

Mock Veal Loaf

¾ pound fresh carrots
1 cup raw peanuts (skinless)
1 medium onion

1 cup cooked brown rice
2 eggs

Season with choice of kelp or sea salt. Grind carrots with medium blade, then grind nuts and onion. Add to carrots. Add rice, eggs, and seasoning. Pack in oiled 9 × 5 inch loaf pan. Bake about 45 minutes at 375 degrees. Serves 4.

Chinese Steak

1 pound mushrooms
1 cup sliced or chopped onions
1 cup celery
1 cup bean sprouts

2 tablespoons water chestnuts
4 eggs
soy sauce

Braise a pound of tender mushrooms in vegetable oil in a skillet. In another deep pan braise a cup of sliced or chopped onions and a cup of celery. When tender, add drained bean sprouts and water chestnuts (if available). Stir all together and steam a few minutes until tender.

Beat eggs and pour over the whole mixture in a large skillet. Sprinkle soy sauce over this as it sets. Cover. Turn with a pancake turner after cutting into steak size. Add a little more soy sauce and it is ready to serve. Serves 4.

Egg Croquettes

2 chopped hard cooked eggs
½ cup cooked brown rice
2 tablespoons homemade mayonnaise

½ teaspoon grated onion
1 tablespoon water
1½ teaspoons Dill seeds
soy grits for coating

Combine ingredients in order given. Shape into 3 or 4 flat cakes. Roll generously in soy grits which have been crushed a little. Bake on an oiled pan about 10 or 15 minutes until brown. Serves 2.

Walnut-Eggplant Patties

1 medium eggplant
2 cups ground walnut meats
½ cup wheat germ
1 teaspoon sea salt

1 medium onion, chopped
2 eggs, beaten
1 tablespoon chopped parsley

Slice eggplant and cook until tender in small amount of water (approximately ¼ cup). Let cool. Mash and mix all ingredients together; form into patties and cook in oil over medium heat to a golden brown. Yield: 6-7 4-inch patties.

Eggplant-Potato Souffle

2 cups cubed, pared eggplant
2 cups cubed, pared potatoes
1 onion, peeled and sliced
2 cups cold water
1 sprig parsley
1 bay leaf

sea salt to taste
½ cup soy milk
3 egg yolks, beaten
2 tablespoons wheat germ
3 egg whites, beaten stiff

In a saucepan place eggplant, potatoes, parsley, onion, bay leaf, salt, pepper and water and cook until potatoes are soft, about 10 minutes. Remove bay leaf and force vegetables through a ricer. Add soy milk, yolks of eggs, wheat germ and mix together well. Let cool 10 minutes.

Preheat oven to 375 degrees. Fold egg whites gently into vegetable mixture and pour into a 1½-quart souffle dish (lightly oiled). Bake for 40 minutes and serve immediately upon removal from oven. Serves 4.

Almond Loaf

Pour 1 cup of hot stock or potato water over 1 cup of oatmeal, blend together, cover and let stand until cool. Add the following:

2 eggs
1½ cups ground almonds
½ cup ground sunflower seeds
1 medium onion, chopped
½ cup diced celery and tops

½ chopped bell pepper or pimiento
1 teaspoon marjoram (fresh or dried)
1 tablespoon sea kelp
1 tablespoon cooking oil

Blend and add as much more of the stock or potato water as is needed for loaf consistency. Pour into an oiled bread tin and bake from 30 to 45 minutes, or until done, at about 350 degrees. Turn out on a meat platter and garnish with red pepper and parsley. Serve hot or cold. Serves 4.

Nutty Burgers

1 cup local nuts, ground fine
½ cup sunflower seeds, ground fine
½ cup grated carrots

1 stalk celery, ground
1 small onion, ground
½ green pepper, ground
1 sprig parsley, ground

Put the above ingredients through the food grinder or in the blender with enough liquid (a tomato or ½ cup broth) and then add the following:

2 eggs
1 teaspoon sea kelp

1 pinch of sage or marjoram

Any nuts may be used. We choose the local ones because they are much less expensive. Blend the ingredients and if they are too dry, add broth or tomato pulp; if too moist, add rice polishings. Shape into patties, roll in brewer's yeast powder or flakes and broil until browned on each side. Serves 4.

High Protein Loaf

1 cup chopped nuts
1 cup cooked brown rice
1 cup wheat germ
2 eggs, beaten
2 onions, chopped
¼ cup celery and tops, chopped
½ green pepper, chopped
1 cup water

½ cup soy flour
2 tablespoons brewer's yeast
½ teaspoon sea salt
½ teaspoon sage (or 2 teaspoons fresh sage)
a few grates of fresh peppercorns

Blend all ingredients, and turn into a greased loaf pan. Bake at 350 degrees for 45 minutes. Serve with tomato sauce or your favorite sauce. Serves 6.

Walnut Loaf

Cover 1½ cups of wheat germ with nut milk and let the wheat germ absorb all the liquid it will take up. Drain slightly. Place in mixing bowl and mix with:

1 cup chopped walnuts
1 chopped onion
1 chopped green pepper
1 chopped tomato

juice of one lemon
1 tablespoon soy oil
1 egg, well beaten

Form into a loaf, place in oiled pan and bake at 325° F. about 30 minutes. Serve with tomato or mushroom sauce. One loaf serves 4.

Mock Turkey

2 cups rolled oats
2 cups hot water
2 green onions, minced fine
4 eggs
2 tablespoons cooking oil

2 cups ground nut meats
  (walnut preferred)
1 cup ground sunflower seeds
2 tablespoons peanut butter
1 teaspoon poultry seasoning
2 teaspoons sea kelp

Pour the hot water over the rolled oats. Add the rest of the ingredients. Oil a baking pan and shape the mixture in the form of a turkey, using stalks of celery for the legs and shaping the mixture around them. Use small oblongs of the mixture for wings. Pat oil over the outside and bake in a moderate oven until done in the middle, probably 45 minutes. Loosen with a spatula and remove to a meat platter. Garnish and serve hot. Serves 4 to 6.

Lentil Loaf

2 cups cooked lentils
½ cup quick rolled oats (raw)
2 eggs
1 teaspoon sea kelp
1 teaspoon fresh or dried thyme

1 stalk diced celery
1 small onion, chopped
1 cup homecanned tomato juice
½ cup ground nuts or
  sunflower seeds

Mix ingredients together and bake 35 minutes at 350° in a loaf pan. Cool and cut in slices. They are also delightful baked in tiny loaf tins, which cuts baking time accordingly. Serves 4.

Lentil Stew

1 cup lentils	1 cup brown rice
4 cups vegetable water	1 small onion, chopped fine
¼-½ teaspoon savory	½ cup carrots, diced
1 tablespoon soy sauce	½ cup peas

Place lentils and 2½ cups water into 1½ quart casserole and simmer, covered, approximately 1 hour.

Add remaining water, rice, onion, savory and simmer, tightly covered, approximately ½ hour.

Stir in carrots, a little more water if necessary, and simmer, covered, for 15-30 minutes longer, or until carrots and rice are just about done.

Add soy sauce and peas and simmer until done.

Add kelp, bone meal or dolomite to increase mineral value.

Potatoes may be substituted for rice. Serves 4.

Soybean Roast

Pour 1 cup hot potato water over 1 cup rolled oats, blend. Add the following ingredients:

2 cups mashed cooked soybeans	½ Spanish onion, chopped fine
1 tablespoon sea kelp	2 stalks celery, diced
1 cup chopped mushrooms	2 eggs
1 cup carrot pulp from juicer	1 teaspoon sage

If mixture is dry, add tomato juice. Bake about 45 minutes in an oiled loaf pan at 375 degrees. Serves 6.

Soya Chops

1 cup soya granules	1 cup hot tomato juice
1 cup rolled oats	

The night before, pour the hot tomato juice over the rolled oats and granules, mix and let stand overnight. In the morning add these ingredients:

2 eggs
1 teaspoon sea kelp
1 teaspoon soy sauce
¼ teaspoon celery seeds

1 teaspoon minced onion
2 teaspoons minced bell pepper
½ cup rice polishings

Blend and add enough tomato juice to form mixture into patties. Shape and arrange in an oiled baking dish and bake 25 minutes at 400 degrees. Serve piping hot with waffles. Serves 6.

Soybean Souffle

3 cups cooked soybeans, mashed until very smooth
3 eggs, separated

1 tablespoon minced onion
2 tablespoons minced parsley
season to taste

Beat egg yolks until light and combine with mashed beans, onion, parsley and seasoning. Mix thoroughly. Fold in stiffy beaten egg whites. Pour into a lightly oiled (oiled with safflower oil) souffle dish and bake in a 350 degree oven for 30 minutes. Serve immediately. Serves 4.

Delicious Squash Flowers

8 freshly picked squash flowers (more or less)
1 egg (beaten)

2 tablespoons water
½ cup soy flour
corn oil

Wash flowers, let drain. Meanwhile beat egg and water together. Dip flower in egg mixture . . . then in soy flour. Brown both sides in corn oil and serve. Serves 4.

Squash Patties

1 pound white squash (cooked and mashed fine)
½ cup wheat germ
½ cup coarse grated pecans
1 egg

1 small onion (grated)
1 small green pepper (grated)
¼ teaspoon kelp
1 teaspoon honey

Mix ingredients into cooked squash in order in which they are listed. Drop from spoon and bake on a hot oiled griddle. Brown lightly on each side. Serves 4.

Sunflower Goulash

1 cup chopped sunflower seeds
2 cups mushrooms, halved
2 onions, sliced
1 cup fresh sprouts
1 cup cooked and cooled millet

2 cups fresh or home-canned tomatoes
1 cup lima or butter beans
1 teaspoon chili powder
sunflower seed oil

Sauté the onions in sunflower seed oil until tender. Add all other ingredients, season, pour in casserole dish and bake about ½ hour, and serve. Serves 4.

Sunburgers

1 cup ground sunflower seeds
½ cup grated raw carrots
½ cup celery, chopped fine
2 tablespoons chopped onion
1 tablespoon chopped parsley
1 egg

1 tablespoon soya oil
½ teaspoon sea salt
1 tablespoon green pepper, chopped
¼ cup tomato juice
a pinch of basil

Combine with enough tomato juice so the patties hold a good shape. Arrange in a shallow baking dish and bake at 350° until browned, turn and brown on other side. Serves 4.

Seedburgers

1½ cups sunflower seeds
1 carrot cut in chunks
2 eggs (shells, too, for calcium)

1 stalk celery, cut in pieces
1 onion (small)
1 sprig of parsley
¼ bell pepper

Whiz until eggshells are reduced to powder. Add seasoning and conditioner as follows:

One half teaspoon each of sea kelp and mace, and enough tomato juice and wheat germ to make the mixture into patties which will hold their shape. Dip each patty into brewer's yeast powder or flakes and place on a hot oiled griddle or skillet. Place under the broiler just long enough to brown, turn and brown on the other side. Serve hot with vegetables to garnish nicely. Serves 4.

Chick Peas and Vegetables

1 pound chick peas, cooked and drained
1 small onion, sliced
1 clove garlic, minced
2 tablespoons pure olive oil
1 cup home-canned tomatoes

¼ cup cooked brown rice
1 sweet potato, peeled and cut into 1-inch cubes
1 cup cold water
½ teaspoon sea salt
1 teaspoon minced fresh parsley

Sauté onion and garlic in olive oil until soft; add tomatoes, chick peas, rice and sweet potato cubes. Add water and sea salt. Cover pan and cook about 20 minutes or until potatoes are tender. Add parsley a minute before removing pan from the stove. Serve piping hot. Serves 4-6.

Vegetarian Nutty Loaf

Combine the following ingredients and soak overnight in a covered granite or glass dish:

1 cup millet (use the seeds for this)
½ cup sunflower seeds

1½ cups home-canned tomato juice (or fresh if it is available)

When ready to make the loaf, add:

1½ cups ground walnuts
1 cup chopped mushrooms
2 eggs
1 tablespoon sea kelp

1 tablespoon fresh basil (diced)
1 small chopped onion
2 tablespoons cooking oil

If the mixture isn't thick enough, add wheat germ until you have a formed batter. Bake in an oiled bread tin for 1 hour at 350° or until done in the middle. Serves 4.

Vegetarian Sukiyaki

In a Dutch oven type (stainless steel or enameled iron) put the following, cover tightly and simmer gently:

1 tablespoon cooking oil
1 large onion, chopped
1 cup diced celery
2 cups shredded Chinese cabbage
½ cup slivered green pepper

2 cups fresh mushrooms
1 cup cubed Tofu (Soybean milk curd or cheese, available at health stores)
1 tablespoon soy sauce

Stir as little as possible for the steam cooks the vegetables. Season to taste. Serve with bean sprouts. Serves 4.

Vegetables

Cook Vegetables Properly
to Insure Nutrition and Flavor

Even if you carefully heed a good value chart in attempting to prepare well-balanced meals, your foods very likely suffer nutritional depletion in your own kitchen, unless you prepare them for the table as carefully as you select them.

Though raw fruits and vegetables are generally the richest in nutrition, cooking is often an essential part of food preparation. The enzymes and the many microorganisms, which help plants to grow, are also responsible for breaking them down. As a result, plants decay. Proper cooking not only destroys these two kinds of spoilers by its intense heat but also makes many kinds of food more palatable.

Heating foods often enhances proteins, fats and carbohydrates by chemically changing them into foods that man absorbs more quickly. But it does play havoc with vitamins and minerals.

Proper Cooking

Leave vegetables unpeeled wherever possible, and cover bruised surfaces with a dab of oil; displace oxygen in the utensil with steam; cook in the shortest time possible; save and use all the cooking liquid which now contains much of the vital nutrients; serve these hot foods immediately after preparation to avoid unnecessary nutrient loss.

The water soluble vitamins, C, P, and B complex, suffer most from cooking, and hence from improper cooking. Many minerals are also lost in the cooking water.

While water is by no means the only depleting influence upon nutrients during preparation and cooking, it is by far the most common one. Foods that are washed, soaked, or boiled stand to lose much of their vitamin and mineral value—especially the water soluble ones.

Provided you keep an eye on the cooking time, steaming in the pressure cooker is a good method of preparation. The length of time that each kind of vegetable should be cooked is included in the directions with the equipment. Only a few tablespoons of water need be used, and the remaining liquid should be served with the vegetable.

The best method of cooking vegetables is the waterless method. Fresh vegetables contain 70 to 95% water, which is sufficient for cooking them if the heat is controlled so that no steam escapes. The utensil must have a tight-fitting lid, and the heat should be evenly distributed. A tablespoon or two of water should be put into the preheated utensil to make steam that will drive out any oxygen that is present. The important thing to remember in this method is to keep the heat low after the first few minutes so that no steam escapes.

If you must boil your vegetables, keep them refrigerated until you bring the water to a rolling boil. Then drop in the vegetables and keep them there only long enough to soften them; don't overcook them.

Stir-Fry Cooking

The simple "stir-fry" method of the Cantonese people produces some of the healthiest and most beautiful meals known anywhere. "Stir-fry," in fact, can be called a masterpiece of culinary technique, ranking with the inventive genius of the French.

The basic method is unbelievably easy, considering the delightful results. Dice, slice or shred vegetables. Heat a small amount of oil in a large heavy frying pan. When very hot, add vegetables, stir constantly and continue to cook on a high heat until the vegetables are just done (by Chinese standards), still crunchy, but neither browned, nor raw, nor soggy. Green vegetables should still be emerald-hued, not grayish. Leafy vegetables takes 1-2 minutes, fibrous vegetables like broccoli and string beans must steam at a lower heat for an extra few minutes. *Serve immediately.*

This is a classically simple method that preserves the best in food value in a highly appetizing form. Everything is eaten: no juices are thrown away. Cooking time is quick, but effective. Even the cooking oil contributes to the good effects. Only the unsaturated fatty acid types like corn, soy, or sunflower oils are recommended. (Avoid olive oil because it has a strong flavor of its own.) Don't use hydrogenated oils (the solid kind).

Proper cutting of the vegetables is a most important step in the preparation, second only to your skill in judging cooking time. The smaller you cut them, the quicker they cook—and therefore, the more healthful the dish.

Choose only young, fresh vegetables. Aging vegetables suffer from hardening of the arteries, making them stringy. You will find that the cooking time is greatly lengthened. Prepare the vegetables just before cooking.

You will get the best results from stir-fry method if you use the traditional Chinese "wok," a very wide iron pan with a curved bottom. It sits on a metal collar a couple of inches above a gas flame or fire. (A heavy cast iron frying pan is an acceptable substitute for the wok.)

The key to successful stir-fry is the chart shown here, from which you can easily compose your own recipes. Most vegetables are good to eat stir-fried alone, but try combining two or more for flavorful variations.

Wok Cookery

Preparation Chart

Green Vegetables	Cutting Preparation	Cooking Time
Parsley (only leaves)	Chopped fine	1 min.
Scallions	Tops chopped coarse	1 min.
	Bottoms: ½" lengths	2 min.
Snow peas	Whole or cut in half	2 min.
Watercress	Cut in half	3 min.
Spinach	Whole	3 min.
Green peppers	Shreds	2½ min.
	1" squares	3 min.

Asparagus (tender stems)	Diagonal slices 1" long by ⅛" thick	3 min.
Peas	Shelled	Sauté 1 min., add a few T water, cover, braise 4 min.
Okra (small pods)	½" lengths	4 min.
	Whole	Sauté 1 min., add a few T water, cover, braise 5 min.
Broccoli (very young and small)	2" flower head lengths, separated	Sauté 1 min., add a few T water, cover, braise 5 min.
	Peeled stems sliced diagonally ¼" thick	Braise 1 min. longer than flower heads
String beans	Frenched (cut in half length-wise)	Sauté 1 min., add a few T water, cover, braise 6-7 min.
	1" lengths	Add 2 min. to braising time.

Basic Vegetables (white or gray)	Cutting Preparation	Cooking Time
Mushrooms	⅛" thick	2 min.
Mung Bean sprouts	Whole	3 min.
Cucumbers	Peel, quarter, remove seeds (if large) and slice into 1" squares	3-4 min.
Celery (tender stalks)	¼" shreds—diagonal	3 min.
	1" pieces	4 min.
Onions	Halve and slice ⅛" thick	4 min.
Cauliflower	1/16" thick, 1" square	Sauté 1 min., add a few T water, cover, braise 4 min.
Celery cabbage	Leaves: ¼" shreds	2 min.
	Stalk: ¼" diagonal shreds	Sauté 1 min., add a few T water, cover, braise 4 min.
Cabbage, head	¼" shreds	Sauté 1 min., add a few T water, cover, braise 4 min.
	1" pieces	Add 1 min. to braising time.
Zucchini (unpeeled)	⅛" dice	Sauté 1 min., add a few T water, cover, braise 6 min.
	¾" dice	Add 3 min. to braising time.

Red or Yellow Vegetables	Cutting Preparation	Cooking Time
Tomato (ripe but firm)	Large dice or sections (8 from a large tomato)	1 min.
Corn	Cut kernels from cob	4 min.
Carrots	Diagonal slivers	2 min.
Summer Squash	⅛" slices	Sauté 1 min., add a few T water, cover, braise 6 min.
	¾" dice	Add 3 min. to braising time.

When combining two vegetables needing steaming, sauté only the longer cooking one. Steam the second vegetable for its full cooking time.

Peeling, Undesirable But Necessary

Next to soaking of foods, peeling is considered the second greatest threat to nutrition. Unfortunately, because pesticide spraying has become so widespread, peeling food has become a sensible health precaution, even though it means throwing a lot of good nutrition into the garbage. It is an important reason why you are often better off to lose some of the nutritive value of food and take a vitamin supplement instead.

Mass-distributed fruits and vegetables may be nipped off their plants before they ever get the chance to ripen and grow into their full nutrient potential. The foods displayed in supermarkets may never come close to the food value specified on charts.

Foods that are processed and packaged before they reach you lose a lot more of their nutritional content. The inviting pictures on the packages may well be the best things about them.

How can *you* avoid these pre-serving pitfalls? Shop for the freshest foods available, and when you get them home waste no time in storing them. Then follow the above suggestions for cooking and preparing your foods, and don't waste vitamins and minerals on the kitchen counter and stove. Above all, don't cook foods to death.

Good judgment on your part can boost your nutritional intake substantially.

Artichoke Recipes

Dieter's Dream—Artichoke

2 tablespoons cold-pressed oil
1 medium onion
1 clove garlic, minced or run
through garlic press

2 cups sliced raw carrots
1 cup sliced raw Jerusalem
artichokes

Over medium heat, sauté diced onion and garlic until the onion is golden in color.

Add carrots and Jerusalem artichokes, mixing well with sautéed onions and garlic.

Cover tightly, lower heat, and steam until tender. Do not overcook.

Variations: Add any or all of the following ingredients in step 2:

1 small handful sliced mushrooms	diced broccoli stems thinly sliced celery
½ cup shredded cabbage	diced green pepper

Serves 4 to 6.

Stuffed Artichoke Salad

1 package frozen lima beans	homemade mayonnaise
1 avocado	pimientos
1 teaspoon minced onion	mushrooms
1 tablespoon broth seasoning	3 artichokes, cooked
1 stalk celery	

Cook and mash lima beans. Mash avocado, add onion and broth, chop celery, add mayonnaise. Stuff ingredients between leaves of artichoke and top with pimientos and mushrooms. Serves 3.

Fresh Artichokes

Take one dozen fresh Jerusalem artichokes (small—one to two inches in diameter), prepare by removing hard leaves and tops, shape stem with sharp knife. Slice in quarter inch slices.

Heat two tablespoons olive oil in heavy skillet, add artichokes, handful of chopped parsley, one clove minced garlic, pepper.

Simmer covered till tender, very short time. Serves 3 or 4.

Artichoke Medley

Through the food chopper put the following:

2 cups scrubbed artichokes, cubed	2 sprigs parsley
1 onion	½ cup pignolias

Grind them into a refrigerator dish and cover immediately. Serve at once. Dressing may be added if desired. Serves 4.

Recipes Using Asparagus or Beans

Marinated Asparagus

12 asparagus spears, steamed
    till tender, crisp, drained
2 tablespoons olive oil
2 tablespoons cider vinegar

¼ teaspoon sea salt
1 teaspoon honey
1 bay leaf, broken

Beat last five ingredients together, pour over asparagus in a shallow dish, cover and refrigerate several hours, turning asparagus once. Remove from refrigerator a while before serving. Serves 4.

Riviera Green Beans

2 cups tender green beans
    cut in inch lengths
1 tablespoon chopped green
    onions
1 young carrot sliced thin on
    a grater

1 cup tiny red or yellow
    tomatoes
½ cup shelled peas
    salad greens and fresh
    herbs

All ingredients are raw. Line a salad bowl with the salad greens. Dice the fresh herbs over them. Toss the other ingredients together with your favorite dressing and pour them into the salad greens. Garnish with rose hips and paprika. Keep covered in the refrigerator until serving time. Serves 4.

Almondine Green Beans

Put a tablespoon of cooking oil in a heavy saucepan, heat and add ¼ cup of minced onions. Cover and steam 5 minutes, add ½ cup slivered almonds and a package of thawed green beans from the freezer. Heat thoroughly, season to taste and serve. Serves 4.

Soy Baked Beans

Use 1 pound of the marvelous Bansei type soybeans for this dish. Cook them with lean veal, the same as you would navy beans, withdrawing from the fire about 30 minutes before they will be done.

Add:

1 small chopped onion   1 tablespoon honey
1 tablespoon blackstrap
  molasses

Bake for the remaining 30 minutes or until the beans are tender and browned. The beans will have been seasoned with sea kelp and a dash of paprika early in the cooking process. Serves 6.

Special Green Beans

Put a Dutch oven type utensil on medium burner and cover the bottom with cooking oil. Dice in chives or green onions, then add 4 cups green beans and steam until done. Season in your favorite way as you stir them during the steaming process. When ready to serve, garnish with strips cut from red bell peppers. Serves 4.

Bansei Boiled Beans

Pick 2 cups ripe Bansei soybeans, shell, wash and cook until almost tender, seasoning with salad oil, sea kelp and a shake of paprika. Add 1 onion, quartered, and 2 quartered tomatoes, and boil gently for another 30 minutes.

Not only the soy variety, but ordinary navy beans can be fixed this way. Serves 4.

Saturday Beans

Soak *1 pound of navy beans* overnight and boil one hour the next day.

Add:

1 cup diced potatoes
1 cup carrots
⅔ cup chopped onion
1 tablespoon parsley

2 cups tomatoes, peeled and
chopped
½ cup oil
1 small clove garlic, minced
sea salt to taste

Brown in moderate oven approximately 1 hour. Serves 6.

Herbed Green Beans

1 pound green beans, cut into
1-inch pieces
2 tablespoons safflower oil
1 tablespoon finely minced
onion

½ teaspoon basil
½ teaspoon rosemary
dash of garlic powder
sea salt, to taste
¼ cup cold water

Place all ingredients in a sauce pan, cover the pan and cook lightly until beans are crisp-tender. Serve with a sprinkling of minced fresh parsley. Serves 4.

Green Beans Scandinavia

2 cups cut green beans,
uncooked
½ cup early onions, sliced
¼ cup apple vinegar
1 clove garlic

½ cup olive oil
1 teaspoon chopped dill weed
1/16 teaspoon clove
Dash of paprika
12 radishes, sliced

Combine vinegar, garlic, oil, dill, clove and paprika in a jar. Let sit while green beans, onions, and radishes are prepared and placed in salad bowl. Remove garlic from dressing, then shake well and pour over salad. Toss, chill and serve. A crunchy accompaniment for any meal.

This recipe may also be used with leftover green beans. Serves 4.

Minted Beans

Wash and coarsely shred 2 cups green beans.

Steam briefly over small amount of water until they are *crisply* tender. Chill.

Add a dash of sea salt and season to taste with apple cider vinegar and finely chopped fresh peppermint. Serves 4.

"A Heavy Duty Bean Pot"

Cook about four pounds neck bones till the meat falls away. Take meat up, cool and refrigerate. Put bones back in broth and boil 2 hours more. Remove from fire, put through strainer, cool, take off fat.

Add to broth in pot:

1 large onion	2 pounds northern or navy
1 cup blackstrap molasses	beans
	1 teaspoon sea salt

Turn heat to high till the broth is almost boiling (late evening). Turn to warm until morning. (It is this long very slow cooking that makes the beans delicious.)

In the morning add:

The meat you put in the refrigerator	2 tablespoons bone meal powder
2 tablespoons dolomite powder	2 tablespoons brewer's yeast powder

Give good stir, turn off the heat and serve. Serves 8.

Baked Beans

Cook 1 pound dry beans until soft. Do not soak them. After they are cooked soft, prepare the sauce for them in the blender.

2 cups home-canned or raw tomatoes	¼ cup molasses
1 tablespoon cider vinegar	½ cup onion, green pepper, parsley pieces
⅓ cup honey	season to taste
½ cup cut-up celery pieces and leaves	

Blend together only enough to blend the vegetables. If the tomatoes are raw blend them smooth first before adding the rest of the ingredients. The tomatoes may be strained but this is not necessary. Lay bacon pieces or bacon strips over the top of the beans. Bake on low heat, 300°, until done. Serves 4-6.

Delicious Beans

1 cup dried lima beans (or any dried beans)
1¾ cups water (more if a thicker bean is used)
2 tablespoons oil
2 teaspoons grated onion
¼ teaspoon sea salt
⅛ teaspoon thyme
1 small bay leaf
2 tablespoons blackstrap molasses

Wash beans and soak overnight. In the morning, bring to a boil and simmer until tender. Twenty minutes before serving time, add the remaining ingredients and simmer. Serves 4.

Savory Lima Beans

2½ cups cooked lima beans
2 tablespoons minced onion
1 tablespoon oil
3 tablespoons green pepper, minced
1 cup tomato sauce or strained tomato

Heat oil, add onion and green pepper. Cook over moderate heat for 5 minutes. Add tomato sauce and cook for 5 minutes. Add lima beans and simmer over a low fire until thoroughly heated. Serves 4.

Recipes Using Beets and Broccoli

Harvard Honey Beets

2 tablespoons arrowroot starch
1 cup beet juice
3 tablespoons cider vinegar
4 tablespoons honey
1 tablespoon soy oil
2 cups cooked sliced beets

Mix arrowroot starch with the beet juice in a medium size sauce-pan, add vinegar, honey, and oil. Stir over medium heat until thickened. Add the cooked beets and stir. Let stand with heat off to blend flavors for about 10 minutes. Reheat and serve. Serves 4.

Western Beets

8 medium beets   1-2 tablespoons corn oil
6-8 large lettuce leaves

Oil the bottom of a large skillet. Clean lettuce leaves under run-ning water. Do not drain. Place half of the lettuce leaves to line the bottom of the skillet. Slice the raw beets very thin and place on top of the beets. Cover pan and simmer slowly for 30 minutes until beets are tender. To serve, chop lettuce leaves fine and toss with beets. Season to taste. Serves 4 to 6.

Stuffed Beets

4 large steamed beets   ½ tablespoon lemon juice
1 cup steamed peas   ½ tablespoon honey
1 tablespoon oil

Cut slices off top of beets having beets as hot as can be handled. Scoop out center, leaving cup. Mix part scooped out with hot steamed peas and refill cups. Add a few drops of lemon juice to oil and half a teaspoon honey, and pour over the stuffed beets. Serves 4.

Herbed Broccoli

Sprinkle mace and basil over washed broccoli heads, then steam until tender. Season with sea kelp just before serving.

Cabbage and Carrot Recipes

Cabbage-Rice Casserole

1 head of cabbage, steamed and
  chopped
1 cup brown rice

1 tablespoon chopped parsley
1 teaspoon fennel seed
½ cup chopped nuts

Oil a baking dish, line the bottom with half of the chopped cabbage. Lay the rice, nuts and seasoning over the cabbage, moisten with 2 tablespoons of apple cider. Add another layer of cabbage, then the rice and nuts and the cider. Lay several coarsely chopped apples on top and bake for about 30 minutes at 325 degrees. Serves 4.

Crisp Cabbage Medley

2 tablespoons homemade
  mayonnaise
1 onion, chopped
1 green pepper, chopped

1 cup thinly sliced celery
3 cups shredded cabbage
2 teaspoons sea salt

Add all the ingredients and mix well. Put the mixture in a large saucepan, cover, and let steam for five minutes. Serve immediately. Serves 4.

Hungarian Sauerkraut

Use a deep earthenware pot. Put in about 2 inches raw cut cabbage; on top place 2 bay leaves, few slices of quince apples, few grapes, very small bag of caraway seeds (the bag made out of cheesecloth), a pinch of salt. Repeat layers until container is filled. Cover with double fold clean cheesecloth, place a small piece of hardwood board on it; for weight, use a large glass jar, filled with water.

As fermentation starts, a film of bubbles will appear over the cloth, which has to be removed by washing the cloth and the board. Repeat the cleaning process a few times. When cabbage turns glassy and yellowish in color, take off the cloth, the board and the weight, cover and place on lowest shelf in refrigerator. The sugar in apples and grapes helps the natural fermentation.

Use raisins and sweet apples, when grapes and quince are not in season.

Mushroom Stuffed Cabbage

1 head cabbage	½ cup raw rice (brown)
3 tablespoons cold-pressed oil	1 cup boiling water
½ pound mushrooms, sliced	1 teaspoon sea salt
½ cup chopped onions	1 cup strained tomatoes

Cover cabbage with boiling water and let stand 10 minutes to soften. Carefully remove 16 leaves. Heat 1 tablespoon of oil in a skillet and sauté the mushrooms and onions 10 minutes.

Heat another tablespoon oil in saucepan, stir in rice and cook slightly. Add boiling water, cover and cook over low heat until tender and dry. Mix in the vegetables and salt. Place a heaping tablespoon of the mixture on each cabbage leaf, turn in the ends and roll up. Shred the remaining half of cabbage and spread in a casserole; arrange cabbage rolls over it. Add tomatoes and remaining oil. Cover and bake at 350°, 1 hour, removing cover the last 15 minutes. Serves 4.

Red Cabbage and Apples

One head red cabbage cut fine. (Cook in a very small amount of water until tender.)

Three apples peeled and sliced.

Sauté apples in three tablespoons oil until tender. Then add one-third cup honey and one-half teaspoon vegetable salt.

Combine the cooked cabbage and sautéed apples. Keep hot on slow flame and serve. Serves 4.

Red Cabbage and Mung Bean Sprouts Saute

3 tablespoons safflower oil
4 cups shredded red cabbage
2 cups mung bean sprouts

1 tablespoon caraway seeds
sea salt and paprika to taste

In a large heavy skillet, heat the oil and sauté cabbage and sprouts for about 5 minutes or until tender-crisp. Add caraway seeds and seasonings and toss lightly. Serve hot. Serves 6.

Panned Cabbage and Carrots

1½ cups thinly sliced carrots
½ cup water
1 quart coarse knife-shredded green cabbage

2 scallions (green onions), thinly sliced with tops included
2 tablespoons cooking oil

In a 10-inch covered skillet, boil the carrots in the water until almost tender; there should be several tablespoons of water left, if not, add that amount to the skillet. Add the cabbage and oil, scallions, mix well and cook gently until cabbage is wilted and as tender as you like. Makes 4 servings.

Carrot Puff

4 large potatoes
6 carrots
3 eggs, separated

1 teaspoon sea salt
¼ teaspoon paprika

Wash, peel and grate potatoes. Scrub and grate carrots. Beat egg yolks until thick and lemon colored. Mix in potatoes and carrots, salt and paprika. Beat egg whites stiff, then fold into vegetable mixture.

Turn into a well-oiled casserole and bake for about 30 to 40 minutes at 350°. Serves 6.

Minted Carrots

2 cups coarsely grated carrots
1 cup blanched, slivered almonds

½ cup chopped sunflower seeds
1 teaspoon minced mint leaves

Moisten with homemade French dressing, put in a nest of late spinach in a glass casserole. Garnish with ripe olives, and cover tightly. Refrigerate until serving time. Serves 4.

Baked Stuffed Carrots

6 large, uniform-sized carrots, cooked

¼ cup finely chopped green onions, plus tops

2 tablespoons finely diced celery

2 tablespoons finely diced green pepper

1 tablespoon homemade mayonnaise

Skin carrots: hollow out centers with sharp end of vegetable peeler; combine onions, green pepper, celery and mayonnaise; stuff carrots with mixture. Brush lightly with olive oil. Place in a 8 × 8 × 2-inch dish. Bake at 325 degrees F. for 30 minutes in oiled baking dish. Serves 6.

Carrots with Herbs

Clean carrots with a stiff brush and slice crossways. Tie dill seeds, mint leaves and fennel seeds in a cloth sack and simmer all in a small amount of water about 10 minutes, or until the carrots are tender. Remove the bag, drain the water into your covered "stock" can, and dust the carrot slices with paprika and serve hot.

Dilly Carrots

Scrape 1 pound fresh carrots, then cut them into 1-inch slices. In a medium saucepan, simmer carrots:

¼ cup cider vinegar

¾ cup water

½ teaspoon dried dill weed

½ teaspoon sea salt

½ teaspoon poultry seasoning

½ teaspoon oregano

¼ teaspoon garlic salt

Cover and simmer 20 minutes or until carrots are tender-crisp. Cool; refrigerate until serving time. Drain and serve cold. Makes 4 servings.

Baked Carrots

8 carrots, washed and cut into strips
½ cup chopped onion
½ cup white or dark raisins
1 apple, cored and cut into cubes
2 tablespoons honey
2 tablespoons sunflower seed oil

Place all ingredients in shallow casserole. Cover tightly.
Bake at 375 degrees about 40 minutes, or until carrots are tender. If carrot strips are thin, less time is needed. Serves 6.

Carrot Patties

½ cup raw ground carrot
½ onion, cut up fine
1 egg, well beaten
Dash of garlic powder
Seasoning to taste

Combine all ingredients and cook slowly on both sides in skillet on top of stove. Makes 4 patties.

Recipes Using Cauliflower, Corn or Cucumbers

Baked Eggs with Cauliflower

2 cups cauliflower (cut very fine)
1 onion grated
6 eggs

Add one cup of water to the cauliflower and onion. Cook on quick flame 7 or 8 minutes. Add beaten eggs. Broil or bake just before serving. Serves 4-6.

Cauliflower A La Polonaise

1 medium-sized cauliflower
4 tablespoons safflower oil
2 hard cooked egg yolks
parsley
¼ cup soybean nuts

Crisp-cook fresh cauliflower flowerets in boiling water three to six minutes. Drain. Add safflower oil and top with sieved egg yolk, fresh cut parsley and crushed soybean nuts. Serves 4 to 6.

Cauliflowerlets with Avocado Dip

Separate a fresh cauliflower into little flowerlets. Wash, place in a covered dish in the refrigerator to crisp. Make a dip as follows:

1 ripe avocado, mashed
1 teaspoon minced onion

1 tablespoon homemade
  mayonnaise
1 teaspoon pure cider vinegar

Blend together. Put the dip in a little bowl in the center of a fancy plate, with the flowerlets around it.

Corn on the Cob

Strip the outer husks off the corn, saving the 3 or 4 very inside ones. Remove the silks. Put the clean inner husks in the bottom of a big kettle, add hot water, lay the ears on the husks, cover and steam the corn tender. This has a better flavor than just boiled corn on the cob.

Corn Puffs

1 pint soy milk

⅓ cup yellow cornmeal

Combine and put over low heat. Simmer until they are fairly thickened, or in a thin mush stage. Remove from heat and beat in 1 tablespoon of soy flour. Let cool. Then put under electric beaters and add these ingredients and beat until very light:

4 eggs
1 tablespoon chopped pimiento
  or sweet red pepper

1 teaspoon sea kelp

Place custard cups on a cookie sheet. Oil them well and fill partly full of the batter. Bake at 375 degrees for about 20 minutes, or until a sharp knife in the center shows that the custard is set. Cool and turn out of the cups on to a platter.

Stuffed Cucumbers

4 large cucumbers	2 cups boiled or steamed rice
1 tomato	1 teaspoon sea salt
1 tablespoon chopped onion	2 tablespoons safflower oil

Peel the cucumber and cut into halves. Peel the tomato and cut into small pieces. Mix with the chopped onion, add the cooked rice, sea salt and oil. Fill the scooped cucumbers with the mixture and bake, covered, in a hot oven 400 degrees until they are tender, or about 45 minutes. Remove the cover the last part of the baking. Four servings.

Recipes Using Eggplants or Mushrooms

Broiled Eggplant

Peel eggplant and slice thin. Baste with: ½ teaspoon garlic powder, ½ teaspoon kelp, pinch of oregano, ¼ cup olive or safflower oil and 1 tablespoon cider vinegar (mixed thoroughly). Place on large baking sheet under broiler, turn eggplant, brush with seasoned oil and finish broiling. Serves 4.

Eggplant Dish

½ cup olive oil	1 large eggplant, diced
1 large onion, chopped	½ teaspoon basil
1 large green pepper, chopped	½ teaspoon oregano
4 tomatoes, chopped	sea salt to taste

Sauté onion and pepper lightly. Add tomatoes and simmer a few minutes. Add eggplant and other ingredients. Cook over medium heat until tender. Serve hot over cooked brown rice. Serves 4–6.

Baked Eggplant Slices

Marinate a teaspoon each of sea kelp and dried marjoram in ½ cup of cooking oil overnight. Slice a small eggplant, leaving the skin on. Brush each side of each slice with the herbed oil and place the slices in an oiled pan (or a cookie sheet) and bake about 30 minutes at 350 degrees. Serve very hot. Serves 4.

Creole Eggplant

2 cups diced peeled eggplant
2 cups chopped fresh tomatoes
1 cup mushrooms
1 medium onion, chopped
1 bell pepper chopped
basil leaf and celery tops

Put a tablespoon of cooking oil in the bottom of a stainless steel saucepan, heat and add the above ingredients. Add 1 clove of garlic if desired and season with sea kelp. Cover tightly and simmer about 30 minutes.

You may use summer squash or zucchini in place of the eggplant if so desired. Other vegetables may also be added. Many herb variations may be used for seasonings. Serves 4.

Eggplant Sauté

1 large eggplant, peeled and
   cubed
   safflower oil
½ cup tomato paste
½ cup cold water
¼ teaspoon sea salt
¼ cup ripe olives, pitted and
   coarsely chopped

Sauté eggplant in oil for 15 minutes. Dilute tomato paste with water and add to eggplant along with salt and olives. Cover and sauté for an additional 5 minutes. Sprinkle with fresh minced parsley and serve hot. Serves 4.

Folksy Eggplant Casserole

1 medium eggplant
1 teaspoon oregano
¼ cup vegetable oil
1 tomato, cut in quarters
1 tablespoon honey
3 tablespoons apple cider
  vinegar

1 teaspoon vegetable seasoning
  or sea salt
¼ cup chopped red or green
  pepper
paprika

Peel eggplant and cut into cubes. Simmer in small saucepan in small amount of water for 10 minutes.

Heat oil and oregano in small pan. Add eggplant and cook 10 more minutes. Add the tomato, honey, vinegar, and seasoning.

Alternate layers of eggplant mixture and pepper in casserole. Top with more pepper. Sprinkle with paprika and bake at 375 degrees, covered, for 30 minutes. Serves 4.

Potted Eggplant

1 large or 2 medium sized
  eggplants
½ cup safflower oil
2 cloves garlic, minced
3 tablespoons fresh parsley,
  minced

1 red onion, minced
4 large ripe tomatoes, quartered
1 cup cold water
sea salt and freshly ground
  pepper, to taste

Peel eggplants and cut into 1-inch cubes. Cook in a saucepan with a little water for 15 minutes. Drain off the liquid. Heat the oil in a large pot and brown the eggplant cubes lightly on all sides. Add remaining ingredients, cover the pot and simmer for 30 minutes. Serve hot. Serves 6.

Baked Mushrooms

1 pound fresh mushrooms
1 medium onion
3 tablespoons soybean oil

3 eggs
⅓ cup soybean milk or water
1 teaspoon kelp powder

Clean mushrooms and slice. Chop onion and sauté lightly with mushrooms for about 10 minutes. Blend together the eggs, soybean milk and kelp. Pour over the mushrooms. Sprinkle top with ½ teaspoon paprika. Bake at 325 degrees F. for 25 minutes. Garnish with chopped chives or parsley. Serves 4.

Stuffed Mushrooms

12 large mushrooms, stems
    removed and set aside
½ cup olive oil (cold-pressed)
½ cup wheat germ

2 tablespoons minced parsley
1 tablespoon minced onion
    season to taste

In a bowl, place mushroom stems which have been finely chopped. Add remaining ingredients and mix well. Stuff mushroom caps with this mixture and broil until caps are tender. Serves 4-6.

Brussels Sprouts and Mushrooms

1 quart of Brussels sprouts,
    steamed

4 tablespoons oil
½ pound mushrooms

Cook mushrooms in oil, add steamed Brussels sprouts and toss lightly. Serve with chopped parsley. Serves 4 to 6.

Groats (Kasha) and Mushrooms

1 cup buckwheat groats
    (ground medium)
1 egg, beaten, raw
1-2 cups mushrooms, sliced

2 tablespoons peanut oil
2 cups fat free chicken broth
1 teaspoon sea salt

Beat egg well and add groats. Mix this very well to coat all the grains. Brown mixture in peanut oil in a heavy skillet. Add sliced mushrooms. Bring to a boil the chicken broth and add to the mixture together with the sea salt. Mix well and cook very slowly, covered, until all liquid is absorbed and kasha is nice and fluffy, adding a little more broth if necessary. Serves 4.

Recipes Using Onions, Peas or Peppers

American Broiled Onions

Slice large onions ½-inch thick. Make a dip of vegetable oil and herb seasonings. Coat the onions well with this dip. Broil on both sides till lightly browned.

Stuffed Onions

6 medium yellow onions
4 ounces cooked mushrooms, stems and pieces
1 tablespoon finely chopped pecans

3 tablespoons oil
sea kelp to taste
1 cup chicken broth
Paprika

Peel and core onions, leaving shells ½ inch thick. Cook the cored onions in boiling water until almost tender. Meanwhile, chop raw onion from coring. Chop mushroom pieces. Sauté raw onion, mushrooms and pecans in oil about 10 minutes. Season with sea kelp, to taste. Stuff onions with mushroom mixture. Arrange onions in shallow pan. Pour chicken broth around them. Sprinkle lightly with paprika. Bake at 350 degrees about 10 minutes or until lightly brown and tender when pierced with fork. Serves 6.

Stuffed Baked Potatoes and Peas

Here's a new way to serve an old favorite.

Scrub 4 medium baking potatoes; rub with oil. Bake in moderate oven (375°) one to 1¼ hours. Take slice from top of each. Scoop out inside; mash. Add oil, sea salt and hot nut milk to moisten. Beat until fluffy.

Fill shells ½ full with mashed potatoes. Combine 1 cup drained, lightly seasoned, cooked fresh peas and 2 tablespoons chopped green onions; divide among potato shells. Pile remaining mashed potatoes atop. Return to oven (375°) 12 to 15 minutes, or until heated through and lightly browned. Serves 4.

Braised Leeks

6 leeks	1 teaspoon kelp
1 small onion, chopped	1 tablespoon cold water
1 tablespoon vegetable oil	2 teaspoons cornstarch
½ cup boiling water	1 tablespoon minced parsley

Clean leeks and cut in pieces about 3 inches long. Sauté onion in oil. Place leeks in pan with onion, heat for a short time. Pour boiling water over leeks. Add kelp. Cover pan and simmer about 30 minutes or until leeks are tender.

Mix 1 tablespoon cold water with 2 teaspoons cornstarch, stir into leeks. Simmer until thickened, stirring constantly. Remove from heat and sprinkle with parsley. Serves 2-4.

Peas Deluxe

When peas become too large to eat raw, fix them in this delightful manner. Heat a heavy saucepan, add 1 tablespoon cooking oil and the following ingredients:

1 cup sliced mushrooms	½ cup sliced celery
1 chopped onion	several branches fresh savory

Simmer with the cover on for 10 minutes, then add:

2 cups shelled peas	¼ cup boiling water

Simmer about 8 minutes and garnish with home-canned pimiento slivers. Season to the family's taste during cooking. Serves 4.

Almond-Stuffed Peppers

4 medium bell peppers, cut off top and clean out seeds	½ cup ground almonds
	2 tomatoes, peeled and mashed
2 cups barley, cooked	¼ cup parsley, chopped
4 garlic cloves, chopped	2 teaspoons kelp

Mix well. Stuff peppers. Cover peppers with their own tops. Put peppers in baking dish and add 1 cup water mixed with 1 tablespoon soy oil. Cover baking dish and bake until peppers are soft. Serves 4.

Surprise Pepper Buns

Instead of the traditional "hamburger buns" let us live dangerously and try a vegetable bun. Use 1 large green bell pepper for each hamburger. Slice in half, lengthwise, and remove the inner portions and seeds. Leave the stem on it. Put a hamburger and 1 onion slice in a pepper half—then put the other half over it and skewer together with toothpicks. Put these back on the hot broiler rack until time for serving, letting them heat through.

Stuffed Green Peppers

Halve 3 large green bell peppers lengthwise, remove stems and membrane. Make a filling as follows:

Heat a heavy skillet and add cooking oil to cover the bottom. Slice in a small onion and cover tightly. When it has steamed a bit add 1 pound of ground beef. Cover and heat through until the red color disappears. Then add the following:

3 shredded basil leaves
⅔ cup boiled brown rice
  sea kelp to taste

1 cup home-canned tomato
  pulp or juice

Stuff the peppers with this filling and bake in a covered baking dish to which a small amount of hot water has been added. When done, garnish with parsley sprigs. Serves 3 to 6.

Potato Recipes

Broiled Potato Slices

3 medium potatoes
⅓ cup salad oil

½ teaspoon sea salt
  dash of paprika

Scrub potatoes, but do not peel. Cut into ¼ inch crosswise slices. Dip slices in oil and place one layer deep on broiler rack. Season with sea salt and dust with paprika. Broil until potatoes are golden brown, about 7 minutes. Turn and continue broiling until brown. Serve hot. Serves 4.

Irish Potato Salad

6 cups boiled, diced potatoes
4 eggs, boiled 4 minutes
½ cup vegetable oil
1 teaspoon sea kelp

½ cup plums
1 teaspoon honey
1½ cups chopped parsley

Put potatoes in bowl with eggs cut in small pieces, sea kelp and oil. Mix well. Add honey to plums and stir well with chopped parsley. Mix all ingredients thoroughly. Serves 6.

If plums are not available, nearly green white grapes are a good substitute.

Potato Carrot Casserole

3 medium sized potatoes peeled, grated on medium blade
2 medium carrots grated, washed, unpeeled or scraped, grated on medium blade

1 small onion chopped
1 egg
½ cup water or carrot juice

Mix all and put in oiled casserole, cover and bake, can be uncovered if desired the last 10 minutes of baking. Bake at 375°. Bake just till potatoes and carrots are done. Serves 4.

Mashed Potatoes and Mushrooms

While six potatoes boil, wash ½ pound mushrooms and cut them in two. Use a chicken fryer or Dutch oven and heat it hot. Put 2 tablespoons of cooking oil in it and add a sliced onion and the mushrooms. Cover tightly, set the heat to moderate and the mushrooms will make their own cooking water. Boil them about 10 minutes, season with sea kelp and boil them another 10 minutes, stirring frequently, until the water is absorbed back into the mushrooms and they are lightly browned.

Mash the potatoes and put their own water back into them in place of milk. Serve the mushrooms spooned over the mashed potatoes. Serves 4.

Potato Kugel (Pudding)

6 medium-size potatoes, pared	1 clove garlic, minced
1 small onion, grated	3 slightly beaten egg yolks
¼ cup potato flour, soy flour or wheat germ	1¼ teaspoons sea salt
	3 stiffly beaten egg whites

Place potatoes in bowl, cover with cold water and refrigerate 2 to 2½ hours. Remove and shred into fine slivers or place in blender. Toss grated potatoes in bowl with onion and flour. Stir in garlic, egg yolks and salt. Blend until smooth. Fold in stiffly beaten egg whites. Place in oiled pan. Bake in moderate oven 350° F. 40 minutes or until brown. Serves 6.

Sesame Potatoes

Wash potatoes, leaving skins on. Cut in ¼″ slices and dip the bottom sides in herbed cooking oil. Lay on the broiler pan and broil. When ready to turn, brush the potato slices with the herbed oil, turn and brush again, sprinkle with sea kelp, then sesame seeds. Broil until crisped. One medium-sized potato per person.

Spinach and Potatoes

4 medium sized potatoes	2 tablespoons olive oil
1 small onion	¼ teaspoon thyme
7 ounces fresh spinach	1 teaspoon kelp

Cube potatoes and cook in boiling water. Mash, using cooking water. Cook spinach in boiling water for five minutes. Drain and chop.

Put olive oil and cut onions in a skillet. Cook onions until slightly browned. Combine spinach, potatoes, and thyme. Heat for two minutes in skillet with onions, then serve warm. Serves 4.

Potatoes Stuffed with Mushrooms

6 baked potatoes

Stuffing:

2-3 tablespoons dried
    mushrooms, chopped fine
1 small onion, minced
1 tablespoon soy oil
2 whole eggs, lightly beaten

1 teaspoon each of chopped
    fresh dill and parsley
2-3 tablespoons of the
    mushroom cooking liquid

Sauce:

1 cup mushroom sauce

Bake potatoes until the skins are crisp—45 to 60 minutes. Cut each lengthwise in half or cut off a thin layer to use later as a cover. Scoop out centers and mash. Brown onion lightly in oil, combine with chopped mushrooms, mashed potatoes, eggs, herbs, mushroom liquid and sea salt, and refill the shells. Cover with their own tops, arrange in shallow baking dish, and pour mushroom sauce over them. Bake in hot oven for 5 to 10 minutes. Serves 6.

Shredded Potato Casserole

3 large potatoes—about 1½
    pounds
1 teaspoon kelp
½ cup wheat germ

2 large eggs
2 medium onions
    chopped parsley

Scrub and grate potatoes (not too fine); grate onions; add other ingredients. Oil very generously a glass pie or cake dish; sprinkle a little oil on top. Bake in 375° oven about 50 minutes or as brown as desired. Serves 4.

Stuffed Baked Potatoes

4 large baked potatoes
2 tablespoons kelp
1 tablespoon sea salt
1 tablespoon chives, cut fine
2 tablespoons safflower oil

Cut off the tops of the baked potatoes and scoop out contents leaving shells intact. Mix contents with rest of ingredients and put back in shells. Bake at 350 degrees for 15 minutes. Serves 4.

Rice Recipes

Fluffy Brown Rice

Put 1 cup brown rice and 2 cups of hot water in a 2 quart heavy stainless steel sauce pan. Bring the rice to a vigorous boil, then turn the heat as low as it will go and leave the rice on this very low heat for 40 minutes. Keep the lid on until you are ready to serve it so the rice will be fluffy. At the beginning, add whatever herbs and kelp, or other seasoning desired as long as the cover isn't lifted during the entire cooking operation. Serves 4.

Chinese Rice

Using a heavy stainless steel chicken fryer with tight high cover, put in the following and simmer 10 minutes:

1 tablespoon cooking oil
1 medium onion, chopped
1 green pepper, chopped
1 cup celery, diced
2 cups mushrooms cut in two

Now add 4 cups of freshly cooked hot brown rice. Blend and drop 4 raw eggs over the simmering mixture, stirring until the eggs are done. Serve this mixture hot over fresh-sprouted Mung beans or alfalfa seed sprouts. Garnish with red pepper slivers. Serves 4.

Cantonese Rice

1 cup long-grain rice
2 tablespoons soybean oil
2 tablespoons chopped onion
½ teaspoon honey

1¾ cups water
3 tablespoons soy sauce
2 tablespoons diced pimiento
1 teaspoon kelp

Place rice and water in covered 2-quart sauce pan. Bring to a boil 20 minutes. Turn off the heat and let rice stand 20 minutes. Break rice with fork to separate grains. Stir in the remaining ingredients. Serves 4.

Indian Pilau

3 cups uncooked brown rice
6½ cups chicken broth
3 tablespoons olive oil
1 teaspoon ground allspice

2 sticks cinnamon
6 tablespoons chopped almonds
¾ cup raisins

Put the rice, chicken broth, olive oil, allspice, cinnamon in a flat baking dish. Mix well. Cover and bake in oven (350 degrees) for 50 minutes, or until the liquid has been absorbed and the grains are separated. Stir in the almonds and raisins. Remove cinnamon sticks. Mix well. Serves 6 to 8.

Persian-American Rice

5 cups water
2 cups brown rice
4 carrots, sliced into thin sticks, one inch long
2 fresh beets, sliced as carrots
⅓ cup raisins
¼ cup almond slices (not slivers)

2 tablespoons safflower oil
2-3 teaspoons honey
dash of onion powder, garlic powder, pepper and saffron (⅛ to ¼ teaspoon)
1 teaspoon sea salt

Sauté almonds in oil and cook over medium-low heat in a large saucepan for a few minutes. Watch and stir and when they begin to brown, add the raisins and lower the heat. Continue stirring and when raisins begin to become puffy, pour water into the saucepan and turn heat up to high. While waiting for water to boil, add the spices to the water. It is best to dilute saffron powder (or crumbled saffron) in a small amount of water before adding it. Add sea salt and one teaspoon honey. When water begins to boil, sprinkle rice into boiling water making sure that water continues to boil gently. Do not sprinkle rice so fast that water stops boiling, on the other hand, do not let water boil madly. Turn heat down to a simmering temperature and cover tightly. Simmer for twenty to twenty-five minutes before removing lid.

While rice is cooking, boil carrots and beets gently in a small amount of water. Try to use just enough water so that you do not need to dispose of cooking water. Cook until vegetables are tender but not limp. When rice is done, fluff gently and pour on to a large platter. Decorate the rice with carrots and beets. Serves 6.

Plantain and Rice

4 cups cooked brown or wild rice	1 medium-size onion
1 plantain (yellow ripe)	¼ clove garlic

In medium oven brown onions and garlic finely chopped in a little cooking oil (preferably cold-pressed). Add rice and mix well with the onion and garlic. Place plantain on top, sliced lengthwise. Let bake in slow oven until plantain is tender and slightly brown or deep yellow—about 5 minutes. Season to taste. Serves 4.

Variation:

For variety, mix in finely cut-up fish or meat left-overs, or mix in a well-beaten egg before placing the plantain slices on top.

Rice and Spinach

1 pound spinach	1 teaspoon mint (optional)
1 cup rice	1 teaspoon vegetable salt
¼ cup oil	1 onion
2 large tomatoes, chopped	

Brown onion and rice in oil. Add tomatoes, spinach and seasoning. Cook until rice is tender, add water if needed. Serves 4.

Rice Colorful

Cook 1 cup brown rice according to directions with 1 teaspoon sea salt. Heat ¼ cup sunflower seed oil in a skillet. Add the cooked rice, ½ cup sliced green onions, and ½ cup diced green pepper. Sauté until vegetables are tender-crisp. Fork toss with 3 tablespoons of diced pimiento and ½ cup sliced ripe olives. Serves 6.

Rice and Sprouts

2 cups brown rice	4 stalks celery
2 teaspoons sea salt	2 tablespoons parsley
1 large onion	1 quart freshly sprouted mung
2 tablespoons safflower seed oil	beans

Cook 2 cups brown rice in six cups water with 2 teaspoons sea salt until water is almost absorbed.

Just before rice is done, slice one large onion in a large pan in which 2 tablespoons safflower seed oil has been placed. When onion is about half cooked, add celery, which has been cut diagonally. Cook five minutes. Then add rice, bean sprouts and parsley. Cook only until bean sprouts are heated. Celery and sprouts should still be crisp. Serve immediately. Serves 8-10.

Vegetable Subgum Fried Rice

3 tablespoons soya sauce	2 eggs

Mix together and add to frying pan that has 1 tablespoon corn oil in it, heated. Stir till the egg is in shreds. Then add:

1 pimiento, sliced	1 cup bean sprouts
2 green peppers, sliced about 2″ by 1″ in size	1 cup largely-diced celery
	1 cup sliced onions

Cook for about 5 minutes so the vegetables are still crisp. Then add:

6 cups brown cold cooked rice

Heat thoroughly. Serve with soya sauce. Serves 4-6.

Saffron Rice

1 cup brown rice   a pinch of saffron
3 cups chicken broth

Simmer together until the rice is tender, then steam with cover on, for another 15 minutes. Add 1 tablespoon kelp and serve hot. Serves 4.

Spanish Brown Rice

2 tablespoons oil	1 clove garlic, minced
1 pound lean chopped beef	½ cup brown rice
2 large onions, chopped	1 cup water
1 large green pepper, chopped	1 pint tomatoes
3 stalks celery, chopped	sea salt, pepper to taste

Put oil in pan and brown meat and vegetables. Add rice and water and simmer for 30 minutes. Add tomatoes and seasoning, continuing cooking for about 30 minutes until rice is tender, adding more liquid if necessary. Serve with fresh green salad. Serves 4.

Sweet Potato Recipes

Hawaiian Sweet Potatoes

Pare 6 sweet potatoes and slice them in an oiled baking dish. Cover with 1 cup raw pineapple chunks. Dribble with cooking oil, cover and bake until the potatoes are tender, about 25 minutes. Serves 4 to 6.

Baked Sweet Potatoes and Prunes

4 sweet potatoes   ½ cup wheat germ
1 pound tart prunes

Pour boiling water over the prunes. Let stand for a while. Remove pits. Peel sweet potatoes and cut into cubes. Place layer of prunes and layer of sweet potatoes in oiled casserole. Add 2 cups of water. Dot with oil and cover with wheat germ. Bake until soft, about 45 minutes at 375°. Serves 6.

Peanut Honey Yams

Peel 4 sweet potatoes and cook in a little water. Mash and blend in thoroughly, 2 tablespoons peanut butter and 2 tablespoons honey. Spoon into serving dish and sprinkle sesame seeds over the top, about 1 teaspoon. Heat and serve. Serves 4.

Sweet Potato Boats

3 large sweet potatoes   ½ cup walnuts
1 cup fresh cranberries   ½ cup sesame seeds
¼ cup raisins

Cook whole sweet potatoes in their jackets just until tender. Cut in half lengthwise. Spoon out center of sweet potato halves and mash. Put remaining ingredients through the chopper. Mix with the mashed sweet potato. Fill the sweet potato with the mixture. Bake at 350° for 30 minutes. Serves 6.

Sweet Potato Casserole

3 cups mashed sweet potatoes   ¼ cup honey
½ cup raw peanut butter   2 tablespoons pure vanilla
⅓ cup hot soy milk   1 teaspoon sea salt

Add hot milk to sweet potatoes and beat until light. Oil baking dish. Mix honey and peanut butter and spread at bottom of dish. Fill with potatoes. Bake 30 to 40 minutes in a 350° oven. Serves 6.

Sweet Potatoes and Apples

8 cooked sweet potatoes
4 apples peeled and cut in rings
½ cup honey

1 teaspoon sea salt
½ teaspoon mace
2 tablespoons oil

Peel sweet potatoes and cut in slices about ½ inch thick. Arrange in layers of sweet potatoes, apples, honey and seasonings in oiled 2 quart casserole. Cover and bake 350 degrees for 50 minutes. Serves 6 to 8.

Squash Recipes

Baked Winter Squash

If you can locate thin-meated winter squashes (or pumpkins taste the same), a delightful new way to bake them is to cut them up in individual servings; around 4″ squares. Lay these pieces on cookie sheets, with skin side down. Brush with cooking oil, then season with sea kelp, a dash of mace and any desired herbs. Bake until tender and serve this way, heaped on a tray or platter.

Yummy Pumpkin

2 cups grated raw pumpkin
1½ tablespoons safflower oil

1 teaspoon pure honey (or more)
sea salt to taste

Combine pumpkin, oil and honey in top of double boiler, cover and cook over boiling water until thoroughly heated. Season with sea salt and serve piping hot. Serves 2-4.

Squash Cups

4 cups mashed winter squash
2 teaspoons oil

4 tablespoons honey
½ teaspoon vegetable sea salt

Beat all the ingredients together. Shape into cups. Fill them with steamed green peas or any preferred vegetable. Serves 6.

Squash Foo Yung

4 medium unpeeled zucchini squash (grated)	3 beaten eggs
1 onion (grated)	1 teaspoon sea salt
	½ cup wheat germ

Mix together. Drop by tablespoon on heated griddle or bake on a cookie sheet in oven. Serves 4.

Recipes Using Tomatoes and Turnips

Avocado Stuffed Tomatoes

Cut the tops off four tomatoes and remove the pulp. (Place it in a covered dish for blender drinks.) Invert the tomatoes in the refrigerator to drain while you make a filling as follows:

2 mashed avocadoes	small amounts of minced onion
a few drops of pure vinegar	homemade mayonnaise

Let your family's taste determine exact amounts of vinegar and onion, but use enough mayonnaise so that the avocado pulp will whip up very light. Fill the tomatoes with the pulp and sprinkle rose hips powder over them. Serve on late salad greens. Serves 4.

Scalloped Tomatoes

3½ cups sliced fresh or home-canned tomatoes	½ teaspoon sea salt pinch of cayenne
¼ cup minced onion	½ cup wheat germ, plus 2 tablespoons soy flour
2 tablespoons minced green pepper	2 tablespoons oil dash of oregano or basil

Combine tomatoes, sea salt, onion, herbs and green pepper. Place in a baking dish alternating layers of tomato mixture and wheat germ, ending with wheat germ. Dot with oil. Bake at 375 degrees F. (moderate oven) 20 to 30 minutes for ripe tomatoes. Serves 4.

Baked Stuffed Tomatoes

6 medium-sized tomatoes
⅓ cup natural peanut butter
¾ cup wheat germ
1 teaspoon sea salt
½ teaspoon oregano
1 tablespoon onion
¼ cup minced celery

Scoop out tomato pulp, dice, and drain. Mix juice with peanut butter, add remaining ingredients, tomato pulp last. Fill tomato shells. Place in oiled flat baking dish and bake at 400 degrees for 25-30 minutes. Garnish with parsley. Serves 6.

Tomato Cups

Cut the tomatoes off the vine, leaving about 1″ of stem for handle. Slice a neat "lid" off the top, lay aside and scoop the pulp out of the tomato, putting it in a tightly covered glass jar to use for a blender drink, later. Fill the tomato "cup" with chopped vegetables and dressing, put the "lid" back on and wrap tightly to keep the vitamins in the cut vegetables. Refrigerate until serving time.

Mashed Turnips

Peel and cook 6 turnips until tender. Drain and mash. Season with salad oil, sea kelp and a shake of paprika. Serve very hot. If the turnip is dry, add some of the cooking water to it; save the rest for soup stock. Serves 4.

Turnip Cups

Steam large turnips. Cut slice off top to even them. Scoop out center leaving cup. Fill with lightly steamed vegetables such as peas, carrots, string beans, lima beans. Pour oil and chopped parsley over and serve, garnished with sprigs of parsley.

Turnip Fluff

6 to 8 medium white turnips,
  pared and diced
2 tablespoons oil
1 teaspoon kelp

2 teaspoons honey
½ teaspoon soya flour
2 eggs, separated

Start heating oven to 350° F. Cook turnips in 1 inch boiling water, 15 to 20 minutes, or until tender; drain. Mash turnips well over low heat. Add oil, kelp, honey and flour. Beat egg whites until stiff. Beat egg yolks until light; stir gradually into hot turnips. Fold in whites. Pour into greased casserole; bake 30 to 35 minutes or until puffy and brown. Serves 6.

Herbed Zucchini Squash

4 zucchini squash
1 fresh large leaf sweet basil
  (dried will do)

6 stalks of onions or chives
a few celery leaves
several sprigs of parsley

Cube the zucchini by cutting both ways the long way, then laying on a bread board and cutting across. Fill a quart utensil and start cooking with only enough water to keep it from burning.

Clean and mince the herbs. As soon as possible, drain off a cup of the liquid and set aside to cool while the squash continues to cook. Put the greens in this liquid to help in cooling just before putting in the blender to blend completely. Mash the squash and add the herbs, stir well and serve in individual dishes. A dash of paprika or vegetable salt adds color and flavor. Serves 4.

Zucchini in Sweet and Sour Sauce

4 sliced zucchini squash
2 tablespoons oil
2 tablespoons sliced onions
¼ cup soy yogurt (homemade)

2 tablespoons honey
3 tablespoons apple cider
  vinegar

Sauté onions in oil. Cool. Mix yogurt, honey and vinegar and blend with zucchini and onions. Serves 6.

Zucchini Boats

4 medium zucchini squash
1½ apples, grated

2 tablespoons grated nuts or seeds
¼ teaspoon sea salt

Steam whole squash in covered pan, with small amount of water until fork pierces (not mushy). Cool and cut out tops lengthwise to make an open "boat." Scoop out centers, mix with apple and sea salt and fill boats. Sprinkle tops of fillings with nuts and bake in oiled pan at 350 degrees for 20 minutes, until lightly brown on top. Serves 4.

Zucchini Mediterranean

¼ cup olive oil
8 medium zucchini, thinly sliced
⅔ cup chopped onions
1 large clove garlic, minced
2 tablespoons parsley

1 teaspoon sea salt
¼ teaspoon oregano
¼ teaspoon rosemary
4 cups peeled chopped tomatoes

Heat oil in large skillet, add all ingredients except tomatoes and sauté 20 minutes, add tomatoes and continue to cook 5 more minutes. May be eaten hot or cold. Serves 6 to 8.

Beverages

Milk For Grown-Ups?

In infancy, of course, every normal mammal from mouse to elephant, has an inborn capacity to thrive on its mother's milk. The milk sugar, lactose, is broken down by the intestinal enzyme, lactase, into two simple sugars (glucose and galactose) which can be absorbed through the intestinal wall. Infant mammals produce the enzyme lactase at high levels. On weaning, however, their lactase levels fall off rapidly.

The degree of milk tolerance varies widely among those determined (through a lactose tolerance test) as lactase deficient. Some can tolerate as much as a daily quart of milk, if taken gradually throughout the day. But there are many who react to as little as the amount added to a cup of coffee. For such super-intolerant individuals, the whole diet must be carefully watched, since many processed foods contain hidden milk solids.

It's an American superstition that a child cannot grow healthy and strong without his daily milk allotment. Of course he can—as his ancestors did for thousands of years. If more calcium and phosphorus are needed, a little powdered bone meal added to the food will do the trick. Nuts and leafy vegetables are also excellent sources of these minerals.

Among the adult population, older people should be particularly alert to intestinal disturbances, and the consequent malabsorption of nutrients, that can be brought about by milk consumption. It is possible for some individuals to maintain high lactase levels throughout their entire lives. But a drop in lactase production apparently can occur at any time in a previously milk-tolerant individual—the timing depending on the genetic code which the person has inherited. Among the older age group a large proportion has passed the point where milk products can be easily accepted.

Of course when you reduce or eliminate milk consumption, at whatever age, you need to make sure that the valuable nutrients previously provided by milk are coming to you from other foods. You may need to eat more of the high quality protein foods—fish, fowl, meat, or eggs. Even more important, since milk is a generous source of calcium, you will want to provide yourself with an alternate intake of this essential mineral. Calcium-rich foods include many greens such as collards, kale, and turnip greens; also egg yolk, molasses, soybeans and soy flour, nuts and seeds, sardines, and agar agar (a vegetable-based gelatin). You will recall that certain processed dairy foods—yogurt, for example—can be eaten by lactase deficient individuals.

What's Wrong With Soft Drinks?

The harmful effects of soft drinks fall under three heads: 1. some of the drinks contain harmful drugs, 2. most of them cause a chemical reaction strong enough to injure certain parts of the body, especially the teeth and 3. their constant use—particularly because of the high sugar content—is bound to have a deleterious effect on other aspects of diet.

The cola beverages contain caffeine—about two-thirds of a grain of caffeine to 6 ounces of the beverage—that is, 3 bottles of "coke" contain about as much of the drug as one cup of coffee. We know many parents who will not permit their children to drink coffee, but permit them, day after day, to drink cola drinks whose total caffeine content may far exceed that of a cup or two of coffee. Most medical men today believe that the use of caffeine is harmful, especially for youngsters. We know that it is a drug which has a stimulating effect.

The American cola beverage has a pH of approximately 2.6. This means that it is highly acid. Erosion of the enamel and dentine in the teeth of experimental animals has been brought about in the laboratory by high consumption of cola drinks. The relation of the consumption of carbonated drinks to the high incidence of tooth decay in America is recognized by a number of highly qualified researchers. A substance which can erode the calcium from the teeth of rats cannot be good for human tooth enamel, particularly when this same substance is in contact with the enamel day after day, year after year, summer and winter.

Perhaps their most dangerous aspect, especially for the health of our children, is the effect of carbonated drinks on dietary habits. As you will see in the chart below, these drinks contain absolutely no food value, except for calories, which produce quick energy and fat. So there is no way to compare the value of milk, or a fruit or vegetable drink with a cola drink. The former contain in varying amounts proteins and fats, along with many, many vitamins and minerals. The cola drink contains nothing the body can use except the calories of its sugar.

When it comes to the comparison of the fruit juices with some popular soft drinks, this table shows the actual difference in nutritive value:

	Lemon Juice	Orange Juice	Grapefruit Juice	Cola	Ginger Ale
Protein, grams per 100 grams	1.0	.5	.5	—	—
Fat, grams per 100 grams	.7	.1	.1	—	—
Carbohydrates, grams per 100 grams	8.5	11.4	9.8	10.5	9.0
Calories	48.	49.	42.	42.	36.
Calcium, milligrams per 100 grams	28.	26.	19.	—	—
Phosphorus, milligrams per 100 grams	7.	14.	18.	—	—
Iron, milligrams per 100 grams	.2	.1	.2	—	—
Vitamin A, I.U. per 100 grams	50.	270.	14.	—	—
Thiamin, milligrams per 100 grams	.060	.080	.028	—	—
Riboflavin, milligrams per 100 grams	4.	80.	90.	—	—
Niacin, milligrams per 100 grams	.15	0.5	—	—	—
Vitamin C, milligrams per 100 grams	45.	45.	30.	—	—

Excessive use of citrus juice also has harmful effects on the teeth. But at least citrus fruit, taken in moderation, is food!

Soft drinks contain carbon dioxide which makes them "fizz." The carbon dioxide used by soft drink manufacturers may be the by-product from some other manufacturing process, such as the brewing or coke industry, or it may be produced by reacting chalk, lime-stone or bicarbonate of soda with sulfuric acid.

As one of the earnest defenders of soft drinks points out, the only sugar used in making these beverages is "sugar of the highest degree of purity." This means, of course, sugar that has been refined until there is not a chance of even one iota of food value remaining in it. This means, too, that all of the other food factors in the sugar cane, beet or corn from which the sugar was made, are omitted in the refined sugar. These factors are important for the proper assimilation and metabolism of sugar in the body. But you don't get them in refined sugar. Sucrose made from cane or beet sugar and dextrose made from corn sugar are the most commonly used sweetening agents in soft drinks. Of course, in many cases a synthetic sweetening agent is used.

The acids poured into the carbonated beverage may be citric, tartaric or phosphoric, depending on what the flavor of the final product is to be.

The sparkling clear green of a lime drink does not mean that the product has been anywhere near a lime. If the luscious purple of a grape drink bears any resemblance to a grape, it is purely coincidental. The coloring agents for soft drinks are, almost without exception, certified coal tar colors.

What About Coffee?

The amount of caffeine in a cup of coffee is quite small. Yet we drink coffee because of the effect of the caffeine, just as we smoke because of the effect of the nicotine. Both are drugs, both are habit-forming. We uncovered some interesting accounts of headaches produced as "withdrawal symptoms" when coffee-drinking was abruptly stopped. We also know that efficiency of work performance decreases when a confirmed coffee-drinker stops taking his daily dose of coffee. These are symptoms typical of addiction. When any drug is taken away from an addict, he suffers "withdrawal symptoms."

Coffee quickens the respiration (that is, makes you breathe faster), strengthens the pulse, raises the blood pressure, stimulates the kidneys, excites the functions of the brain and temporarily relieves fatigue or depression. Individuals who have heart disease, angina, high blood pressure, stomach trouble, skin infections, arthritis, liver trouble should avoid drinking it. Caffeine causes an increase of 3 to 10 per cent in the basal metabolic rate within the first hour after the coffee is taken. Basal metabolism is the rate at which your body makes use of the food you eat. It can be safely assumed that any increased efficiency brought on by artificial stimulation will be temporary and will be followed by a reversal that will drag efficiency to a point far below the norm.

A person who drinks one cup of coffee a day needn't be concerned about giving it up. The individual who is in danger from coffee is the one who finds that coffee is indeed a drug to him, that he feels he needs it often throughout the day.

Tea For You?

It appears that the criterion for excellence in tea is a tea high in caffeine and low in tannin. The best way to achieve this is to infuse the tea only 5 or 6 minutes and then immediately pour it off the leaves. For making tea, the water should be freshly boiled, the water and tea put into a hot teapot, then the brew poured off into another hot teapot. And, of course, teapots should always be of crockery, glass or china, never metal.

Tea contains caffeine, tannin or tannic acid and essential oils. The caffeine is the stimulating element, the tannin gives tea its color and body and the oils give it flavor and aroma. Tea contains 2.5 to 5 per cent of caffeine and 7 to 14 per cent of tannin. The tannin in concentration has an unpleasant effect on the mucous membranes of the mouth and digestive tract, but in the concentration in which it appears in a cup of tea it is not believed to be harmful. It is, of course, the same substance used widely in medicine as an astringent and for skin diseases and burns.

In general, everything we say about caffeine in relation to health applies to tea as well as to coffee, except that the caffeine content of tea is not so high.

What Is the Food Value of Vegetable Juices?

The juices listed in the following chart were kept in a refrigerator for about 12 hours before they were tested. This accounts for the fact there is no listing of the vitamin C present. There was no vitamin C in any of the juices except the kale. It had been oxidized during the time of storage. This is one of the most important facts to remember—the highly perishable quality of vitamin C. Once a fruit or vegetable has been cut, chopped, squeezed or otherwise exposed to the air, you can be pretty sure that much of the vitamin C is lost. This is why we urge readers to eat fresh foods just as soon as they are prepared—don't peel fruit or juice it, don't chop vegetables or juice them until just before you are going to consume them.

Composition of Some Fresh Vegetable Juices Compared to the Vegetable Itself

(The content of the vegetable appears in brackets beside the juice figures)

JUICE	Total Sugars (as glucose) grams per 100 ml. (gm.)	Iron mg. per 100 ml. (gm.)	Calcium mg. per 100 ml. (gm.)	Vit. B.1 mg. per 100 ml. (gm.)
Broccoli leaves	3.00(0.4)	0.60(1.52)	18.70(160)	15.0
Cabbage	4.17(8.3)	1.02(1.0)	16.90(65)	75.0(75)
Carrots	7.11(5.4)	0.30(10.6)	0.49(48)	30.0(60)
Celery	2.06(1.2)	0.43(0.6)	0.62(52)	15.0(30)
Kale	3.71	1.60(2.5)	11.60(200)	15.0(120)
Melon	4.33	0.42	0.40	30.0
Parsley	0.44(8.8)	1.12(8.0)	6.30(325)	30.0(120)
Spinach	1.85(1.2)	1.02(4.0)	0.75(595)	Nil (100)
Tomato	3.06(2.8)	0.08(0.4)	4.05(13)	15.0(60)
Watercress	0.20(0.6)	2.12(1.6)	2.90(222)	30.0(120)

In the chart the amount of sugar is given in grams per 100 milliliters which is about ½ cup. It is worth noting that the spinach juice is not very high in calcium compared with the amount in the fresh vegetable, which seems to indicate that the calcium is simply not released into the juice, possibly because of the oxalic acid content of spinach. None of the vegetable juices contained any significant amount of carotene (vitamin A) except carrots and watercress. So it seems that the other vegetables hold on to their vitamin A, for we know that the whole vegetable contains considerable amounts.

Former investigations have shown that the raw whole vegetable contains more nitrogen, pectin, sodium, calcium, sulfur and phosphorus than the juices. But the potassium content of the juice is higher than that of the whole vegetables. This seems to indicate that these substances are retained by the pulp and do not find their way into the raw juice.

There are, also, certain amino acids, or forms of protein in vegetable juices. Cabbage juice, for instance, contains relatively large amounts of lysine, tryptophan and methionine. What other food elements are present in vegetable juices we can only guess since tests have not been done on the less important vitamins and the trace minerals.

It is well to keep in mind that the very qualities which make juices valuable render them dangerous if they are kept for long in a state in which bacteria could grow in them. Juicing fresh vegetables and letting them stand unrefrigerated can present a grave risk. The main reason why canned and bottled foods must be heated to such high temperatures is to prevent the growth of such bacteria. So if one plans to use raw vegetables (or fruit) juices they should be prepared immediately before eating and consumed at once, *not stored*. Vitamins and enzymes are lost during storage, and toxic bacteria may easily spoil the juice if it stands any length of time.

Why juice vegetables or fruits instead of eating them whole? In general, the average person, anxious to preserve good health and prevent illness, will get more benefit from eating his fruits and vegetables whole rather than by juicing them. As we have seen, considerable amounts of the minerals and vitamins are lost in juicing.

It is well to keep in mind that everything we have said about the healthful properties of juices refers only to raw, freshly made juice. In canned, bottled, cooked or otherwise processed juice the vitamin C will be all, or nearly all, destroyed, enzymes will be nonexistent and the quality of other ingredients will be so changed that one cannot expect the same results one gets from raw juice.

For juicing get organically grown vegetables, or grow your own, since the chemicals and insecticides which pollute most commercially grown foods today contaminate the vegetables you plan to juice. You cannot wash them away, no matter how you scrub. Poisonous residues can nullify whatever nutritional values fresh-squeezed juices can supply to your body.

Soybean Coffee

Use yellow soybeans for this purpose, roast at about 350 degrees until the kernels are brown all the way through (you can split them for testing). Cool. Grind in a food mill to the desired fineness and store as you do coffee. You can probably grind the soybeans in a food grinder or your blender if you don't have a mill. Steep about 1 tablespoon of this mixture to each cup of water for 10 minutes or so, strain and serve.

Blackstrap "Coffee"

Put a teaspoon of blackstrap molasses into a cup of hot water and let steep for a minute. (One teaspoon more or less according to taste.)

Fenugreek Tea

Fenugreek is a legume, and the tea, like comfrey, should never be boiled. Fenugreek seeds are about 30% protein.

Suggestion: grind the seeds and use as little heat as possible in making this tea. In the Mediterranean areas and Far East, fenugreek leaves are used, like comfrey, as a conditioner for animals. The seeds are used as a beauty aid in North Africa, while the people of India use them as food and the doctors use them as an emolient and for poultices.

Oat Tea

1 cup of washed, organically-
grown oats
2 tablespoons raw cranberries
3 whole cloves
6 cups boiling water

Pour the boiling water over the above ingredients, cover and let stand until cool. Strain and sweeten to taste with honey. You may use mint leaves in place of the cranberry-clove seasoning if desired. Serves 6.

Alfalfa Tea

It is a good idea to have an alfalfa plant in your organic garden, maybe in a corner, leaving it there year after year, for the deeper the roots go, the more trace minerals it brings up and stores in its leaves. Then you can put a few leaves in most of your blender and juicer drinks, and you can dry any surplus leaves for winter use.

Gather a handful of fresh leaves, add a few mint leaves for flavor, wash, pat dry and pour boiling water over them. When they have set a few minutes, cut through them with a very sharp knife to release more flavor, then cover again and let steep for around 15 minutes. Serve hot, with a fresh mint leaf on each cup.

Comfrey and Peppermint Tea

Take several comfrey leaves and a handful of fresh peppermint leaves and wash, then cover with boiling water and cover tightly, setting the dish on a hot burner which has been turned off. Let it steep for 10 minutes, strain then serve. Makes 2 or 3 cups.

Tahini Milk

1 tablespoon tahini
1 cup warm water

Blend or stir until tahini is dissolved into a milk. Tahini is a thin butter made from sesame seeds with a 36% protein content. Easily digested.

Soybean Carrot Milk

Mix fresh carrot juice and soybean milk, half and half, and drink immediately. The carrot pulp from the juicer can be used as a filler in vegetarian patties and casseroles.

Sunflower Seed Milk

The night before, put 1 cup of shelled sunflower seeds and 3½ cups water in the blender. Cover. Before breakfast, blend until you have a white milk and seeds are reduced to pulp. Pour into a fine wire strainer or strain through a thin cloth. The seeds can be soaked only a few hours, if you need the milk during the day.

Manchurian Milk Drink

Mix the required amount of soya milk for your family. Put about a cup in the blender and add dates and almonds and blend fine, then add this to the full amount of soy milk and serve. Use about 3 pitted dates and 1 tablespoon of almonds for each cup of soy milk.

Soybean Milk

Wash soybeans and soak them overnight in plenty of water. Put 1 cup of soaked beans and 3 cups of water in the blender and whiz until pulpy. Use up the beans in this proportion.

Put the blended mixture in a large stainless steel kettle and simmer gently for 15 minutes. Strain through a very fine sieve or stout cloth.

Refrigerate the milk until used.

If you don't have a blender, drain the beans and grind through a food chopper, add the water and simmer and strain as before.

Seed Milk

The seeds may be watermelon, cantaloupe, muskmelon, ripe cucumber, summer squash, zucchini or any fresh vegetable seeds.

In the blender put the following and blend into liquid:

3 cups of fresh seeds and membrane
2 cups of cold water
1 cup of mint leaves, or 1 cup of fresh herbs and dill seeds, depending on which flavor you want. You can also use nasturtium leaves, peppergrass, or any pungent seasoning.

Whiz and strain, then thin with water to desired strength. Serves 6.

Peanut Milk

In the blender put ½ cup shelled, skinned peanuts and 2 cups of water. Blend until the nuts are mostly reduced to fine pulp. Add blackstrap molasses or honey if desired, but peanut milk is so perfectly delicious just as it is that sweeteners are unneeded.

You can strain the peanut milk through a wire strainer or cloth. The chunks which remain are fine to eat with a spoon.

You can get hard nuts reduced quicker if you put ¼ cup of nuts and ½ cup water in the bottom of the blender and reduce the nuts to pulp this way, then add the remainder of the water and blend it again.

Another way to make peanut milk is to take a tablespoon of homemade peanut or nut butter and stir it into a cup of warm water. This is for those who don't have blenders and who make their peanut and nut butters with a food grinder.

Magic Milks

These substitutes can be used in any recipe asking for milk.

No. 1

3 eggs   ½ cup oil

Turn blender on and keep adding water gradually. When blender is full, pour into a jar and add water to make about 4½ to 5 cups of milk.

No. 2

½ cup sunflower seeds   3 cooked eggs
½ cup sesame seeds

Add hot water gradually until thick and smooth. Keep adding water to thin and when blender is full, pour into jar and add enough water to make 4 or 5 cups of milk. Sunflower alone is the mildest tasting. Use all sunflower seeds for sunflower seed milk.

1 cooked egg	⅓ cup water
¼ cup oil	⅓ cup brown rice

Blend until smooth. Add water to make 2 cups of milk.

This one is given in a smaller quantity to get the rice blended well. It can be strained through a small fine strainer to get it perfectly smooth. This one won't separate as fast as the other two.

"Nut Milk" Yogurt

1 cup nuts, local variety, cashews or almonds	2 cups of warm water ½ cup yogurt starter

Liquefy the nuts in the warm water. Add hot water, enough and of the right heat to make a quart of liquid of 115 degrees temperature. Stir the starter in, blend and keep at this temperature for 8 hours or until as sour and thick as is desired. We suggest a heating pad for this purpose as the simplest method. Then refrigerate.

Almond Milk

In the bottom of the blender, put ½ cup almonds, ½ cup pure water and supplements. Blend until you have a paste, then add 3 cups of warm water and blend again. You may strain this milk if you wish, but we like the nutty taste of any of the almonds which haven't been reduced to paste. Serve warm in winter, cold in summer.

Cashew Milk

In the blender, put 1 cup of cashews, 1 cup of warm water and ½ cup of unsulphured raisins. Blend until the nuts are reduced to fine pulp, then add 3 cups of warm water and blend. You may strain it if you wish.

Coconut Milk

1 cup fresh coconut chunks   2 cups pure water
  (or 1 cup coconut meal)

Whiz in blender until pulp is fine (or meal is dissolved). Store in a covered jar in the refrigerator.

Banananut Milk

In the blender put 1 cup of locally-grown nuts and ½ cup water. Blend until the nuts are reduced to liquid. Add 1 banana and 2 cups of water and blend together. This is one of the most nutritious drinks you can make and you may thin it down more if you desire. Use whatever supplements are needed, of course.

Carob Milk

For each serving, put the following ingredients in the blender and whiz smooth. Serve hot or cold, depending on the weather and the children's taste.

1 cup nut milk   1 tablespoon carob powder
1 teaspoon honey   ½ teaspoon pure vanilla

Tropical Milk Shake

In the blender put 1 cup of locally-grown nuts and 1 cup of coconut milk. Whiz until the nuts are reduced to liquid. Add a shake of mace, 2 bananas and fill the blender with coconut milk and blend together. Keep covered until serving time.

Hot Soya Shake

In the blender put the following:

2 cups hot water	½ teaspoon cinnamon
1 tablespoon carob powder	½ cup pitted dates
1 tablespoon honey	½ cup soya milk powder

Blend until smooth, thin with more hot water if desired.

Soyafig Shake

Mix up soya milk according to the directions on the package. For each cup of milk, stem 3 figs. Put a cup of the milk, the figs and 1 heaping teaspoon brewer's yeast per serving in the blender and whiz into a liquid. Mix the rest of the milk and serve with a shake of mace on the top of each glass.

Breakfast Banana-Shake

This is a meal in a glass—great for a quick "must run" breakfast.

1 pint soy yogurt or buttermilk	3 tablespoons brewer's yeast
2 large or 3 medium ripe bananas	2 tablespoons lecithin
	½ teaspoon vanilla extract

Liquefy all ingredients to make delicious "Milk Shake." For variation try adding carob powder, or an egg. Serves four.

Apricot Shake

2 cups pitted fresh apricots (or soaked dried apricots)	½ cup honey
4 cups soy milk	¼ teaspoon mace

Prepare the soy milk according to directions on the container. Put 1 cup of it in the blender and add the other ingredients. Blend, then add the remainder of the milk and blend again with the cover held tightly on. Serve chilled or room temperature, as desired. 4-6 servings.

Banana Milk

In the blender put the following ingredients: 3 cups warm water, 4 tablespoons instant soy milk (powdered), 2 bananas, 1 tablespoon honey, 1 teaspoon pure vanilla extract and supplements. Whiz and serve in 4 glasses.

Delicious Health Drink

16 ounces soya bean milk
1 teaspoon brewer's yeast
1 teaspoon blackstrap molasses
1 teaspoon rose hips powder
1 teaspoon bone meal
1 teaspoon clover honey
1 or 2 teaspoons sunflower seeds
¼ teaspoon sea kelp

Blend all ingredients well together. For different flavors you can add walnut kernels or prunes or bananas. This recipe serves two.

Grape-Yogurt Drink

Take the late fall grapes and put 2 cups of water and 2 cups of the whole grapes in the blender. Whiz until you have the grapes reduced to liquid. Strain through a fine wire strainer and add honey to taste. Store in a tightly-covered glass jar.

Grape-Yogurt Drink is made by stirring a half cup of yogurt thin, then adding a half cup of the grape juice.

Cantaloupe Shake

A refreshing beverage—high in flavor—low in calories.

½ cup unsweetened pineapple juice
2 cups sliced or cubed cantaloupe (ripe)

Put juice into blender to start, drop sliced or cubed cantaloupe into blender a few pieces at a time, blending thoroughly. Add more cantaloupe if you desire a thicker shake. Serves 3.

Sweet "Port Wine"

Here's a wine that's legal for children—delicious too! Serve in a beautiful wine glass; it looks and tastes better that way.

Pour in each glass, one tablespoon of a good apple cider vinegar. Fill with a good Concord grape juice and stir.

Voilà! You have a delicious Port "wine."

Vitamineral Green Drink

4 young comfrey leaves
1 cup young dandelion leaves
1 cup young mint leaves
  (spearmint preferred)

1 cup sunflower seeds
1 cup fresh pineapple

Put this through a clear juicer, adding sweetening or seasoning, and thinning to your family's taste. Any greens can be used.

Strawberry Mint Nectar

In the bottom of the blender, put a handful of young mint leaves and 1 cup of cold water. Liquefy. Add 2 cups strawberries, 2 more cups of water, ½ tray of ice cubes and blend. Then dribble in honey to taste and thin the drink down with additional water. Supplements may be added, and alfalfa leaves, pea pods and many nourishing little extras may be "snuck in" without anybody being the wiser, for the strawberries and mint cover for them.

Raspberry Pineapple Juice

In the blender put these ingredients:

2 cups cold water
1 cup frozen black raspberries
  (thawed first)

1 cup fresh pineapple

Whiz until the pineapple is reduced to pulp. Add honey to sweeten and whiz again, then fill the blender with cold water and blend with the cover tightly in place, or remove from blender and dilute to individual taste. Garnish each glassful with a tiny pineapple slice floating on top.

Purple Cow

Gather wild elderberries which are away from any spray activities. Pick the berries off the stems after they have been washed carefully. Use equal parts pure water and berries in the blender, then put through a wire strainer. Now sweeten to taste with honey or maple syrup and spice the drink with cloves. Add ice cubes. Keep in a covered glass jar until used up. Mint can be added to the blender mixture and the leaves strained out, or other spices may be used.

Pineapple Tonic

In the blender, put the following, whizzing between additions:

1 cup water
½ cup dandelion leaves
½ cup alfalfa leaves

1 stalk rhubarb (cut in inch
  lengths)
1½ cups pineapple chunks
  (fresh)

Water to thin and honey to taste. Keep covered until served.

Pineapple Mint Julep

1 tablespoon tender new mint   1 tablespoon unprocessed honey
  leaves

Put these in the bottom of the blender and whiz for 30 seconds, then cover the blender and let stand a few minutes for the honey to extract the essence from the mint. Now add:

1 cup fresh pineapple chunks   2 cups cold water
½ cup honey

Blend until the pineapple is reduced to liquid. Add more water and ice cubes and keep blender covered until the Julep is served.

Peachy Fruit Flip

In the blender put ½ cup each of almonds and water, whiz until they are reduced to paste. Then add 2 cups cold water and the following fruits:

1 peach, pitted   1 apple, cored
1 pear, halved   1 cup soaked figs for sweetening

Thin down to desired consistency. Add supplements if desired. Serves 1.

Peach Nectar

Make pineapple juice by whizzing ½ cup of frozen (thawed) pineapple with 2 cups of water. Add a pared and pitted peach and honey to taste, plus several ice cubes. Serve with a mint leaf on each glassful of nectar. Serves 1.

November Punch

In the blender put the following ingredients and whiz until all are reduced to liquid. Keep covered until they are served, to preserve the vitamins.

1 cup frozen or fresh pineapple
3 cups cold water
½ cup raw cranberries
   honey to taste

¼ cup sunflower seeds
½ tray ice cubes, added
   gradually

Serves 2.

Hot Mulled Cider

1 quart pure apple cider
1 teaspoon whole cloves

1 inch stick cinnamon

Tie spices in a small square of cheese cloth—add to cider—simmer covered for 15 minutes. Garnish mug with a cinnamon stick. Honey may be added if desired. Serves 5.

Mustang Juice

1 cup fully ripe grapes

⅔ cup honey

Put in a quart jar. Fill with boiling water, and seal. Use after 4 to 6 weeks.

Hot Fruit Peppo

1 raw apple (cored and
   quartered)
1 cup pineapple pulp
   (from freezer)

½ cup fresh sprouts
1 tablespoon powdered soy
   milk
1 cup hot water

Put the above in the blender and run until you have a fine consistency. Add honey to taste and 3 cups of very hot water. Run the blender a second and serve. Serves 4.

Holiday Punch

2 cups sweet cider
½ cup raw cranberries
1 banana

½ cup sunflower seeds
Blend and serve in clear
goblets

Serves 2.

Homemade Sweet Cider

It seems strange, but putting raw apples through a juicer gives APPLE JUICE, while putting them through the blender and a pressing process, which we will describe, makes APPLE CIDER just like the kind we get from cider mills in the autumn.

Besides the blender, you will need a large wire strainer sitting in a large granite kettle. Then find a plate which will fit inside the strainer and line the strainer with a stout clean cloth. The bottom of an old pillowcase is fine.

For each "batch," prepare about 3 cups of apple quarters, leaving the skins on, and all of the core but the seeds. Put them in the blender, with 1 cup of cold water. Blend until they are reduced to a thick pulp, which is poured into the cloth-lined strainer and the 4 sides of the cloth are brought over from each direction and arranged to hold the pulp neatly in the bottom of the strainer. (Wet the cloth so that it doesn't take up the cider.)

Now place the plate on the cloth folds and weight it all that you dare. A heavy scrubbed stone is a good weight. Cover the kettle to keep out all air and drip out all of the juice. Get the cider in a closed jar and repeat until you have the desired amount.

Hawaiian Dash

1 cup pineapple (fresh)
4 egg yolks
½ cup honey

mint leaves which have been
soaked
2 cups cold water

Whiz in the blender until the pineapple is reduced to liquid, then fill the blender full of cold water, cover tight and whiz again. Keep covered until served. Serves 2.

Grape Punch

In the blender put these ingredients:

1 cup grape juice
1 pear, cored

1 handful of mint leaves
2 cups sweet cider

Honey to taste and water to thin to desired strength, after the mixture has been blended and removed to a larger container. Serves 2.

Grape Juice

In the blender put:

1 cup fresh-picked grapes
½ cup honey

2 cups of water

Blend until you have the grapes reduced to pulp. Strain through a wire strainer, add more water and supplements, and keep in a tightly covered glass jar until serving time. Serves 2.

Fruit Blender Drink

In the blender put the following:

1 cup raw pineapple (fresh or
   frozen and thawed)
3 cups water

½ cup honey
4 washed and pitted peaches

Blend, adding ice cubes until you have a thin, chilled drink. You may add supplements and sunflower seeds if you wish. Serves 4.

Frosty Fruit Shake

2 cups pineapple juice
½ raw apple, peeled
½ cup honey

½ teaspoon pure vanilla
   (optional)
1 tray ice cubes

Place all ingredients except ice in blender. Add ice gradually, and beat until ice is slush—looks like shaved ice. Serves 2.

Fruit Drink

2½ cups unsweetened grape juice
½ cup dried apricots
½ cup dates
½ cup raisins
¼ cup almond meal
¼ cup sunflower seed meal

All ingredients organic. Mix in blender until ingredients are well blended. If it is a little thick, more grape juice can be added, or apple juice. Serves 2.

Fresh Apple Juice

This is made with a juicer. Wash and core the apples and put them through the juicer, catching the juice and sealing it immediately to preserve the vitamin and mineral content until ready to drink.

Blackberry Cordial

2 cups fresh or frozen blackberries
2 cups pure water
3 comfrey leaves

Blend and put through a wire strainer.

Now add honey plus a pinch of cloves, and thin with water and ice cubes. A tiny pinch of spice adds greatly to fruit drinks. Serves 2.

Blender Benedictine

In the blender put:

1 cored apple cut in chunks
1 cup frozen (thawed) strawberries
½ cup honey
6 almonds
4 cups hot mint tea

Blend until the nuts are reduced to liquid. It is usually best to put half of the liquid in first, for the blending process, then add the remainder and blend a few seconds. This keeps the nuts in the bottom of the blender for a quicker job of blending them up. This drink is served hot, being reheated if need be. Serves 4.

Autumn Fruit Punch

For this punch, hunt up all of the cull fruit in season, any time of year. Especially any that is almost overripe, as this is the sweetest fruit of all. For October use very ripe peaches, pears and grapes in the north, other fruits in the south and west. If you have a juicer, make them into clear, rich juice. Otherwise peel and pit, blend with pure water and add honey if needed, also supplements, nuts, sunflower seeds, mint leaves, comfrey and any other desired additions.

Garden Cocktail

In the blender, put the following:

1 cup fresh carrot juice
several sprigs of young carrot tops
handful of fresh mint
½ cup sunflower seeds
1 cup fresh berries
2 tablespoons raw honey
½ tray ice cubes

Whiz the seeds and greenery up before adding the ice cubes. Serve at once. Serves 1.

Floral Punch

In the blender, put the following:

4 large yellow tomatoes, cut up
celery tops
sea kelp to taste
12 nasturtium leaves and stems

Blend until reduced to liquid, add ice cubes and blend again. Serve in tall glasses with a nasturtium flower floating in each glass. Serves 4.

Hot Tomato Tonic

For each serving, use the following ingredients:

1 cup home-canned tomato juice
1 tablespoon desiccated liver
1 teaspoon sea kelp

½ teaspoon dried marjoram
supplements as desired

Heat most of the tomato juice quite hot. Add the rest of the ingredients to the hot juice, stir well, and serve very hot. This is a wonderful drink on a cold wintry morning, and a most healthful one.

Herbed Tomato Punch

3 cups tomatoes
1 cup water

½ cup fresh herbs, nasturtium
leaves, parsley, and dill

Blend, strain, and add ice cubes. Float slivers of parsley on the top of each glass. Serves 2.

Blender Raw Cabbage Juice

Start blender—push 1 cup down with rubber scraper to keep cabbage going into blade. After cabbage is like cole slaw—turn blender on and off to work it into a mush. When it starts to juice, let it run until it's good and mushy. This doesn't take long. For juice pour into wire strainer. Press juice out with rubber scraper. This is a real green juice. Honey may be added.

Artichoke Flip

Put scrubbed Jerusalem artichokes through a juicer which makes clear juice for this drink. They don't need any flavoring, whatever, but you may add herbs or parsley snipped up fine on top of the glass for adornment. Serve immediately.

Breads and Spreads

Breads

Bread is not the staff of life even though it be made of whole wheat. It is fattening, constipating for many, causes alarming symptoms in some heart patients, contributes to celiac disease in susceptible children, and is a factor in colds and many other ailments. Try a wheatless diet for a month and see what it will do for you.

Those who think they cannot do without some form of bread made with wheat are in for a pleasant surprise when they try the following substitutes:

Recipes for Breads and Muffins

Carrot Corn Bread

1 cup cornmeal	½ teaspoon sea kelp
1 cup grated carrots	2 tablespoons oil
1 teaspoon honey	2 eggs, separated

Mix thoroughly: cornmeal, carrots, oil, honey and kelp. Stir in ¾ cup boiling water. Add 2 tablespoons cold water to egg yolks and beat until thick. Add to above mixture.

Fold in stiffly beaten egg whites. Pour into warm oiled pan. Bake at 400 degrees for 25 minutes or until done. Serves 4.

Dixie Corn Bread

4 cups soy milk	2 tablespoons cooking oil
2 cups yellow cornmeal	1 teaspoon sea kelp
4 eggs separated	

Heat the milk hot, add the cornmeal gradually, stirring constantly. Stir and cook until very thick. Remove from fire and cool to warm.

Beat the 4 egg whites stiff, then put the cornmeal mixture, the egg yolks, oil and sea kelp under the beaters and blend them thoroughly. Fold in the whites and pour the batter in an oiled oblong cake tin. Bake at 375 degrees until done, about 45 minutes.

Indian Corn Bread

1 tablespoon dry yeast granules	1 tablespoon maple syrup
1 cup warm nut milk	1 cup yellow corn meal
1 egg, separated	½ cup potato flour
3 tablespoons cooking oil	½ cup wheat germ flour

Put the yeast in the warm milk. Beat the egg white stiff and set aside while you mix the other ingredients. Beat the egg yolk in the milk mixture, then add the corn meal and beat, then the oil and the remainder of the flours. Fold in the egg white and pour the batter in a 9 × 9″ tin. Let rise in a warm place while the oven preheats to 350°. Bake about 30 minutes, or until the bread is nicely brown.

Raised Cornbread

1 tablespoon yeast granules	2 beaten eggs
2 tablespoons honey	2½ cups unsifted corn meal
4 tablespoons cooking oil	1 cup unsifted brown rice
2 cups soy or nut milk, scalded, cooled to lukewarm	flour

Dissolve yeast and honey in warm milk. Add eggs, oil, corn meal and flour which has been sifted after measuring. Beat well and pour mixture into an oiled pan about 9 × 18. Let rise in a warm place (on a heating pad, covered, if you don't have a better place) for one hour. Bake at 375 degrees until done, 25 or 30 minutes. Serve hot.

Sunbaked Fruit Bread

This should be made about 2 hours before the meal, and on a sunny, hot, day. The time of baking depends on the temperature in the sun, of course.

In a bowl, chop together:

1 cup dates	2 cups sliced bananas
1 cup figs	4 cups raw peanut flour
1 cup nut meats (local variety)	

Shape into wafers and bake 1 hour in hot sun, then turn and bake a while longer. Store in a covered dish and keep refrigerated.

These are delightful "bread slices" and make good *hors d'oeuvres*.

Health Bread

1½ cups cooked brown rice	2 teaspoons soy or corn oil
2 cups whole kernel yellow cornmeal	1 cup cold water

Mix well. Add one beaten fresh egg and mix again. Turn mixture into oiled baking pan. Bake at 350 degrees for 60 minutes.

Millet Bread

1½ cups millet flour	3 tablespoons cooking oil
1 cup grated carrots	3 eggs
1 tablespoon honey	¾ cup boiling water
1 teaspoon sea kelp	

Separate the eggs and beat the whites very stiff. Set aside. Pour the boiling water over the millet flour, then add the carrots, honey, kelp, and oil. Beat the egg yolks and add 3 tablespoons cold water. Add to the millet mixture. Fold in the egg whites last, pour the batter in a very hot oiled bread tin and bake about 45 minutes at

350 degrees. The oven should be preheated while the bread is being stirred up, and the oiled tin put in the oven to heat. This bread must start baking immediately. It tastes and looks like corn bread, but is a richer yellow because of the carrots.

Nut Bread

1 cup warm potato water	2 teaspoons honey
1 tablespoon dry yeast granules	1 cup corn flour

Blend together and let rise until light, about 45 minutes. Then add the following to make a stiff loaf:

½ cup sunflower seed meal	1 cup peanut flour
1 cup raisins	1 cup wheat germ flour
1 egg, beaten	1 teaspoon sea kelp
1 tablespoon safflower oil	

This batter needs no kneading as it contains no gluten. Stir with spoon, then put into an oiled bread pan.

Let rise while oven heats and then bake 10 minutes at 400° F. Lower heat to 350° F. and bake 50 minutes longer.

Oatmeal Bread

2 cups hot potato water	½ cup warm water
2 cups oatmeal	1 tablespoon yeast granules
¼ cup honey	1 tablespoon corn oil

Pour hot potato water over oatmeal. Blend and cool to lukewarm. Blend honey and warm water and add the yeast cake, then add this mixture to the warm oatmeal plus the tablespoon of oil. Let rise in warm place until light and doubled in bulk.

Add:

1 cup pitted dates	2 eggs
1 cup raisins	1 cup corn flour
½ cup chopped nuts	½ cup wheat germ
½ cup chopped sunflower seeds	½ cup rice polishings

Stir until blended and spoon into 2 oiled bread tins. Spread dough with bowl of spoon. Let rise until light, about 1½ hours. Bake 50 minutes at 350 degrees.

Southern Spoon Bread

1 cup yellow cornmeal   4 eggs
2 cups soy or nut milk

Cook corn meal and milk together until mixture is quite thick. Remove from fire and let cool about 5 minutes, stirring often. Then beat in 4 egg yolks, one at a time while the 4 whites are being beaten stiff in the electric mixer.

Now fold the stiffly beaten egg whites carefully and pour the batter into an oiled oblong glass baking pan.

Bake at 300 degrees for 30 minutes or until a toothpick comes out clean.

Wheat Germ Bread

5 tablespoons vegetable oil
1 cup soya flour
1 cup rice polishings
7 cups wheat germ
4 egg yolks

1½ cups water, more if required to make fairly stiff batter
4 egg whites, beaten very stiffly

Mix in order given and divide into two oiled and floured loaf pans. Let stand for ten to fifteen minutes, then bake about one hour in 325° oven, or until nicely browned. Test with toothpick.

Do not have oven heat too high, as the bread burns easily.

Blueberry Muffins

2 tablespoons cooking oil
3 eggs, separated
¾ cup nut or soy milk
½ cup honey
1 teaspoon sea kelp

½ teaspoon cinnamon
½ cup potato starch flour
½ cup low-fat soy flour
½ cup rice flour
1 cup frozen blueberries

Separate the eggs and beat the whites stiff and set aside. Put all of the ingredients except the whites and berries in a deep bowl and beat at medium speed for about 5 minutes to lighten the starch flours. Then fold in the blueberries and egg whites, bake in oiled muffin tins at 400 degrees for about 30 minutes. This makes 12 muffins. Be sure they are done, the frozen berries slow up the baking process a little.

Buckwheat Muffins

1⅓ cups home-ground
    buckwheat flour
⅔ cup nut flour (grind
    nuts in blender)
½ teaspoon sea salt
2 tablespoons wheat germ
1 teaspoon bone meal
2 heaping teaspoons whey

1 tablespoon blackstrap
    molasses
1 tablespoon oil
3 eggs, separated (whip
    whites stiff)
½ cup raisins (soaked)
1 cup water (more, if
    necessary)

Combine ingredients, whipped egg whites last (folded in carefully). Bake in muffin pan 20 minutes at 425°. Makes 12 muffins.

Caraway Millet Muffins

1 cup hot soya milk   1 cup millet flour

Blend together and let cool to lukewarm. Then add:

1 tablespoon dry yeast granules
    dissolved in ¼ cup warm water

Let this rise about 30 minutes and add the following ingredients:

1 tablespoon honey
1 tablespoon cooking oil
1 egg

1 teaspoon caraway seeds
1 teaspoon sea kelp
¾ cup brown rice flour

Blend the batter and pour in 9 oiled muffin tins. Bake about 25 minutes, or until done, at 400 degrees. These are surprisingly good considering that there is no gluten on which the yeast can act to produce resilience and lightness. Makes 6 muffins.

Coconut Muffins

2 eggs, separated
2 tablespoons cooking oil
2 tablespoons honey

1 cup coconut meal
½ cup sifted potato flour

Beat the egg whites stiff enough to hold peaks. While this is being done, sift the potato flour and coconut meal 3 times. Put the egg yolks under the beaters, start beating at medium speed and add the other ingredients in their order. Clean off the beaters, and fold in the egg whites. Pour batter in oiled muffin tins and bake about 25 minutes at 350 degrees. Makes 6 "different" and very good muffins.

Cranberry Muffins

The night before, wash, stem, and cut in two, 1 cupful of cranberries. Cover with ½ cup of raw honey and let stand over night. When ready to make the muffins, add these:

4 egg yolks (and 4 whites)
4 tablespoons cooking oil
1½ cups unsifted peanut flour

1 cup wheat germ
½ teaspoon cloves

Blend ingredients and fold in the stiffly beaten egg whites. Bake 30 minutes at 350 degrees in well-oiled muffin tins. This recipe makes 12 muffins of excellent flavor and texture. Serve with raw red raspberry jam which can be made quickly by draining the juice off frozen red raspberries, mashing the berries and adding enough honey for sweetening.

Peanut Muffins

2 eggs, separated
2 tablespoons cooking oil
½ cup chopped raw peanuts (optional)

1 tablespoon maple syrup
½ cup sifted peanut flour
½ cup sifted wheat germ flour

Beat the whites and set aside. They should be stiff enough to hold peaks. Put the egg yolks under the beaters, add the other ingredients in order, beating well after each addition. Fold in the egg whites and pour batter in oiled muffin tins. Bake about 25 minutes at 350 degrees. Makes 6.

Rice Muffins

3 eggs, separated
2 tablespoons maple syrup
1 cup soya milk
1 teaspoon sea kelp

½ cup almonds
2 tablespoons cooking oil
1 cup brown rice flour
1 cup rice polishings

Beat the egg whites until stiff and set aside. Combine the other ingredients and beat until very light. Fold in the egg whites, pour the batter in oiled muffin tins and bake about 25 minutes at 400 degrees. Makes 12 muffins.

Soya Muffins

2 eggs, separated

Beat the whites very stiff and set aside. Put the bowl with the yolks under the beaters and continue with the following:

½ cup soy milk
1 tablespoon honey
2 tablespoons oil

1 teaspoon sea kelp
½ cup potato starch flour
½ cup soy flour

Sift the last 3 ingredients several times before adding to the mixture and beating it. Fold in the egg whites gently, pour in oiled muffin tins and bake at 400° for 20 to 25 minutes. Makes 6 muffins.

Sprout Muffins

At last, a muffin made without flour that has a toasty, crunchy goodness.

Blend together:

1 cup sunflower seeds
1 teaspoon dolomite
¼ cup brewer's yeast
1 tablespoon desiccated liver
3 tablespoons cold-pressed oil
1 cup sprouts

½ cup coconut
1 teaspoon bone meal
1 teaspoon kelp
1 tablespoon molasses
4 egg yolks

Add enough buttermilk or soy milk to make a thick batter. (Will vary because of egg size.)

Fold in stiffly beaten egg whites. Bake in greased muffin tins 25 minutes at 400° F. Makes 12 small muffins.

Variations:
1. Add 1 cup raisins, currants or dried apricots (chopped).
2. Add nut meats.
3. Put two pitted dates in each muffin tin.

Sunflower Seed Muffins

3 eggs, separated
2 tablespoons oil
2 tablespoons honey
½ cup coconut
¼ cup wheat germ
1 teaspoon sea kelp

1 cup sunflower seed meal
½ cup rice polishings, sifted
½ cup apple juice or other unsweetened fruit juice
1 cup raisins

Beat the egg whites and set aside. Blend other items and fold in egg whites last. Pour batter in oiled muffin tins and bake about 25 minutes in a 350 degree oven. Makes 12 muffins.

Waikiki Muffins

4 eggs, separated
1 cup chopped pineapple, fresh, frozen or home-canned
4 tablespoons cooking oil

2 tablespoons honey
1½ cups yellow cornmeal
½ cup wheat germ flour

Beat the egg whites stiff and set aside. Blend the other ingredients and fold in the egg whites. Pour in oiled muffin tins and bake about 25 minutes at 350 degrees. This recipe makes 12 large muffins.

Corn Popovers

1 cup unsifted corn flour
1 cup nut milk

2 eggs
1 teaspoon salad oil

Blend the ingredients together, then put under the electric beaters and beat hard for 5 minutes. Place 6 heated glass custard cups on a cookie sheet and fill half full with the batter. Bake for 15 minutes (without opening the oven door—or they won't pop) at 450 degrees F. then bake another 30 minutes at 350 degrees F. Serve immediately. This makes 6 large popovers.

Corn Squares

2 eggs, separated
2 tablespoons raw honey
3 tablespoons cooking oil
1 teaspoon sea kelp

1 cup soya milk
¾ cup wheat germ
¾ cup yellow cornmeal

Beat the egg whites stiff and set aside. Put the other ingredients under the beaters and beat, until light. Fold in the egg whites, pour in a 9×9″ pan and bake at 400 degrees until browned, about 20 minutes. Cut in squares and serve hot.

Corn Sticks

You will need corn stick pans for these. The pans are iron and should be oiled well and put in the oven and heated very hot before filling.

This batter may also be baked in an 8×8×2″ pan.

⅔ cup sifted wheat germ flour
1¼ cups sifted cornmeal
1 teaspoon sea kelp
2 egg yolks

1 tablespoon honey
3 tablespoons cooking oil
1 cup soy milk

Turn on the oven at 425 degrees, then combine the dry ingredients. Separate the eggs and beat the whites very stiff and set aside; add yolks, oil, honey and milk to dry ingredients, beat just until blended, fold in the whites and fill the corn stick pans the first time and bake about 8 minutes for each batch or until nicely browned. Makes about 12.

"Cornflower" Buns

½ compressed yeast cake
1¼ cups lukewarm water
1 beaten egg

1 teaspoon honey
1 cup corn flour

Dissolve yeast in warm water, add other ingredients and stir in the flour. Let rise about 30 minutes, or until bubbly.

Add these ingredients:

1 tablespoon salad oil   1 tablespoon honey

Enough corn flour to make a soft yet firm dough. Stir well but do not knead. Oil the top and let rise. Shape into small buns and let rise for 2 hours, then bake 15 minutes at 400 degrees. Makes 6.

Corn-Caraway Gems

2 eggs, separated   2 tablespoons cooking oil
1 tablespoon honey   ½ cup wheat germ
1 teaspoon caraway seeds   ½ cup coconut or nut milk
1 teaspoon sea kelp   ¾ cup yellow corn flour

Blend all ingredients except the egg whites, which you beat stiff and fold in last. Bake in the tiny muffin tins if possible, or in small custard cups. Have baking dishes well-oiled and bake about 10 minutes at 400 degrees, or until brown and done in the middle. Makes 6.

Peanut Corn Sticks

1 cup yellow cornmeal   ½ cup boiling water

Pour the boiling water over the cornmeal, blend and cool.
Add the following ingredients to the cornmeal mixture:

1 teaspoon sea kelp   1 rounded tablespoon brown
1 egg yolk   rice flour
1 tablespoon honey   ½ cup soy milk
1 rounded tablespoon peanut
  butter

Blend together and fold in 1 stiffly beaten egg white. Have the oven preheated to 425° and have the oiled corn stick pan in it, very hot. Fill it with the mixture and bake until done, about 10 to 12 minutes. Makes 6.

Spreads and Jams

If it comes down to a choice, it is butter over margarine every time. For one thing we need a limited amount of the kind of animal fat butter contains, and butter is also extremely rich in vitamin A and carotene. Because the vegetable oils from which margarine is made do not contain the vitamin, synthetic vitamin A must be added to margarine.

It is true that butter contains little vitamin F (unsaturated fatty acids) but margarine generally is a conglomeration of fats that are at least as bad as the butterfat they substitute for, with a bewildering array of chemicals added to furnish texture, flavor and color.

But if you are concerned about using either of these, there are delicious alternatives. Nut butters make tasty spreads, even for people not particularly attracted to health foods. Sugar-free preserves make another interesting possibility in this area.

Experiment with some of the suggestions that follow. Your family will be pleasantly surprised.

Recipes for Butters and Honeys

Cashew Butter Spread

Pour 1 cup raw cashew bits into the blender with 1 tablespoon sesame seeds. Blend. Pour mixture into a mixing bowl and mash lumps with a tablespoon. Spoon mixture into a glass container with a screw top.

Add ⅓ cup soy oil and mix thoroughly. Refrigerate at least overnight before serving. For variation add ½ cup fresh crushed pineapple and ¼ cup honey.

Coconut Butter

Cut off meat from coconut and cut into strips. Put through a meat grinder and soak for two or three hours in several times its bulk of warm water. A rich cream will rise to the top. Skim off this cream and work into a butter-like mass with an ordinary butter ladle.

Raw Grape Butter

This is from the freezer, of course. During grape season, sort the grapes, wash them, then "jump" them, putting the pulp into the blender and the skins in a basin. Blend the pulp and strain out the seeds (wire strainer is best for this). Now blend the skins until they are whizzed fine and put with the pulp. Add honey to taste and freeze immediately.

If grape butter is too rich for you, add a few cored apples to the skins when you whiz them. This mixture is superb if you add a bit of cinnamon and allspice to it. Use less honey than for the whole grape butter.

Nut Butter

Take any kind of nuts you have, whether a local variety, peanuts, walnuts, pistachios, or whatever. Grind them through the nut knife of your food chopper, or in a nut mill, or even in the blender, a half cup at a time. Then put the desired amount in a deep but small-diametered bowl. Take a tool like a wooden potato masher and start pounding the ground nuts. Add a few drops of salad oil, then pound, then a few more drops of oil, then a thorough pounding and keep this up until you have the kind of fine nut butter you want, and of the consistency you want.

Peach Butter

½ cup almonds   1 cup honey
½ cup water   1 teaspoon cinnamon
 6 peaches, peeled and pitted

Put the nuts and water in the blender and run it until they are reduced to liquid paste. Then add the other ingredients and whiz until you have a well-blended butter. Keep covered and refrigerated.

Peanut Butter

Put a cupful of shelled peanuts and 1 tablespoon of peanut oil in the blender. Blend with motor on and off to prevent overheating until you have the consistency you want. You can have anything from chunk-style to sloppy. Keep in refrigerator. If you don't like unroasted peanuts, then roast them for 20 minutes at 300 degrees *in their shells*, and cool before making them up.

Pineapple Butter

In the blender, put 2 cups of pineapple chunks and 2 cored apples, with just enough pineapple juice to blend them into a thick butter. Remove from blender and add honey to taste. Keep in a covered dish in the refrigerator.

Plum Butter

Pick over and wash clean 1 pound plums. Put into kettle and cover with water. Cook until tender. Put through colander to remove skins and pits. To 1 cup pulp add ½ cup honey. Mix well. Cook until thick. Seal in sterilized jars.

Seed Butter

1 cup ground sunflower seeds	¼ cup soy oil
¼ cup ground pumpkin seeds	2 tablespoons honey

Mix well, then add:

¼ cup peanut butter	¼ cup tahini

Mix well. Very good with fruit.

Soya Butter

Using a small-diameter, high bowl, so the beaters will come as high as possible, put 2 cups of full fat soy flour into the bowl. Drop the beaters in place and fit a piece of clean paper over the top of the bowl around the beaters so that the flour won't fly. Have a small opening for a funnel and start the electric mixer, running a tiny stream of soya oil into the flour and beating it on medium speed. When you get a peanut-butter consistency, pack the soy butter in a covered dish and keep refrigerated.

You can hand-beat the oil into the flour and make a good butter but it is a lot of work.

Orange Honey

Scrub the skin of an organically-grown orange, quarter it, and blend until it is fine. Add it to 3 cups of raw strained honey. Keep it in a covered can in the refrigerator between meals. This is good on waffles, pancakes and corn bread.

Mint-Honey

1 cup crystallized honey (preferably 2 years old as crystals
are needed for texture)

20 fresh spearmint leaves
20 fresh peppermint leaves
40 fresh alfalfa leaves

Whiz in the blender from 1 to 2 minutes, depending on how fine or coarse you want it. Refrigerate 48 hours before using.

Peanut-Honey

Take 1 cup of crystallized honey and beat it (preferably with an electric mixer) until it is the whiteness and consistency of lard. Then beat in homemade peanut butter until you have the flavor as you want it. Probably a cup of peanut butter would be about right for most people.

Recipes for Jams and Jellies

Apricot Conserve

Pit and mash fresh apricots. Stir in the desired amount of honey and thicken with blanched, ground almonds. This is food for the gods, both in nutrition and taste.

Raw Blackberry Jam

Mash ripe blackberries and add the amount of honey needed for your family's taste. Stir it in and keep the raw jam in a covered dish except during the meal. This makes a fine jam for waffles or any of the corn bread recipes we have given you.

Blueberry Jam

In the blender put the following and blend into mush:

2 cups blueberries (thawed)   ½ cup nuts
1 stalk rhubarb

Pour the jam into a dish which can be covered tight. If too thin, stir in rice polishings to thicken and add honey to taste. Comb honey is better than the liquid type for raw jams.

Dewberry Jam

Wild dewberries are one of Nature's offerings that haven't been tampered with as yet. They are a most delightful berry. If you don't like the seeds, whiz the berries in the blender and strain through a wire strainer. Then add as much honey as is needed and thicken with rice polishings or wheat germ if you want the jam thick. Keep covered in the refrigerator until used up. You can freeze it for winter use, also.

Raw Marmalade

To make raw marmalade, use fresh fruits, wash and crush; or crush frozen and thawed fruits.

Any of the following fruits can be made up this way, as well as combinations of two or more fruits: Peaches, plums, strawberries, raspberries, blackberries, cherries, currants.

For each cupful of fruit, use about ⅓ cup honey. If you have honey which is crystallized, here is a good place to use it up.

Thicken the marmalade with wheat germ flour, using only as much as is needed. Keep refrigerated and covered.

Part Cooked Jam

1 cup honey   2 cups whole cranberries
1 box pectin powder

Boil slowly 1 cup honey with 1 box of pectin powder. Add ½ cup of whole cranberries to cook with it. Chop up 1½ cups raw cranberries in the blender and add to the jell after it has boiled for a few minutes. Chill.

Raw Pear Conserve

In the blender (or through the food grinder) put these ingredients:

2 cups diced pears   ½ cup honey
½ cup organically grown   ½ cup nut meats
  unsulphured raisins   ¼ cup pineapple

Blend until you have a thick jam. Put in tightly covered glass jars and refrigerate.

Pear and Cranberry Conserve

Core 6 ripe pears and put in the blender. Thaw 2 cups of cranberries and put in the blender with the pears. Whiz them into fine pulp. Add honey to taste, and a pinch each of cinnamon and cloves. Whiz again and store in a covered glass dish until serving time. Red raspberries may replace the cranberries. Nuts may be added, or sunflower seeds, for added protein.

Pineapple Jam

½ cup cold water   2 cups fresh pineapple

Put in the blender and whiz until smooth. Remove from blender and add honey to taste, then ground nuts and sunflower seeds until you have a thick jam. Keep refrigerated in a covered dish until used up.

Raw Strawberry Jam

Wash the desired amount of strawberries, then hull. Mash and add honey to taste. If the berries are very juicy, as they are some years, then stir in either wheat germ flour or rice polishings, raw, and add enough to thicken the jam as you want it. Tiny new mint leaves may also be shredded up in the jam for an extra-special flavor.

Sugarless Jelly

3 quarts blueberries (or any fruit in season)

4 cups apple cider (for sweeter you may add more)
1 box pectin

Place washed blueberries in pan on low heat with cover till blueberries cook well. Boil till thickened slightly. Add apple cider, continue boiling without cover, add pectin available at health store. Continue boiling until slightly thickened.

Pack in hot jars. Process in hot water bath for 5 minutes. Seal tightly for winter.

Tutti-Frutti Jam

Mash the following fresh fruits:

½ cup red raspberries
½ cup black raspberries
½ cup blueberries

1 ripe avocado
2 very ripe bananas

Add honey to taste, and thicken if necessary with rice polish. Add a pinch each of cinnamon and allspice. Keep in a covered dish, refrigerated, until used up.

Avocado Spread

1 ripe avocado, peeled and pitted
1 small yellow tomato

2 green onions, minced
1 teaspoon pure vinegar
1 teaspoon sea kelp

The quickest way to make this spread is with a potato masher as there is hardly enough to use the blender. This spread has a cool, clean taste which makes the "high priced spread" seem too rich and greasy. You can use it as a salad dressing, a dip, or fill peppers and tomatoes with it if you live where avocados are plentiful and inexpensive.

Carrot Spread

1 cup grated carrots   kelp or sea salt to taste
1 teaspoon chopped onion   ¼ cup chopped celery
¼ cup finely chopped peanuts   1 hard boiled egg, chopped

Mix the above. Add 2 tablespoons of homemade mayonnaise.

Chicken-Pecan Spread

2 cups cooked chicken, minced   ½ cup chopped pecans
¼ cup finely chopped celery   1 tablespoon fresh lime juice
1 pimiento, finely chopped   homemade mayonnaise

Combine all ingredients and add enough mayonnaise to suit individual taste. Place mixture in a glass bowl and sprinkle liberally with parsley flakes. Four servings.

Seed Spread

Put the following seeds and nuts in the blender and whiz up, one half cup at a time, emptying between each batch:

½ cup sunflower seeds   ½ cup pumpkin, squash or
½ cup sesame seeds   melon seeds
½ cup peanuts (shelled but
  not skinned)

Blend the seeds together and add just enough sunflower seed or peanut oil to make a spreadable paste. Keep refrigerated in a glass jar. You can substitute other seeds or nuts for those given above.

Sumptuous Spread

⅓ cup honey
½ cup coconut, ground

½ cup tahini (ground sesame seed)
½ cup sunflower seed meal

For variety use peanut butter, or cashew or almond butter in place of one of the above.

Keep the spread refrigerated until ready to use.

Sunshine Spread

1 cup wheat germ
2 cups honey

1 cup sunflower seed meal
1 cup pumpkin seed meal

Shake dry ingredients in wide-mouth mason jar to distribute evenly. Cut in honey with knife, or tighten cap and turn jar sufficient times for honey to be absorbed thoroughly. Refrigerate.

Vitamin Spread

4 medium carrots
½ green pepper
3 stalks celery
2 tablespoons wheat germ
2 tablespoons chopped nuts

1 teaspoon horseradish
3 tablespoons mayonnaise
1 teaspoon kelp granules
sea salt to taste

Mince vegetables finely. Mix with wheat germ. Add other ingredients; blend well. Serve on celery stalks.

Walnut-Seed Spread

Whiz the following nuts and seeds in the blender, a half cup at a time (to keep the blender from heating up):

1 cup walnut meats
1 cup shelled peanuts

1 cup sunflower seeds

Mix just enough peanut or sunflower seed oil into the ground mixture to make a spreadable consistency. Store in the refrigerator in a glass jar.

Desserts

Some Plain Talk About Sugars

Sugar is a carbohydrate, which means that it is made from carbon, hydrogen and oxygen. The way these elements are combined makes the basic difference in sugars such as glucose, fructose, lactose, maltose, etc.

We should try to confine our consumption to natural sugars which occur in foods along with all the nutrients that appear there, as opposed to white sugar and similar products, which are nothing but pure carbohydrate without a single particle of mineral, vitamin, enzyme or anything else that makes them food.

Refined white sugar is not only worthless as food, but dangerous to health in the quantities in which Americans consume it. Because of its easy solubility, it rushes through the stomach wall, creating imbalances in the blood, thereby inviting viruses and other infectious organisms to get a stronger foothold.

Sugar, besides leading to overweight, can be dangerous for heart cases as it distorts the calcium-phosphorus relationship in the blood. Strange as it may seem, if consumed in large amounts, sugar creates low blood sugar which could lead to physiological and emotional troubles. So there should be no candy, cake, pie, ice cream or soft drinks in the well-planned diet. These foods contain a great deal of refined white sugar. The best way to obtain sugar is in the natural state, as found in fruits and some vegetables. Honey is a valuable food, in moderation. We do not favor brown sugar; it is highly processed and bereft of most nutritional values.

Pure glucose is made from cornstarch and is sold as corn sugar. Health-conscious people shouldn't use it for it is "pure," which means that whatever nutritional values were present have been processed out of the final product, leaving "pure" carbohydrate. Other forms of sugar are used in processed foods for various reasons:

Lactose is used as a coating agent for olives, preserved fruits and sugared almonds and a flavoring agent for chocolate products. This form of sugar appears in many bakery products and confectionery products. It is an ingredient of baking and biscuit mixes, some cheeses, and baby foods. Sometimes lactose is used as a substitute for other sugars in jams. It is used as a preservative in meat products.

Maltose is used in beer and malt production, in making beverages and soft drinks, in bread doughs, confectionery products, jams, milk and coffee substitutes, tea extracts and in corn syrup.

This gives you some idea of the many, many ways sugars are hidden in food. It is difficult to find a processed food that does not contain "hidden" sugars, in addition to the many chemicals that may be there.

But sugar does give you energy. How then can you be sure you are getting enough if you eliminate white sugar from your diet?

Do you have any idea how much sugar, in various forms, you get in a well-planned diet which does not include a single grain of white sugar? Eating fruits, whole grains, vegetables, eggs, meat, nuts and milk, you would get the equivalent of close to two cups of sugar as a total for the day! Do you think anyone could possibly *need* more than that?

Here is a list of fruits and vegetables along with their carbohydrate content. We use the word "carbohydrate" here rather than "sugar," for in some of these foods the carbohydrate is in the form of starch rather than sugar. But the starch is changed into sugar almost as soon as you eat it, so in considering the total of your sugar intake, you should count this starch as sugar. *These foods contain only about 5 per cent carbohydrate:* carrots, cauliflower, okra, onions, peppers, pumpkin, radishes, string beans, watercress.

These foods contain about 7 per cent carbohydrate: avocado and olives (quite high in fat), grapefruit, lemons, strawberries, watermelon.

These foods contain about 10 per cent carbohydrate: parsnips, peas, Hubbard squash, turnips, berries, cantaloupe, muskmelon, oranges, peaches, pineapple, raspberries.

These foods contain about 15 per cent carbohydrate: apples, apricots, cherries, currants, grapes, huckleberries, nectarines, pears.

These foods contain about 20 per cent carbohydrate: corn, lima beans, navy beans, sweet and white potatoes, rice, bananas, fresh figs, plums and prunes. Dried fruits may contain as much as 75 per cent carbohydrate.

The amount of carbohydrate absorbed in a given individual at a particular time depends on the healthful condition of his digestive tract and of his glands, and the amount of B vitamins he obtains along with the sugar or starch.

Processed sugar or starches contain little or no vitamins or minerals. Nowhere in a natural food can you find starches or sugars without some of the vitamins or minerals accompanying them.

We say a positive and unequivocal "no" to any and all sugar substitutes—that is, the various chemicals you can buy labeled saccharin, sucaryl, dulcin, sodium cyclamate and so forth. All these are many times sweeter than sugar. A small amount of one of these chemicals dropped into your coffee or dissolved in your pudding gives you no calories, hence no energy, and nothing else, either, except a sweet taste. These chemicals provide nothing that is needed nutritionally, and can be harmful.

Cake Recipes

Banana Nut Loaf

1 cup chopped nuts	1 cup honey
2 cups soy flour	2 eggs, beaten
½ teaspoon brewer's yeast	3 mashed bananas
½ teaspoon sea salt	3 tablespoons soy milk or water
½ cup safflower or soy oil	½ teaspoon vanilla

Blend all ingredients. Turn into a greased loaf pan. Bake at 350° F. for one hour.

Blackberry Shortcake

1 quart fresh or frozen blackberries	1½ cups water
	1½ cups honey

* ❋ ❋

Shortcake:

4 cups quick cook oats
1⅜ cups soy flour, sifted twice
1 cup vegetable oil

1 cup honey
3 tablespoons water

Put blackberries in sauce pan, add water and cook until tender. Then put through a blender and pour in a fine sieve strainer over a large bowl and mash pulp through with spoon to get seeds out. Put back in sauce pan, add honey and boil enough to dissolve honey well.

Mix oats and soy flour thoroughly, add oil and mix until crumbly. Add honey, mix well, then add water and mix in. Put one half dough in greased shallow side of a 7½ × 14½″ iron griddle and cut twice to make three layers. Bake in moderate oven until a nice brown color. Bake the remainder of dough likewise. Put in shallow dish with the berry pulp between the layers. Let stand about twelve hours in refrigerator before cutting.

Date Delight

1 cup chopped pitted dates
1 cup chopped nuts (local)
½ cup maple syrup

2 egg yolks
2 heaping tablespoons wheat
germ flour*

Cream the above ingredients together while the egg whites are being beaten stiff in the electric mixer. Then fold in the stiffly beaten whites and pour the batter in a small cake tin, preferably 9×9.

Bake at 300 degrees for 30 minutes or until a toothpick comes out clean.

* You can buy wheat germ flour at Health Food Stores or make your own by putting the wheat germ in the blender, ½ cup at a time, and whizzing until it is a fine flour.

Eatmor Vitality Fruit Cake

12 ounce package dried apricots
2 cups prunes
¾ cup raisins
1 cup pecans
1 pound dates

1 cup figs
1 cup fresh cranberries
1 cup wheat germ
2 cups ground coconut
(unsweetened)

Cover apricots and prunes with cold water and put in refrigerator overnight. Soak raisins in cold water ½ hour to soften.

Run pecans through blender. Chop mixed nuts coarsely. Grind dates, figs and cranberries. Cut apricots and prunes. Mix all the fruits in a large bowl. Add wheat germ, pecans, mixed nuts and coconut. Mix all together and put into cake pan, or mold into little balls, and cover with more coconut, if desired.

Holly Berry Fruit Cake

Grind the following ingredients through the food chopper and place in a large mixing bowl:

1 cup pitted dates	1 cup sunflower seeds
1 cup pitted prunes	1 cup raisins
1 cup stemmed figs	1 cup raw coconut chunks (optional)

Now add the following ingredients and blend together:

4 egg yolks	1 cup Thompson seedless
1 cup raw honey (and more later if needed)	grapes or plumped raisins
	1 cup whole nut meats
1 cup red cherries (frozen and thawed)	½ cup pignolias

Now add enough raw peanut flour to make a very stiff raw dough. Pack in oiled bread tins, wrap in towels and put in a cold place to ripen a few days before Christmas. The cherries serve as red and the Thompson grapes or raisins as green, but garnish still more before serving by cutting holly leaves out of salad greens and cutting small berries out of thawed red cherries. These should be on the top of the cake.

Little Imp Cake

1½ cups wheat germ flour	⅓ cup water
⅓ cup carob	½ cup oil
2 teaspoons cinnamon	1¼ cups honey
1 teaspoon kelp	2 teaspoons pure vanilla
6 egg yolks	1 cup raisins
6 egg whites, beaten stiff	

Sift dry ingredients into large bowl. Add oil, honey, egg yolks, vanilla and water. Beat egg whites in small bowl until stiff. Set aside. Beat first mixture 4 minutes at high speed with electric mixer. Add raisins, then fold in egg whites. Bake at 350° for an hour.

Nuts or sunflower seeds may be added.

Maple-Nut Passover Sponge Cake

6 eggs, separated	½ cup potato starch flour
¾ cup matzo meal	½ cup finely chopped nut
½ teaspoon each of cinnamon,	meats
mace and allspice	1½ cups maple syrup

Beat the 6 egg whites very stiff. While you are doing this, sift the matzo meal, potato flour and spices at least 3 times. The potato flour is very heavy at first. Sifting with the meal and spices lightens it.

Set the egg whites aside and beat the yolks until light and lemon colored. Add the nuts and syrup gradually and beat light again. Fold in the flour mixture carefully, then the egg whites. Put in an ungreased tube pan and bake for 1 hour at 325 degrees. Invert to cool.

Pineapple Nut Torte

5 large fertile eggs, separated	3 cups ground nuts (walnuts
¼ cup Tupelo Honey (¾ for	or pecans)
normal diet)	20 ounce can unsweetened
1½ cups wheat germ	crushed pineapple

Beat yolks until light, add honey, beat again. Add wheat germ and nuts, beat. Add crushed pineapple, stir. Fold in stiffly beaten egg whites. Bake at 325 degrees for 30 minutes in two greased cake pans or in one large greased baking pan.

Quick Carob Fudge Cake

1 tablespoon safflower oil
4 tablespoons rice polish (not sifted)
8 tablespoons carob flour (not sifted)
¼ cup water

3 teaspoons clover honey
3 teaspoons pure vanilla extract
3 extra large eggs, beaten separately

Put the first six ingredients in a bowl all at once. Blend until smooth. Then add the egg yolks beaten until thick, about four minutes. Fold in the egg whites which have been beaten stiff. Blend until smooth. Pour in a greased eight-inch pie dish, that has a six-inch bottom.

Bake in a moderate oven about a half hour, until it is crisp around the edges.

Candy Recipes

Apricot Marbles

The kids will enjoy rolling these—right into their eager mouths.

1 cup sun dried apricots
½ cup nut meats

½ pound coconut
4 tablespoons lemon juice

Put apricots, nut meats and coconut through a food grinder. Add lemon juice, shape into balls and roll in grated nuts. Refrigerate. Makes 1 to 1½ dozen.

Carob Candies

1 cup sifted carob powder
1 cup freshly-grated coconut
1 cup ground nuts

½ cup chopped dried prunes or apricots (soaked), or dates
Honey or maple syrup to taste

Blend these together, roll into balls and roll in wheat germ, chopped nuts or sunflower seeds.

Carob Nut-Seed Clusters

Break up brick carob and place the chunks in a basin which is set in hot water. Melt the carob just as you would brick chocolate.

Stir the melted carob full of chopped sunflower seeds and nut meats, then drop spoonfuls of the mixture on an oiled pan. Let cool.

Carob-Peanut Clusters

Beat 3 egg whites until stiff. Add:

¼ cup honey   ½ cup carob flour
½ cup peanut butter

Beat together lightly and drop by spoonfuls onto a greased cookie sheet and bake for 10 to 12 minutes at 300°. Ground nuts or seeds may be added to mixture if desired.

Coating for Seed Candies

First step: Chop *walnuts, peanuts* and *coconut* in the blender separately. Pour these into deep cereal bowls for rolling and coating the candies.

To chop nuts: Turn the blender on and off quickly until they are the way you want them.

To chop coconut: You will have to keep pushing it down on the sides of the blender with a rubber spatula until it is as fine as you want it.

Separate the nuts into two bowls—leave one plain, add cinnamon to another.

Separate the coconut into two bowls—leave one plain, add carob powder to the other.

Have carob in one bowl plain.

Stuffed Dates

Remove seeds from dates and stuff with peanut butter fondant made as follows: Mix ⅓ cup homemade *peanut butter*, ⅓ cup *honey* and add ½ cup *soya milk* powder. Chill until firm enough to handle, make into small rolls and insert in seed cavity of dates. Dates may be rolled in coconut meal.

Fruit Balls

Grind or chop the following ingredients:

1 cup pitted dates
1 cup stemmed figs
1 cup soaked dried apricots

1 cup nut meats (local variety)
½ cup sunflower seeds
½ cup pignolias

Add ½ cup wheat germ, honey to taste, and enough peanut flour to make the right consistency. Shape into balls, roll in peanut flour and store in the refrigerator until used.

Fruit Candy

1 cup dried peaches
½ cup raisins
1 cup figs
½ cup dates
¼ cup honey

1 cup dried apples
1 cup raw almonds
½ cup sunflower or sesame seeds

Grind the fruit before measuring and the nuts after measuring. Use just enough honey to hold the fruit together. Pat small bits out flat and roll in ground sunflower seeds or sesame seeds. Makes about 2 pounds.

Fruit Nibbles

1 cup pitted dates
1 cup pitted prunes
1 cup dark raisins
1 cup white raisins

1 cup apricots
1 cup black figs
1 cup white figs

Grind in a food grinder, using a fine blade. Add:

2 tablespoons honey
1 cup shredded coconut

1 cup natural crunchy peanut butter

Mix thoroughly. Form into small balls and roll in fine shredded coconut. Makes 1 dozen balls.

Stuffed Fruit Energy

1 cup unsulphured raisins
1 cup shredded coconut
¾ cup sunflower seed or
   nutmeats (or mixture)
1 tablespoon lemon juice
   (more or less as needed)

dried prunes, slightly cooked
and drained
pitted dates
dried apricots, slightly cooked
and drained

Put raisins, coconut and nuts or seeds through grinder. Blend with lemon juice. Use about ½ teaspoon to stuff prunes, dates and apricots.

No Cook Fudge

½ cup honey
½ cup peanut butter
½ cup walnuts
½ cup carob
½ cup sesame seeds

½ cup coconut
½ cup ground sunflower seeds
⅛ cup lecithin
1 teaspoon pure vanilla

Melt honey in double boiler, add peanut butter and the rest of the ingredients. Roll into balls and roll in coconut. Cool.

Health Candy

2 cups thick honey
2 cups peanut butter
2 cups fine coconut

1 cup brewer's yeast flakes
2 cups raisins
2 cups sunflower seed meal

Warm honey and peanut butter over hot water just enough to handle. Mix all ingredients, except sunflower seed meal, in large bowl till well blended.

Spread a cup of sunflower seed meal on a large wax paper. Pat the mix over it, about ¾ inch thick. Spread another cup of the sunflower seed meal over this. Chill and cut in squares.

Roll each piece in the meal. Keep in a cool place to keep firm. This candy is like fruit cake; gets tastier as the flavors blend. Makes 5 pounds.

Lollipops

1 cup raisins
1 cup dried prunes
1 cup nut meats

1 cup coconut chunks
1 cup figs

Put the above ingredients through the food grinder and shape into balls, then flatten into oblongs. Roll each one in either ground coconut meal, ground nuts or ground sunflower seeds and put a wooden paddle in each lollipop. These are the children's own treat.

Marshmallows

1 cup water (cold or
  lukewarm)
3 heaping teaspoons gelatin

½ cup corn oil
  pure vanilla
3 or 4 tablespoons honey
  berries or juice to be added

Method: Put one cup water in blender. Add the remaining ingredients and blend until it looks like whipped cream. The gelatin will melt in.

Pink Raspberry

Make basic recipe. Add box of frozen raspberries. This thickens fast. Keep blending and helping with spatula. Stiff gelatin mixtures become liquid again in the blender, and will set fast after they are poured out. Drop by spoonfuls on plate. If raspberries are already sweetened omit the honey. Also omit the vanilla. A drop or two of almond can be added.

Pale Pink Strawberry

Follow same instructions as for raspberry, using strawberry as the fruit.

Purple Grape

Add can of frozen grape juice—omit honey and vanilla. Pour in pan and cut in squares.

Peanut

Make basic recipe. Add a cup or two of chopped peanuts. Peanut butter for a stronger flavor. Without peanut butter it stays nice and white. Pour in pan.

Let these set at room temperature. These can be cut up and frozen as they freeze well. Thaw completely before serving.

Nutty Confections

Put ¼ pound of brick carob to melting. Meanwhile, chop the following ingredients and form the mixture into thin cookies:

1 cup locally grown nuts
1 cup shelled peanuts
½ cup sunflower seeds

1½ cups pitted dates
1 cup grated coconut
supplements

Dip the thin cookies into the warm carob mixture on both sides, then place on an oiled pan until the carob is reset. Serve as cookies.

Peanut Patties

Mix together 1 cup homemade peanut butter, ½ cup each of honey and brewer's yeast and shelled raw peanuts. Form into balls and flatten with a fancy cut glass dish dipped in ground nuts or peanut flour. Keep refrigerated.

Popcorn Balls

1 cup honey
1 teaspoon vanilla

¼ cup water
bowl of freshly popped corn

Put honey and water together. Put on high heat stirring constantly till it boils. Change heat to medium and stir. If it starts to rise, blow it down. When it balls in cold water, take it off. Mix in vanilla. Pour over popcorn and form balls. Roll in ground nuts, wheat germ or sesame seeds.

Potato Nip Candy

¾ cup potatoes cooked in as little water as possible and then mashed to smooth paste in their own water
⅓ cup honey
¾ cup pure peanut butter
¾ cup raw mixed nuts and sunflower seeds
½ cup coconut

Mix well the potatoes, honey and peanut butter. Then stir in chopped nuts and seeds and coconut. Place on wax paper in refrigerator until firm. May be made into any shape desired.

Potato Carob Bonbons

2 cups cold mashed potatoes
2 tablespoons carob powder
¼ teaspoon kelp powder
1 cup medium ground coconut
2 tablespoons honey
1 teaspoon vanilla
1 teaspoon liquid lecithin (optional)
⅛ teaspoon ginger
¼ cup chopped dates
1 tablespoon rice polish

Combine thoroughly the potatoes, carob powder and kelp, using wooden spoon. Add remaining ingredients in order given and mix well.

Dough should become of consistency to handle with fingers; if too moist, add more rice polish.

Shape into bite-size balls and roll in finely ground coconut.

Refrigerate for about 8 hours before using. Makes about 40 bonbons.

Pumpkin Seed Candy

In blender:

2 cups pumpkin seeds
2 tablespoons honey
½ cup of sesame oil
Dash of pure vanilla

Drop by teaspoons into coating mixtures. Chill.

A heaping tablespoon of honey in these recipes means swirling the spoon until you can lift it to the bowl without dripping. This actually is more than a level tablespoon.

Freeze all of these separately on a cookie sheet. Then put them into freezer containers to store in the freezer.

Raisin and Almond Candy

1 large tablespoon honey
2 big teaspoons lecithin granules
2 big teaspoons almond meal

2 big teaspoons wheat germ, toasted
2 big teaspoons sunflower meal
1 tablespoon raisins, seedless

Place honey in large cup, add lecithin granules, wheat germ, sunflower meal, almond meal, blend in cup till it forms a ball. Then add raisins, mix well. Press in a plate until flat. Set in the refrigerator until cold. Cut.

Raw After School Snacks

1 cup raw wheat germ
½ cup soy grits
1 cup soy lecithin granules
½ cup date sugar
½ cup organic honey
1 cup carob powder
1 cup grated fresh coconut

½ cup sesame or sunflower seed oil
2 teaspoons vanilla
1½ cups chopped dates
1 cup seedless raisins
1 cup sunflower meal or sesame meal or almond meal

Mix dry ingredients; add oil, honey and vanilla. Add to dry mixture. Add dates, raisins, coconut and sesame meal. Mix with enough water to be able to lightly knead the mixture. Divide it in thirds. Sprinkle coconut on sheet of waxed paper and shape into a 1½ × 10 inch roll. Store the rolls in the refrigerator. Then cut small portion off to make individual rolls.

St. Nick Candies

Thaw large red sweet cherries, drain and pat dry. Put the following through the food chopper:

½ cup nuts
½ cup sunflower seeds
1 cup pitted dates

1 cup figs
1 cup raisins

Add enough honey to make a mixture which will pack in a small square tin. Cut in squares, place a cherry in the center of each one. Dip sides and bottom in sesame seeds.

Sesame Seed Candy

In blender:

2 cups sesame seeds   ½ cup oil

Start blender with cover on and run it awhile. Take the cover off and help push seeds down and under. Add 2 tablespoons *honey* and a dash of *vanilla* to running blender. Blend until smooth. Divide into three bowls. Add 1 tablespoon *peanut butter* to one, 1 tablespoon *carob* to the other. Leave one plain. Shape into balls. Do not coat these. They resemble fudge.

Sesame Taffy

In blender:

1 cup sesame seeds   vanilla and a bit of almond
½ cup oil   flavoring
   enough honey to sweeten,
   if desired

Start blender and keep seeds turning down and under with rubber scraper. Let it run a long time until mixture gets hot and looks glossy. Turn out into bowl. With rubber scraper knead up on side of bowl, squeezing out the oil. Finish kneading with your hands, squeezing out the oil. Roll this dough into a log and slice.

Sesame Treats

½ cup fine ground fresh   ¼ cup tahini (ground sesame
   coconut   seed)
½ cup sunflower seed meal   ¼ cup honey
½ cup natural wheat germ

   Mix all together.
   Separate into two portions. Place each on a piece of waxed paper

and form into a one-inch roll. Wrap in the paper and keep in the refrigerator. Cut into one-inch pieces as needed.

Sunflower Seed Candy

Blend 2 cups *sunflower* seeds to a fine meal. Start with cover on and then remove cover and push seeds down with spatula. Always do this carefully, keeping far away from the knife. Add 1 heaping tablespoon *honey* to one cup of the ground seeds, 1 heaping tablespoon *peanut butter* and dash of *vanilla* to the other cup. Stir into dough, form into balls or desired shapes and roll in coating mixtures.

Sweet Treat

1 cup raw peanuts, ground fine in food chopper or seed grinder
¼ cup brewer's yeast

¼ cup wheat germ, raw or toasted
½ cup honey
4 teaspoons peanut oil
add raisins, if desired

Stir and mix thoroughly. Roll into balls the size of a walnut. Coat with additional wheat germ, unsweetened coconut shreds or sesame seeds. Makes about 20.

Uncooked Candy

1 cup honey
1 cup raw peanuts
1 cup carob powder
1 cup sunflower seeds
1 cup pumpkin seeds

1 cup sesame seeds
1 cup black walnuts
1 fresh coconut
½ cup coconut milk
¼ cup brewer's yeast powder

Melt honey over low flame. Cut up coconut including brown outer skin and run through blender. Also blend raw peanuts, carob powder, sunflower seeds and pumpkin seeds.

If coconut milk is less than ½ cup, make up the difference by adding soy oil.

Mix all the ingredients except coconut. Spread coconut on a

piece of waxed paper. Spread ingredients over coconut patting down with hands and form into squares. Refrigerate overnight before serving.

Uncooked Taffy

½ cup homemade peanut butter   1 cup peanuts (shelled from
½ cup honey   whole unroasted peanuts)
                                  instant soy milk powder

Blend the first four ingredients together. The peanuts may be chopped if desired. Then use only enough of the soy milk powder to make a stiff dough. Roll it in a long roll and place on a cookie sheet and chill overnight. In the morning, whack off inch pieces for the lunch pail, or for the children for special treats.

Vim Candy

⅔ cup soy flour   2 tablespoons dulse (dried
¼ cup peanut butter   seaweed)
½ cup carob flour   2 tablespoons brewer's yeast
¼ cup rice polish   2 tablespoons wheat germ
 2 tablespoons bone meal   2 tablespoons vegetable oil

Add enough *cream honey* to make of consistency to knead. Press *chopped nuts* over top. Chill and cut in pieces.

Recipes for Cookies

Angel Food Cookies

6 egg whites   2 cups popcorn flour
4 tablespoons honey   1 teaspoon pure vanilla

Put egg whites and honey in top of double boiler. Beat until light and fluffy over boiling water. Add vanilla. Fold in popcorn flour and drop by spoonfuls on heavily buttered pan, so they don't stick.

Bake in 325 degree oven until brown.

To make popcorn flour—pop popcorn with as much oil as popcorn. This adds the shortening to the cookies. However, they are good made with dry popcorn too. Fill the blender with popcorn. Let it whiz and push popcorn down with a wooden spoon until it's all caught in and blended well. This takes a little practice. You can sift it thru the flour sifter if you like. It's easier to handle made with oil because it doesn't get so powdery while you're blending and produce a miniature snow storm in the kitchen. Makes 2 dozen.

Apple Sesame Cookies

1 cup grated apple (tart)
1 egg
2 tablespoons safflower oil
2 tablespoons honey
    pinch sea salt

¾ cup raisins
¾ cup sunflower seed meal
    (sesame meal to sprinkle
    tops of cookies)

Mix egg, oil, honey and apple together. Add remaining ingredients. Spoon-drop on oiled cookie sheet. Bake about 15-20 minutes in moderate oven 350°. Makes 1 dozen.

Breakfast Cookies

1 cup raw bran
1 cup soaked prunes
1 cup soaked figs

1 cup soaked dates
1 cup soaked raisins
1 cup soaked sunflower seeds

Pit the dates and prunes, and stem the figs. Chop ingredients together and add blackstrap molasses if they need more wetting. Shape into balls and roll in coconut meal, sunflower seed meal or sesame seeds. Makes 2 dozen.

Brownies

½ cup honey
½ cup oil
½ cup carob powder
2 eggs, beaten
1⅓ cups oat flour

⅓ cup rice flour
⅓ cup soy flour
½ cup chopped nuts-walnuts
1 teaspoon pure vanilla extract

Blend honey, oil and carob powder. Gradually add eggs. Stir in flour. Add nuts and vanilla.

Turn into oiled 8 × 8 inch pan. Bake at 350 degrees for 25 to 30 minutes. Cool and cut into squares.

Carob Brownies

Have three sizes of mixing bowls.

Mix as follows:

In large bowl:

½ cup honey	¼ cup sunflower seed oil
2 tablespoons blackstrap molasses	2 eggs separated. Beat yolks, add to mixture

In small bowl:

beat the whites; set aside

In medium bowl place:

½ cup soybean powder	1 teaspoon cinnamon (optional)
½ cup sunflower seed meal	
½ cup carob powder	1 teaspoon pure vanilla can be used in place of spices
½ teaspoon allspice (optional)	
½ teaspoon ginger (optional)	

Now add this mixture to large bowl, a little at a time. This will be very stiff.

Add:

½ cup of chopped raisins or dates; mix well

Add the whites of eggs (beaten stiff but not dry)

Pour into oiled 9 inch square pan. Bake in oven heated to 350° for 25 minutes. Cool; cut into squares.

Unbaked Carob Brownies

In a bowl, mix together the following ingredients:

2½ cups quick cooking oatmeal	1 teaspoon of either cardamom seeds or pumpkin pie spice
½ cup chopped nuts	(Cardamom seeds are, of course, ground fine)
1 teaspoon pure vanilla	
¾ cup raw honey	

In a saucepan, mix these ingredients:

¼ cup cooking oil   ½ cup nut milk
⅓ cup carob powder

Heat this mixture until hot, but not to the cooking stage, shut off the heat and pour the other mixture in with this one and stir constantly until it is blended, then take the pan from the heat. Pour the mixture in an oiled brownie pan, spread it evenly and chill. Cut the brownies and serve. Caution: the saucepan mixture should be stirred constantly while it is being heated. Makes 1 dozen.

Bone Meal Cookies for Babies

2 eggs
1 cup pitted dates, blend smooth   ½ cup oil

Pour in bowl, add:

3 tablespoons carob   1 cup bone meal powder

Bake at 325° until done or set. Cookies will be soft. Makes 1 dozen.

Christmas Cookies (unbaked)

Melt about 6 ounces of brick carob over hot water, then stir in ½ cup of nut meats and ½ cup of sunflower seeds. Drop in teaspoons on an oiled cookie sheet and set in a cool place to harden. Serves 6.

Santa Claus Cookies

1 cup nut meats (local variety)   ½ cup dried and soaked
1 cup dates   apricots
1 cup prunes   ½ cup honey

Grind fruit and nuts through the food chopper, add the honey. Using coconut meal in place of flour, pat the mixture out on a board and cut with Santa Claus cutters. Roll each Santa cookie in more coconut meal, shake off excess, and place cookies on a red or green plate to serve. Makes 1 dozen.

"Cocodate" Raw Cookies

2 cups pitted dates   ½ cup maple syrup or honey
2 cups coconut meal

Caution: Be sure the dates are unsulphured and unsprayed.

Put the above ingredients in the blender and whiz until blended fine. Or grind the dates through the food grinder and add the other two ingredients.

Shape into balls and roll in the coconut meal. Store in a covered container and keep in a cool place.

You can press whole pecans or black walnuts into the tops of the balls for added interest and food value. Makes 1 dozen.

Date Carob Bars

4 eggs, separated, whites   ¾ cup ground almonds
     beaten stiff   ¾ cup wheat germ
⅓ cup honey   ⅓ cup carob powder
¾ cup chopped dates

Blend the egg yolks with other ingredients, fold in the whites last and bake in a small cake tin about 45 minutes at about 325 degrees until done. Cut in bars while warm.

This recipe may be varied by changing the fruit and nuts and by adding different spices with the different combinations. Makes 1 dozen.

Date Dandies

½ cup maple syrup   2 eggs
½ cup cooking oil

Cream together. Then put in the blender, small amounts at a time, and whiz them fine:

½ cup raisins   1 cup oatmeal (old-fashioned
½ cup dates   large kind)

Add the remaining ingredients:

1 teaspoon ground cardamom   ½ cup wheat germ
½ cup brown rice flour

Blend and drop by spoonfuls on an oiled cookie sheet and bake
12 or 15 minutes at 375 degrees. Store in cookie jar while warm.
(½ cup nuts may be added if desired.) Makes 18.

Date or Raisin Nuttle

In blender:

1 cup dates or raisins   1 egg

Turn blender on and off until fruits are chopped and partly
blended. Stir the mixture in a bowl with 1 cup of large nut meats.

Spread in well oiled pyrex pie plate. Bake at 350° until browned.
(About ½ hour.) Break up into pieces.

Sprinkle some of them with cinnamon if desired.

Raw Fruit Cookies

1 cup soaked figs
1 cup soaked prunes
1 cup raisins
1 cup dates

1 cup sunflower seeds
1 cup rice polishings
1 teaspoon nutmeg

All fruits should be unsulphured. Chop all ingredients except
dry ones, which are added last. Form into little cakes and roll in
sunflower seed meal. You can decorate the tops with nut meats.
Makes 3 dozen.

Ginger Snaps

Blend together:

½ cup blackstrap molasses
¼ cup honey

¼ cup sunflower seed oil
   (or other oil)
1 egg

Sift together:

1⅔ cups soy-carob flour
⅓ cup arrowroot starch
1 tablespoon bone meal
   powder
3 or 4 tablespoons brewer's
   yeast

½ teaspoon cloves
1 teaspoon cinnamon
1 teaspoon ginger
1 teaspoon kelp

Mix dry ingredients with others adding 1 or 2 tablespoons water if too dry. Chill. Roll in balls, then press flat on greased cookie sheet. Bake 12 minutes at 375°. Makes 2 dozen.

Raw Icebox Cookies

1 cup figs, stemmed

1 cup dates, pitted

1 cup raisins

1 cup local nut meats

Run these through the food grinder then add:

2 egg yolks

½ cup maple syrup or honey

½ teaspoon pumpkin pie spice

1 cup whole nut meats

Enough peanut flour to make a stiff dough. Roll as for icebox cookies dough and refrigerate. Cut off slices and serve raw. You can add a whole nut meat to each cookie at serving time, or a segment of a red home-canned cherry. Makes 1½ dozen.

Oatmeal Cookies

¾ cup soy flour

2 cups oatmeal, uncooked

1 teaspoon cinnamon

½ teaspoon nutmeg

1 cup raisins

1 egg, beaten

½ cup raw wheat germ

1 tablespoon brewer's yeast

½ teaspoon bone meal

½ teaspoon cloves

⅔ cup oil

1 cup honey

1 tablespoon blackstrap molasses

Combine oil, egg, honey and blackstrap. Add dry ingredients and mix well.

Drop by teaspoonfuls on baking sheet. Bake at 350° for 8-12 minutes. Makes 3 dozen.

Nut Macaroons

Here's a confection that will invite raids on the cookie jar. But, who cares? They're packed with nutrition.

3 eggs, separated

1 cup coconut meal

1 cup almonds, ground

½ cup honey

¼ cup potato flour

1 teaspoon pure vanilla

Beat egg whites until very firm and set aside. Place other ingredients in another bowl and beat until light. Fold in egg whites and drop them on oiled cookie sheet. Bake about 12 minutes at 350° F. until delicately browned. Loosen soon after removing from oven. Makes about 20.

Peanut Cookies

1 cup chopped organically-
  grown peanuts

½ cup homemade peanut
  butter
1½ cups peanut flour

Mix the ingredients together. If too dry, add drops of salad oil. If too sticky, add soy milk powder. Shape into small cookies and roll in sunflower seed meal. Store in the refrigerator. These cookies satisfy the peanut lover's taste for peanuts, and are easily digested: Even the children and aged can eat them safely and they are a high protein dessert or snack. Makes 1½ dozen.

Peanut Hootenannies

½ cup peanut butter
  (homemade)
½ cup honey (unprocessed)

½ cup chopped sunflower seeds
½ cup chopped English walnuts
½ cup wheat germ

Mix together and shape into balls, then flatten with fork tines, first in one direction, then over them in the other direction, so you have grillwork on top of the cookies. Dip them in coconut meal, pack in a glass jar and keep refrigerated. Makes 1 dozen.

Peanut Raisin Cookies

½ cup wheat germ
½ cup soy flour
2½ cups oatmeal
1 tablespoon baking yeast
½ teaspoon sea salt
¾ cup chopped raw peanuts

⅓ cup vegetable oil
⅔ cup honey
2 eggs
½ cup apple or pineapple juice
1 teaspoon pure vanilla
½ cup raisins

Mix dry ingredients well (wheat germ, soy flour, oatmeal, yeast, sea salt, chopped peanuts).

In a large bowl beat together oil, honey; add eggs, beat again. Then add juice, vanilla, and raisins. Mix well. Add dry ingredients to liquid mixture, and mix well. Let batter rest 20 minutes before baking. Bake at 375° 10-15 minutes or until golden brown. Drop by teaspoon onto oiled cookie sheets. Makes 3 dozen.

Pecan Macaroons

4 egg whites
   few grains of sea salt
1 tablespoon honey (optional)

½ pound honey grated pecans
   pecan halves

Beat egg whites until stiff. Slowly drizzle in honey if desired and continue to beat. Add grated pecans. Shape into little balls and top with pecan half on each ball. Bake on oiled cookie sheet at 350 degrees until light brown. Makes 2 dozen.

Persimmon Cookies

1 cup persimmon pulp
¾ cup sunflower seed meal
¼ cup oil
¼ cup organic honey

1 teaspoon kelp
1 egg
¾ cup walnuts
1 cup raisins

Mix all ingredients except sunflower seed meal, walnuts and raisins. Mix in dry ingredients. Place cookie batter on well oiled cookie sheet. Bake at 325° for 10 to 12 minutes or until done. Makes 2 dozen.

High Protein Cookies

1 cup soy flour
½ cup brown rice flour
½ cup sunflower seed meal
½ cup wheat germ
½ cup rolled oats
½ cup raisins
½ cup apple juice

2 eggs
¼ cup vegetable oil
½ teaspoon sea salt
½ cup honey
¼ cup blackstrap molasses
½ cup peanut butter

Combine dry ingredients and raisins. Stir in apple juice. Beat together: the eggs, vegetable oil and sea salt, and add to mixture. Combine the honey, molasses and peanut butter and add to mixture. Spoon onto greased cookie sheet and bake 12 minutes in oven preheated to 350 degrees. Makes 2½ dozen.

No-Bake Protein Cookies

Chop:

22 organic dates   1 cup pecan nuts

Grind and add to date mixture:

1 cup almond nuts

Then add and mix well:

½ cup organic honey   2 raw egg yolks
¼ teaspoon kelp   2 teaspoons vanilla

Add and mix well:

1 cup carob powder   ½ cup rice polishings
¾ cup raw wheat germ   1 cup sesame-sunflower meal
½ cup soy lecithin granules

Add about 1 cup unsweetened coconut to absorb moisture and roll into 2½ inch roll. Then wrap in wax paper. Refrigerate. Cut in convenient slices. Makes 1 dozen.

Sesame Raisin Squares

Combine in large mixing bowl:

2 eggs   ½ cup honey
⅓ cup tahini (sesame seed
  butter)

Then add:

1 cup broken walnuts   ½ cup fine ground unsweetened
1 cup oatmeal   coconut
¼ cup rice polishings   ¼ cup sesame seed
¼ cup wheat germ   1 cup raisins

Spread in oiled 9″ × 9″ glass baking dish. Bake about 20 minutes at 350° or until light brown. Cut in squares and remove to cooling rack. Store in cookie jar. They get better with age. Makes 16 squares.

Soybean-Walnut Cookies

½ cup honey
½ cup blackstrap molasses
4 egg yolks
4 egg whites, beaten

1 cup raisins
2 cups broken walnuts
¾ cup soybean flour
1 tablespoon cinnamon

Cream honey, molasses, yolks, fold in raisins, walnuts, and flour and cinnamon. Fold in beaten egg white. Spread on oiled cookie sheet. Bake 20 minutes—350° oven. Cut in strips when cool. Makes 1 to 1½ dozen.

Sunflower Fig Cookies

3 cups unsulphured dried figs   1 cup sunflower seeds

Put through food grinder together.

Add the following:

1 tablespoon brewer's yeast powder   1 tablespoon rose hips powder

Enough maple syrup, honey, or blackstrap molasses to hold the ingredients together. Shape into balls, flatten with a tumbler, roll in chopped nuts or sesame seeds and store in a covered container in a cool place. Makes 1½ dozen.

Tahini Cookies

6 tablespoons tahini (sesame seed butter)
¾ cup honey

½ cup chopped walnuts
1½ cups oatmeal (minute)

Stir honey and tahini together. Add nuts. Add oatmeal till blended. Drop by teaspoonfuls on an oiled cookie sheet. Bake at 350 degrees for about 10 minutes or until edges are brown. Delicious! Makes 3 dozen.

Ambrosia

2 cups fresh pineapple chunks
2 cups sliced bananas

segments from 1 orange

Dress with yogurt and honey.
Serves 4.

Raspberry Ambrosia

2 cups red raspberries
½ cup honey

½ cup freshly grated coconut

Serve in sherbet glasses.
Serves 4.

Applesauce

All the nutrients of your apples are retained in applesauce—if it is uncooked.

4 medium size apples
½ cup raw honey

⅛ cup lemon juice

Wash and core apples, place all ingredients in blender and whip.

Apri-Applesauce Dessert

Wash ½ pound sun-dried apricots; place in saucepan with water to cover; simmer 45 minutes or until tender; drain. In medium bowl, mix apricots, 2 tablespoons honey, 3 cups homemade applesauce, ½ teaspoon ground ginger, 1 teaspoon pure vanilla, 1 teaspoon cinnamon. Refrigerate, covered, until served. Makes 4 servings.

Hot "Grapple" Sauce

Make applesauce the usual way. After it is taken from the fire, sweeten with honey and add ½ cup of grape juice. Add ¼ teaspoon each of cinnamon and cloves. The combination of grapes and apples is a new taste treat. You can also make a cold raw "Grapple" sauce in the blender, and without any cooking. Mint leaves may be added in place of the spices. Serves 4.

Harvest Moon Applesauce

Put ½ cup pure water and ½ cup spearmint leaves in the blender and whiz until the leaves are reduced to liquid. Add:

1 cup honey   2 cups pure water

Blend this mixture, covered. Then pare and core and cut small enough harvest apples to whiz in the mixture until it makes thick raw applesauce. Remove from blender and store in a covered dish.

Raspberry-Applesauce

In the blender put 2 cups of frozen (thawed) red raspberries and whiz until they are reduced to liquid. Add 4 cups of cored apple chunks and whiz into sauce. Remove from blender and season with ½ teaspoon of cinnamon and honey to taste. Keep covered until serving time.

Apricots and Almonds

The night before, put the dried apricots in a dish that has a tight cover and pour very hot water over them. If they are very sour, add honey to taste and cover tightly. They will be soaked out by morning. Soak it in hot water, overnight in a covered dish. Add unprocessed whole or chopped almonds to the apricots and serve for dessert.

Arabian Makoud

Stem dried figs, cover with hot water and let stand all night in a covered dish. In the morning chop them with walnuts or blanched almonds. Sprinkle with pignolias (pine nuts) and serve as dessert. Honey may be added if desired.

Avocado Dessert

2 peeled, ripe avocados	3 tablespoons fresh orange
2 bananas	juice
1 cup seedless grapes	2 teaspoons grated lemon rind
1 cup yogurt	1 tablespoon fresh lemon juice
2 tablespoons honey	1/8 teaspoon sea salt

Chop the avocados and bananas into bite sized pieces and combine with grapes. Beat yogurt for about a minute and stir in the honey, orange juice, lemon juice, lemon rind and sea salt. Pour this sauce over the fruit mixture and serve immediately. Serves 4.

Bananas Plus

Mix 2 tablespoons raw wheat germ with 2 teaspoons of coconut meal. Slice in a banana and toss lightly so that each slice is coated. Dribble a little honey over the top. Serves 2.

Banana Surprise

Stem 2 cups of dried figs. Put them in a dish which can be covered, chop fine and cover with hot water. Cover and let stand overnight or several hours. Then mash fine. Slice 4 bananas in a casserole-type dish. Pour the mashed figs over them. Sprinkle with chopped English walnuts, peanuts or pignolias. Keep covered until serving time. This dessert is better if not chilled. Serves 6.

Berry Melee

1 cup strawberries	1 cup cherries
1 cup red raspberries	1 cup early blueberries
1 cup black raspberries	

Combine them carefully, without starting juice, and keep refrigerated in a covered dish until serving time. You don't need sweetener. Savor the lovely blended flavors instead. Serves 6.

Cantaloupe Circles

Peel a cantaloupe, slice into circles about one inch thick. Remove seeds. Place fruit on crisp lettuce leaves, fill the center with sweet, red, pitted cherries and top with mayonnaise mixed with sunflower seeds.

Cold Fruit Compote

3 cups thinly sliced bananas
1 pint crushed fresh or frozen
  strawberries

1 quart frozen pineapple (freeze
  your own in small chunks and
  add no sugar)

Thaw the frozen fruit slightly. Add bananas and serve, within 15 minutes. Cherries may be used instead of strawberries. Serve in sherbet dishes. Drizzle honey on top if sweetening is desired. Serves 6.

Fiji Fruit Cocktail

1 cup sliced bananas
1 cup fresh pineapple

1 orange cut in small segments

Mix and put in small individual covered containers. Serves 4 to 6.

Fruit Medley

2 cups crushed pineapple—
  unsweetened
½ cup walnuts

½ cup coconut—unsweetened
1 pound of seedless grapes
2 oranges

Drain pineapple. Peel and section oranges. Mix all ingredients together. Garnish with a few orange sections. Add a little honey or any good natural jam sweetened with honey if you need a little more sweetness. Let flavors meld in refrigerator for a few hours before serving. Serves 4.

Peach Surprise

Open the tops of peeled, fresh peaches just enough to get out the pit, then fill the cavity with crushed raw strawberries or red raspberries. Wrap tightly to hold in the juices.

Pineapple-Paradisio

Remove leaves from large fresh pineapple with a twist of the wrist. Peel with a sharp kitchen knife. Do not remove any of the eyes that remain on the pineapple. Slice in half lengthwise. Without removing the core, cut each half of pineapple in half-inch slabs lengthwise. Stack the slabs and again cut half-inch pieces lengthwise. Finally, cut these strips to a half inch, thus cubing the whole pineapple. This should yield about 1½ quarts of cubed pineapple, so put this into two clean glass quart jars.

Into a porcelain sauce pan put two cups of water, one cup of tupelo honey and one tablespoon of thyme. Bring to a boil and stay with the pot, stirring occasionally. Let it boil for five seconds and remove from flame. Pour this hot mixture into the two jars of pineapple, dividing the liquid evenly. Put the lids on and let cool sufficiently to put into the refrigerator. This will last for weeks without fermentation, but is at its prime in 3 days. Serve as a dessert or instead of a side vegetable with fish or chicken. Anyone not knowing how this is done will be intrigued, mystified and delighted with the flavor. Serves 6.

Pineapple Sticks

1 fresh pineapple   ½ cup raw sunflower seeds
¼ cup honey

Prepare pineapple, slicing into sticks. Brush with honey, place under medium broiler for approximately two minutes (using a cookie sheet). Sprinkle with sunflower seeds. Serves 6.

Raspberry Supreme

Serve a dessert like this and who needs cake?

1 cup cooked brown rice (hot)	2 eggs
1 cup nut milk	1 tablespoon honey

Mix together and cook on low heat until thick, stirring constantly. Add 1 cup fresh or frozen raspberries. Serve hot or cold in 4 portions.

Yogurt-Fruit Dessert

For each person to be served, allow:

½ banana, firm ripe	1 tablespoon grated coconut
⅛ cup fruit juice (pineapple, or other naturally sweet juice)	1 tablespoon ground sunflower seeds
½ cup thick yogurt	1 tablespoon wheat germ may also be added

Mash the banana with a fork. Add other ingredients and stir together till lightly blended.

Serve in individual compote dishes. Good for any meal, or as an in-between-meal snack.

Variations:

(1) Use ½ ripe mealy type apple (if fruit is large) such as Golden Delicious, instead of ½ banana, for each portion. If apples are small, use 1 whole apple. Shred the apple, or chop coarsely.

(2) Ripe peaches, sliced; strawberries, partly mashed, partly sliced; or other fresh fruit in season may be used instead of the banana.

Recipes for Frozen Desserts

Apricot Ice

1½ cups chopped fresh or home-canned apricots	1 large cup of water
¾ cup honey	1 tablespoon fresh lemon juice or 1 teaspoon pure lemon extract

Blend all ingredients together and freeze in a refrigerator tray until firm.

You may use peaches or plums in place of the apricots for this fruit ice. Serves 4.

Banana Bars

Blend:

1 cup dates, ¾ cup water to make date butter.

Peel and cut 4 bananas in 2 inch pieces. Cover with date butter and roll in fine coconut or chopped nuts. Freeze and remove a few minutes before serving. Serves 4.

Banana Ice Cream

1 egg, separated
1 cup pineapple juice
½ cup powdered soy milk
2 mashed bananas
1 tablespoon honey

Beat the egg white stiff and set aside. Beat the other ingredients until well blended, and fold in the egg white. Pour into a refrigerator tray and freeze about 30 minutes, then beat well and finish freezing. Serves 4.

Banana Pineapple Sherbet

1 banana, chopped
1 cup banana milk
2 egg yolks, beaten
4 tablespoons pineapple juice
1 cup chopped pineapple

You may want it sweeter, in which case add honey to taste. Nuts may be added if desired. Blend the mixture and pour into a refrigerator tray.

Freeze until mushy, beat with a fork until creamy, then freeze until ready to serve. Serves 4.

Blackberry Ice

1 tablespoon pure gelatin
¼ cup cold water
1 cup boiling water

Dissolve the gelatin in the cold water, then melt it in the boiling water and set aside to cool. Whiz up about 2 cups of blackberries in the blender, then put them through a wire strainer to get out the seeds. You will have about 1¼ cups of thick raw pulp.

1¼ cups blackberry pulp   ¾ cup raw honey

Blend and stir until the honey is dissolved, then add the gelatin mixture and freeze. Serve cut in squares and garnished with whole blackberries and other fruits.

This recipe can be used with any berries or small fruit, and it can be frozen with wooden paddles inserted for the children to have "paddle-pops." Serves 4.

Cranberry Sherbet

1 pound cranberries   ½ cup honey
4 cups sweet apple cider   1 sprig mint

Simmer cranberries in cider. Cool. In blender, blend all ingredients until smooth. Turn into ice tray of refrigerator and freeze until mushy. Beat thoroughly. Finish freezing. Serves 6.

Grape Juice Ice

Put a handful of ice cubes in the blender; add pure grape juice. Blend until ice is fine. It takes one can of frozen grape juice to make one blenderful. Keep adding ice cubes until the blender is full.

Papaya Date Ice Cream

Liquefy the following:

1½ cups water   5-6 pitted dates
 ½ cup clover honey   1 cup fresh papaya
 ½ cup raw cashews

After liquefying well the above ingredients, add and whip in ¼ cup coconut juice. Freeze, whip, then freeze again. Serve when firm. Serves 4.

Pineapple "Ice Cream"

1 cup instant soy milk   1 cup cold water

Put these ingredients in the blender or under electric beaters and blend together. Then with blender running fast (or beaters) pour in the following:

½ cup soy oil

When this is well blended and very light, add the following:

1 cup fresh or frozen pineapple   ½ cup honey
bits (unsweetened)   ½ teaspoon pure vanilla extract

Freeze in a refrigerator tray. This makes a very smooth ice cream. The oil takes the place of the usual cream. You may use any kind of fruit. If you use bananas, cut the amount of honey in half. Ground nuts and maple syrup would make a "Maple-Nut Ice Cream." Serves 4.

Minted Pineapple Sherbets

3 cups fresh pineapple chunks   3 tablespoons fresh mint leaves
honey to taste

Wash and shred the mint leaves over the pineapple chunks, add the desired amount of honey and put the mixture in a covered dish at least 2 hours before serving. Serve in sherbet glasses with mint sprigs sticking out of the fruit. Serves 4.

Raspberry Ice

6 cups raspberries, mashed   1 tablespoon pure gelatin
1 cup cold water   ¾ cup boiling water
¾ cup honey

Mash the berries and add the cup of cold water. Run them through a strainer to remove the seeds if desired. Then add the honey and stir until blended. Soak the gelatin in ¼ cup of cold water, then dissolve it in the ¾ cup of boiling water. Cool, add to the berries and freeze until mushy, then beat with a spoon. Beat several times during the freezing process for better texture. Serves 6.

Soya "Ice Cream"

It is now possible to make a delicious ice cream at home, without any cream. Freeze it in an ice cream freezer if possible, if not, then use a blender to whip air into the mixture *before* freezing in the refrigerator, and at least once *during* the freezing process. When it is frozen, pack in a glass jar and cover tightly, and use as desired, out of the freezer.

In the blender, put the following ingredients, whipping hard after each addition:

1 cup cold water	½ cup cold-pressed soya oil
1 cup soya milk powder	1 cup ground nut meats
½ cup maple syrup	2 teaspoons pure vanilla
2 egg yolks	extract

The more times you pour the partly frozen mixture back in the blender and whip air into it, the better textured ice cream you will have. Serves 4.

Strawberry Ice

In the blender put these ingredients:

2 cups fresh hulled strawberries	½ cup honey
2 egg yolks	1 cup pineapple juice

If you don't have fresh raw pineapple juice on hand or in the freezer, then use a heaping tablespoon of raw pineapple and ¾ cup of cold water.

Pour this mixture in a freezing tray and stir it several times while it freezes. Serves 4.

Strawberry "Ice Cream"

It is necessary to have a blender with which to put air into the mixture before (and during) the freezing process, when made in the refrigerator. The more you whip air into the mixture, the better texture the ice cream is. Start whipping with the first two ingredients and whip hard after each addition. Whip at least twice during the freezing if done in the refrigerator tray.

| 2 cups mashed strawberries | 1 cup honey |

Blend together and let stand an hour in a covered dish in the refrigerator. Have all the ingredients very cold.

In the blender, put the following, whipping each time:

1 cup water	½ cup soy oil
1 cup soya milk powder	strawberry and honey
2 egg yolks	mixture

Store any remaining ice cream in covered glass jars in the freezer. This recipe can be doubled or tripled for a big ice freezer. Serves 4 to 6.

Strawberry-Yogurt Freeze

1 cup plain yogurt (homemade)	⅓ cup honey
2 cups fresh or frozen	1 tablespoon lemon juice
strawberries, halved	

Whirl all ingredients in blender until smooth. Pour into ice cube tray and freeze until firm around edges. Turn into chilled bowl and beat until smooth. Put back into tray and freeze until firm. Makes 2¾ cups. (Peaches can be substituted for strawberries.) Serves 4.

Tutti Frutti "Ice Cream"

1 can frozen pineapple juice (undiluted)	¼ cup tahini (approximately)
1 papaya	¼ cup sesame oil (approximately)
2 bananas	¼ cup honey (approximately)
8 soaked dried apricots	3 tablespoons sunflower seeds

Liquefy and freeze to semi-solid state. Serves 4.

Vanilla "Ice Cream"

Beat 4 eggs in the mixer. Add 2 cups nut milk alternately with 2 cups water.

Slowly add ½ cup honey and ½ cup of corn oil.

Add 2 tablespoons pure vanilla. Pour in a quart container with a lid. Freeze. Serves 4.

Vegetable-Fruit Dessert Ices

1 quart fresh carrot juice	3 medium-size bananas
3 large oranges	3 tablespoons honey (if desired)

Put all ingredients into blender and mix at high speed until very smooth. Pour into ice-cube trays and freeze. For smoother consistency—reblend and refreeze. Place in lower portion of refrigerator an hour before serving. Serves 6 to 8.

Recipes for Pies and Custards

Pie Pastry (Barley)

1¼ cups sifted barley flour	3 tablespoons water
3 tablespoons oil	¼ teaspoon sea salt

Mix flour and salt in bowl. Whip oil and water together until well blended and thickened. Pour onto dry ingredients. Mix until well moistened. Press mixture into 9 or 10 inch pie plate. Fill with your favorite filling and bake. Or prick bottom and sides of crust well with a fork and bake in 400 degree oven for about 15 minutes or until nicely browned, then fill with cooked filling. Note: soy milk may be used instead of water.

No-Cook Apple Pie

1 cup wheat germ	4 cups grated apples
½ cup chopped dates	½ cup honey
¼ cup ground almonds	1 cup yogurt (homemade)

Combine wheat germ, chopped dates and almonds. Mix well and press into a pie plate to be used as pie crust. Combine grated apple and honey and put this into the pie crust. Top with the whipped yogurt and sprinkle with chopped nuts.

Apple Crisp

4 cups thinly sliced apples
½ cup wheat germ flakes
½ cup oat flakes
¼ cup corn meal

1 teaspoon cinnamon
½ cup chopped walnuts
½ cup honey
⅓ cup corn oil

Spread apples two layers deep in 12-inch pan. Mix with fork the wheat germ flakes, oat flakes, corn meal, cinnamon and walnuts. Add honey and oil and mix until crumbly. Sprinkle over apples and bake at 350 degrees for 40 minutes. Serves 4-6.

Apple Custard Pie

Fill a large oven-proof casserole with peeled, sliced cooking apples. Stir one cup nut milk, four beaten eggs, one or two tablespoons buckwheat and honey together. Add 1½ cups unsweetened coconut and one cup ground pecans or walnuts.

Bake apples almost done. Cover apples with the egg mixture. Return to oven and bake about 30 minutes longer at 275° F. oven temperature, cool and refrigerate covered. Cut in wedges like pie.

Apple Rice Betty

4 large tart apples
1 cup cooked brown rice
1 cup honey
¼ teaspoon cloves

¼ teaspoon cinnamon
¼ teaspoon nutmeg
¼ teaspoon sea salt
2 tablespoons safflower oil

Mix honey with spices. Grease baking dish. Place a thin layer of rice in dish; add a layer of thinly sliced apples, and sprinkle with honey and spices. Repeat layers until all ingredients are used, saving some honey for the top. Pour oil over all.

Bake in 350 degree oven until apples are soft. Serve hot. Serves 4.

Brown Betty

In small baking dish pour 1 tablespoon or more of safflower oil.
Sprinkle as much wheat germ (not toasted) as desired.
Cut up a large apple in small pieces.
Sprinkle with cinnamon.
Place on low rack under broiler for 15 minutes.
The apple should have cooked nicely and the oil and wheat germ flavors it nicely. Serves 2.

Carob Custard

Take about 3 heaping tablespoons of soya powder and 2 tablespoons carob powder; mix. Add 1 quart water and mix. Heat to boiling point and add 3 well-beaten eggs and enough arrowroot starch (moistened with water) to make a pudding of desired thickness (about 2 tablespoons). Cook a little longer, then add pure vanilla extract and cool. Top liberally with chopped black walnuts. Serves 6.

Carob Pie

Put in blender:

2 eggs
3 tablespoons honey
3 heaping tablespoons carob powder

3 heaping tablespoons soya powder

Blend well.
Dissolve 1 rounded tablespoon plain gelatin in 2 cups hot water. Slowly add to mixture in blender. Add 1 teaspoon pure vanilla. Pour in large pyrex pie plate. Set in refrigerator when well set, cut like pie.

Cherry Cobbler

Cook 1 quart sour pie *cherries* or 1 quart packaged frozen pie *cherries,* in ½ cup *water.*
Thicken with 2 tablespoons *arrowroot flour,* mixed with ¼ cup *water.* Cook until thick only. Add ½ cup *honey. Blend.* Set aside.

Mix with fork:

1 cup oatmeal
½ cup soya flour
½ cup rice flour

⅓ cup soya oil
⅓ cup honey

Divide mixture. Use 1½ quart casserole dish and cover bottom with ½ inch of oil.

Oil hands. Using about a teaspoon of mixture, pat out in rounds. Lay in bottom of casserole dish. Press together to make bottom crust.

Pour in filling.

With remainder of mixture pat in rounds and lay on top.

Bake 30 to 45 minutes at 325 degrees or until nice and brown on top. Serves 4.

Coconut Custard

3 eggs, beaten
⅓ cup honey
1 teaspoon pure vanilla

2 cups coconut milk
¼ teaspoon mace

Beat well and pour in a small baking dish. Set this in a pan of hot water and bake until the custard is set in the center. Cool, then grate fresh coconut over the top. Serves 2.

Coconut Banana Meringue Pie

4 eggs
⅓ cup date sugar
1½ cups crushed almonds
2 tablespoons almond butter

4 bananas
1½ cups flaked, unsweetened coconut
1 teaspoon lemon juice

Blend almond butter with crushed almonds. Then press into a pie plate and refrigerate. Mash bananas with a fork. Stir in lemon juice, then coconut. Pour into crust after crust has been refrigerated half an hour. Separate yolks from whites of eggs and beat whites into meringue, adding the date sugar. Cover pie with meringue mixture. Keep refrigerated until just before serving. Serves 6.

Uncooked Date Pie

Equal parts organic dates
and coconut
1 large grated apple

1 large banana
½ cup almonds

Make a crust of equal parts of cold organic dates and coconut ground through a food chopper. Roll out to a thin layer, spread on glass baking dish. Prepare filling. Blend apple, banana and almonds well and spread over crust. Then sprinkle top with shredded coconut. Add blanched almonds around edge for decoration.

Molasses Custard

Put 1 level tablespoon of blackstrap molasses in a cup and finish with honey to make ½ cup. Pour it in a bowl and add:

3 eggs
½ teaspoon cinnamon

¼ teaspoon ginger or allspice
2 cups of soy milk

Beat until the eggs are completely reduced to liquid.

Pour mixture into custard cups or a small baking dish. Set the custard cups or dish in a pan of hot water and bake at about 350 degrees until the custard is set. Serves 2.

Peach-Maple Pie

Crust:

¼ cup oil
¼ cup honey

1 cup wheat germ
¾ cup sunflower seed meal

Mix all together and pat into bottom and sides of a 9-inch pie pan. Bake at 350 degrees about ten minutes or until lightly browned. Cool.

Filling:

1 quart sliced peaches
½ cup maple syrup

⅓ cup arrowroot starch

Use some of peach liquid to mix with starch until smooth. Bring peaches and maple syrup to boil. Stir in starch mixture. Cook slowly, stirring constantly about five minutes. Pour into crust, piling it up. Makes a deep pie.

Peach Meringue Pie

This pie has a meringue crust, which is made as follows: Beat 6 egg whites until quite high, add ½ cup honey in a thin stream, beating fast all of the time. Continue until the mixture stands in stiff peaks, probably 15 minutes in all. Spread it on the bottom of a fancy pie plate, then pile it up at the sides until you have a well-shaped pie shell. Bake 1 hour at 275 degrees, turn off heat, then leave it in the oven another hour. Cool before filling.

The filling is an ordinary old-fashioned cream pie filling. Heat 2 cups of milk (nut or soya) to the boiling point and stir in a thickening made with ½ cup honey, ½ cup arrowroot flour and 3 egg yolks blended with cold water. Cook until thick. Cool and add 1 teaspoon vanilla and 1½ cups sliced peaches. Pour this in the meringue crust and garnish with slivered almonds.

Mock Pecan Pie

2 eggs, well beaten
⅔ cup rolled oats
⅓ cup cold pressed oil

⅔ cup maple syrup (pure) or part syrup and part honey
¼ teaspoon sea salt
1 teaspoon vanilla

Mix ingredients thoroughly and turn into an 8″ pie pan (pie shell not necessary).

Put in 350° oven, preheated, then turn oven back to 300° and bake 30-45 minutes until knife inserted in center comes out clean.

Blender Pumpkin Custard

1¾ cups cooked pumpkin (sweet potato, or winter squash may be used)
¼ cup cooked brown rice
¼ cup raisins
¼ cup honey
¼ cup molasses

2 eggs
1¼ cups soy milk
1 tablespoon soy flour
⅛ teaspoon each: ginger, cinnamon, cloves
¼ teaspoon sea salt
¼ teaspoon nutmeg

Place in blender: raisins, rice, soy milk, eggs, honey, molasses, pumpkin, spices, sea salt, and soy flour. Blend until well mixed.

Pour into oiled oven-proof pie pan. Place this pan in a larger pan partly filled with water. Place in oven. Bake at 450° F. for 15 minutes. Reduce heat to 350 degrees F. Bake for 45 minutes more or until set. Serves 4.

Soybean Pie

2 cups cooked, ground soybeans
⅓ cup raw honey
1 tablespoon soybean oil
(cold-pressed)
1 egg, slightly beaten

1 cup soy milk
1 teaspoon cinnamon
½ teaspoon ginger
½ teaspoon pumpkin spice
⅛ teaspoon sea salt

Combine all ingredients in the order given and turn into pie plate. Bake at 350° for 45 minutes. Bake until a knife inserted in the middle comes out clean. Serves 6.

This recipe is an excellent substitute for pumpkin pie.

Vanilla Rice Custard

A delicious dessert festive enough for company, easy enough for a family affair.

3 tablespoons cooked brown
rice
1 cup nut milk or soy milk
1 egg, slightly beaten

3 tablespoons honey
1 teaspoon pure vanilla
½ cup raisins

Mix well and sprinkle cinnamon over top. Bake at 325° about one hour or until silver knife comes out clean. Serves 4.

Pudding Recipes

Sour Cherry Pudding

In blender:

1 cup water

3 tablespoons plain gelatin

Blend until gelatin looks like whipped cream. Then, while it is still running, add:

1 egg
½ cup honey
1 teaspoon pure vanilla
    flavoring

½ teaspoon pure almond
    flavoring
½ cup oil

Pour mixture into a bowl and set aside. Put in blender:

1 cup water

1 cup sour cherries (fresh or
    frozen)

Chop and blend until pink. Add to bowl mixture. Add one cup pitted sour cherries (whole) to bowl mixture.

Pour in baking pan and chill in the refrigerator. Cut into bars. Almond is compatible with cherry in any cherry dish.

Fig Pudding

1 cup of unsulphured figs which have been soaked for several hours. Drain and chop the figs with ½ cup nut meats. Add these ingredients:

2 egg yolks
2 tablespoons maple syrup

2 large rounded tablespoons
    wheat germ flour
1 teaspoon vanilla

Fold in 4 stiffly beaten egg whites, bake in an oiled 9 × 9 inch cake pan at 350 degrees until nearly done, then sprinkle sesame seeds over the top and bake another 5 minutes. Serve hot.

Oatmeal-Peanut Pudding

2 cups cooked oatmeal
1 cup chopped peanuts
½ cup raisins
1 cup sliced apples

⅓ cup honey
dash of sea salt, if desired
½ teaspoon cinnamon

Mix all ingredients thoroughly and bake in an oiled baking dish for 30 minutes at 325 degrees. May be served either hot or cold. Sunflower seeds may replace the peanuts. Serves 4.

Peanut Butter Pudding

3 eggs
2 cups sunflower seed milk
½ cup peanut butter

¼ cup honey
1 teaspoon pure vanilla

Scald 1½ cups seed milk in double boiler. Thoroughly mix eggs, peanut butter and honey, beat with fork, add ½ cup cold seed milk. Stir some of scalded milk into this mixture and return all to double boiler. Cook over hot water, stirring constantly, about seven minutes. Stir in vanilla and pour in bowl to cool. Serves 4.

Pineapple Pudding

¼ cup cold-pressed oil
3 to 4 cups crushed pineapple
  (unsweetened)
½ cup honey
1 teaspoon cinnamon

1 cup wheat germ
½ cup pumpkin seeds, ground
1 cup coconut (unsweetened)
2 tablespoons soybean oil

Combine oil, pineapple, honey and cinnamon. Combine wheat germ and ground seeds. Put half of pineapple mixture into a 1½ quart shallow baking dish. Sprinkle with half of wheat germ and ground seeds mixture, and half of coconut. Repeat layers. Dot with oil. Sprinkle with remaining coconut. Bake at 350° F. for 15 minutes. Serve warm or cold. Serves 8-10.

Pineapple Rice Pudding

Have 2 cups of brown rice in the last stages of cooking. Make a sauce of the following.

2 egg yolks
½ cup honey

enough pineapple juice to stir them up

Stir the mixture into the simmering rice and cook until the egg yolks are done. Take from the fire, put in a baking dish, fold in 1 cup of pineapple chunks.

Beat the 2 egg whites stiff, add honey and spread over the pudding. Bake at moderate heat 350° until the meringue is a nice golden brown. Serve either hot or cold. Serves 4.

Pumpkin Pudding

2 cups cooked pumpkin,
　mashed
1 cup mashed bananas
　(3 medium)
5 dates, chopped

1 tablespoon honey
1 teaspoon cinnamon
⅛ teaspoon ginger
⅛ teaspoon allspice

Mix all ingredients and blend in blender for best results. Chill.
Serves 6.

Soy Pudding

4 eggs, beaten
2 cups soy milk
¼ teaspoon cinnamon
½ cup sunflower seed meal
½ cup soy grits (cooked)

1 cup dates (chopped fine)
1 cup raisins
1 cup nut meats (chopped
　fine)

Mix, put in oiled pans, and bake in moderate oven at 375° until
done. Serves 4 to 6.

Soy-Rice Pudding

3 eggs
⅓ cup honey
2 cups cooked brown rice

1 cup organic raisins
2 cups soya milk, scalded

Beat eggs well in large (pitcher type) bowl; beat in honey and
blend well. Beat in scalded soya milk gradually. Blend in rice and
raisins and pour into ungreased casserole. Place in a pan of hot
water and bake at 350°, or until silver knife inserted 1 inch from
edge comes out clean. Serve warm or cold. Serves 4.

Sweet Potato Pudding

Grate sweet potatoes until you have 2 cups. Then add the
following ingredients:

2 beaten eggs	½ teaspoon cinnamon
¼ cup blackstrap molasses	2 tablespoons honey
¼ teaspoon ginger	2 cups soya milk

Blend together and place the custard in the top of a double boiler and boil the water gently until you can insert a silver knife in the middle of the pudding and see that the custard has set. Remove from the heat, cool and chill. It can be served hot also. Serves 4.

Yam and Apple Pudding

2 cups cooked mashed yams	1 cup seedless raisins
2 cups peeled and diced raw apple	½ cup soy milk mixed with 1 tablespoon pure honey
1 cup chopped nuts	½ teaspoon cinnamon

Combine all ingredients and place in a lightly oiled casserole. Bake for about ½ hour or until apples are soft and top of pudding nicely browned. Serves 6.

Apricot-Cranberry Gelatin

(This salad must be made ahead to set.)

In blender:

1 cup hot water	2 tablespoons gelatin

Blend well, add:

½ cup honey	½ cup oil
1 teaspoon pure vanilla extract	1 cup water
¼ teaspoon pure almond extract	1 cup dried apricots
	1½ cups fresh cranberries

Add cranberries and blend only until chopped well. Add any extra you want such as nuts, etc. Pour into cake pan and let set. The chopped fruits will rise to the top and the bottom layer is a creamy-like texture. Serves 4.

Apricot-Prune Souffle

½ pound dried apricots, cooked
¼ pound dried prunes (pitted
  and cooked)

5 egg whites
5 tablespoons pure honey
  pinch of sea salt

Press cooked apricots and prunes through a sieve into a large bowl. Add honey and mix thoroughly. Beat egg whites and salt until stiff and fold gently into the fruit. Lightly oil a souffle dish and put the fruit mixture into it. Bake in a slow oven (300 degrees) until firm, about 45 minutes. Serve immediately. Serves 4.

Baked Apricot Whip

¾ cup cooked dried apricots,
  sieved or put through blender
  (just bring apricots to a boil
  and let stand)

4 egg whites—beaten stiff
  dash sea salt
3 tablespoons honey

Fold apricot puree into egg whites. Add sea salt and honey. Mix lightly. Pile lightly into 1 quart casserole, lightly oiled. Bake 30 minutes or until firm. Serves 6.

Black Cherry Gel

Open a quart of home-canned black sweet cherries and pour off the juice, adding water if needed to make 2 cups of it.

Dissolve 1 tablespoon gelatin in ¼ cup cold water and melt this in ½ cup of the cherry juice which has been brought to boiling. Blend this gelatin mixture with the other 1½ cups of juice. Then add:

1 cup drained black cherries
1 sliced banana

1 cup nut meats (local
  variety)

Cover and chill until set. Serve on salad greens with mayonnaise topped with rose hips powder. Serves 4.

Cherry Cream Mold

Here's a festive gelatin dessert made without sugar.

2 envelopes or 2 tablespoons gelatin
2 cups yogurt
1½ cups cherries, raw, pitted

½ teaspoon vanilla extract
1 sprig mint
2 tablespoons honey

Soften gelatin in ½ cup of water. In blender, mix gelatin and ¾ cup cherries. Add yogurt, vanilla extract, honey, sprig of mint and blend well. Stir in remaining cherries. Turn into mold and chill until set.

Variation: Cranberries or other berries in season may be used in place of cherries. Nuts or sunflower seeds may be added. Serves 4-6.

Cherry Delight

Open a pint can of your own sweet cherries, either pink, red or yellow, and drain the juice in a saucepan. Heat it very hot and add 1 tablespoon of plain gelatin which has been put in ¼ cup of water to dissolve. Stir until clear. Cool. Pour the gelatin mixture into a pretty glass dish, add the cherries, 1 sliced banana, ½ cup chopped nuts, ½ cup chopped sunflower seeds and honey if needed. Chill and serve "as is."

Coconut Cream

Peel and grate the meat of 1 coconut. Tie cheesecloth over a bowl and pour the grated coconut on the cheesecloth, then pour 1 cup of boiling water through the coconut into the bowl. Squeeze the coconut, then put it in the blender and make it up into milk. Put the bowl of liquid into the refrigerator overnight, covered, and a thick cream will rise to the top. This may be used as whipped cream.

Crusted Honey Almond Cream

1 envelope or 1 tablespoon
  unflavored gelatin
2 cups nut milk
2 eggs, separated
⅛ teaspoon sea salt
4 tablespoons honey

¼ teaspoon pure almond
  extract
1½ cups wheat germ
¼ cup almonds, slivered
1 tablespoon oil

Soften gelatin in ½ cup cold nut milk.

Combine remaining milk with egg yolks and salt in top of double boiler and cook gently over hot water until mixture thickens just enough to coat spoon.

Remove from heat. Add gelatin mixture and chill until it begins to set. Beat egg whites stiff. Blend in honey and flavoring. Fold into gelatin-yolk mixture. Turn into shallow pan 8 inches by 8 inches, which has been rinsed in cold water. Mix wheat germ, almonds, and oil and sprinkle over top. Chill until firm. Cut into squares. Makes 9 squares.

Prune Gelatin

1 pound large prunes
1 quart boiling water

2½ tablespoons gelatin
1 cup of cold water

Pour boiling water over prunes and let plump up over night. In the morning, soften gelatin in cold water. Heat water from soaked prunes, pour over softened gelatin and stir until dissolved. Pit prunes and put about half of them in blender with half of the gelatin, blend well. Repeat with rest of prunes and gelatin. Mix both batches and pour into mold. Refrigerate several hours until firm. Serves 8.

Prune Whip

2 tablespoons honey
1 cup soaked chopped prunes
1 tablespoon pineapple juice

¼ teaspoon mace
2 egg whites beaten stiff

While the egg whites are beating, chop the other ingredients together until very fine. Fold-in the beaten whites and put all into a quart casserole, then set this into a pan of boiling water. Put in the oven and bake 40 minutes at about 350 degrees. Serves 4.

Snack Foods

Healthful Snacks

Surveys reveal that one of the factors contributing to the inadequate diets of our country's teenagers is the poor selection of food for those after-school and late-night snacks. Teenagers (and many adults for that matter) tend to skip breakfast, lunch or both, and keep going on snack foods—crackers, candy bars, cookies, potato chips, cupcakes and soft drinks—all high in calories, low in nutrients. The salt and sugar contained in these foods tends to upset the chemical balance vital to good health.

It's difficult to find commercially-made crackers free of all undesirable ingredients, so make your own instead; it's simpler and less expensive. Remove those candy dishes from the coffee table and substitute raisins, stuffed dates, nuts, sunflower seeds, pumpkin seeds and honeylized popcorn around the house for between-meal snacks. Raw carrots, celery and apples are always welcome as snack foods.

Snack-Food Recipes

Bean Sprout Balls

1 cup bean sprouts
1 cup pecans or other nuts
1 cup raisins

1 tablespoon honey
coconut flakes (unsweetened)

Run all ingredients through the food chopper except the honey and coconut. Add honey and mix well. Form into 1-inch balls and roll in the coconut.

Frosted Bananas

Use well-speckled ripe but firm bananas. Break in halves or thirds according to size of bananas. Do not leave exposed to air, but roll in this dip immediately.

Prepare a dip made of carob powder and water. Add water gradually to carob powder to a smooth consistency, not too thin, not too fudgy. A little honey may be added.

Dip bananas into carob mixture, coating well all over. (Use tongs.) Then roll in grated coconut. Put each "frosted banana" in a small air-tight bag and freeze.

Take out of freezer 20-30 minutes before serving.

Fruit Man

To encourage children to eat fruit or to delight a child who has been ill, make a fruit man. It has a pear half for the body, peach slices for arms and legs and banana slices for the head, hands and feet.

Honeylized Popcorn

This requires an old style popcorn popper with a handle on the top for turning it. Put ⅓ cup each oil and honey and ½ cup popcorn in the popper. Turn the burner on high and keep turning like mad to keep it from scorching. If it's an electric stove, turn it off after it starts popping. Turn it out into a bowl fast. This takes a little practice. If you do burn a batch, wash the popper before popping it and sprinkle with cinnamon while it is hot. This is similar to crackerjack and should be made ahead. Once you are successful in making this, it is a real treat. Don't pop it too long as the time between popping and burning is short. Better to leave a few unpopped kernels than to let them burn.

Nahit

Wash dried garbanzos or chick peas, cover with cold water and soak overnight. Season and cook steadily until they are tender. Drain off the water into the soup stock jar and dry the garbanzos by shaking over low heat until they are dry. Serve cold as a healthful food to nibble on in place of the questionable ones so popular in this country. Garbanzos are used in the Orient in this way, probably accounting for the name of "Nahit."

Porcupines

Lay a moist, fresh fig on a plate and stick pignolia nuts in its top, slanting them towards the stem, which will look like the porcupine's tail. Fix a plate of these. If you leave a bit of the opposite end bare and fill the rest of the back and sides you will have quite a presentable porcupine.

Soybean Snacks

¼ cup dry soybeans   1 cup cold water

Soak soybeans overnight in the refrigerator. Next day, drain liquid and reserve as stock. Dry the soybeans with a clean towel. Spread them on a shallow pan. Roast 2 hours at 200°. Then place under broiler and continue to cook, stirring frequently, until soybeans are brown.

They may be used just as they are, or oiled and seasoned.

Leave whole, or grind, if desired, in blender or food grinder. Use as topping in the same way as nuts.

Peachy Prunes

Take soft, fresh dried prunes and open enough to get out the pit. Insert a slice of dried peach and pinch the prune back in its natural shape.

Seed-Stuffed Celery

½ cup sunflower seed meal   ½ cup sesame seed meal

Season to taste with *sea kelp* powder; mix to spreading consistency with *oil*. Stuff crisp celery or Romaine.

Zucchini Sandwiches

Pick zucchini squash when they are about 4 inches in length. Cut them in thin slices crossways and spread with nut butter and put together like sandwiches. They can also be diced and put in all kinds of raw salads, or cut fancy for canapes.

Canape Crackers

1½ cups soya flour
1½ cups corn flour
1 teaspoon sea salt
¼ cup soya or corn oil

½ cup water (least bit less than ½)
2 eggs

Sift flour and sea salt into mixing bowl. Make a well in center and pour in oil, water and beaten eggs. Stir until it forms a ball of dough. (Should be slightly moist, not dry. If necessary, add bit of water.) Pinch off pieces and shape into 1-inch balls; set on greased or oiled cookie sheet and flatten. Bake at 325° for 10-12 minutes. Makes 2 dozen.

High Protein Crackers

Beat 2 eggs slightly. Add:

½ cup tomato juice or water
2 tablespoons safflower oil
1 cup soya granules
½ cup instant soya milk powder

¼ cup sesame seeds
½ teaspoon celery seed
¼ teaspoon cayenne

Mix, forming a heavy paste. Spread on very heavily oiled cookie sheet. Cover with a sheet of oiled paper and roll to size of the cookie sheet. Bake for 15 minutes, or until edges turn medium brown, at 325 degrees. Cut into small portions. Dry for an hour or longer in a slow oven.

When crisp, these crackers will keep indefinitely. They are a good substitute for bread in open-face sandwiches, or as snacks. The taste may be varied by adding chopped onion or other seasonings, such as dill, oregano, sage, thyme, etc. The sesame seeds may be omitted or replaced by ground sunflower seeds. Makes 1 dozen.

Corn Meal Crackers

1 cup yellow corn meal
½ teaspoon sea salt
1 tablespoon soy oil

⅞ cup boiling water
¼ cup sesame seeds

Combine ingredients, drop by tablespoons on oiled baking sheet, spread in 3 or 4 inch rounds. Bake at 400 degrees until golden. Poppy or other seeds may be substituted for the sesame seeds. Makes about a dozen.

Corn Crisp Crackers

1 cup stone ground corn meal
1 tablespoon oil

½ teaspoon kelp
⅞ cup boiling water

Combine all ingredients; make balls using one tablespoon mixture for each. Place on oiled baking sheet, and pat or mash into three-inch rounds. Bake in hot oven (400 degrees) for 30 minutes. Makes 2 dozen.

Oat-Corn Crumbles

These are delicious as a substitute for crackers in soup or as a cereal. You can bake a large amount and freeze the cooled crumbles.

2⅔ cups oatmeal
⅓ cup wheat germ
1 cup whole grain cornmeal
¾ teaspoon sea salt
2 tablespoons honey

1 tablespoon each sesame and sunflower seeds
3 tablespoons oil
⅔ cup hot water
¼ cup coarsely shredded coconut

Mix well oatmeal, wheat germ, cornmeal, sea salt, and seeds. In large bowl put oil and honey. Mix. Add hot water. Mix well. Add coconut.

Pour bowl of dry ingredients into wet ingredients. Mix well, till crumbly.

Place in large oiled pan. Bake at 350° for 1½ hours, more or less, or until brown and crisp. Stir occasionally while baking.

Oatmeal Crackers

Blend together:

1 cup potato water

½ cup cooking oil

1 teaspoon sea kelp

4 cups quick-cooking oatmeal

(You can use the old-fashioned rolled oats and whiz it up fairly fine, a cup at a time, in the blender, if you wish.) Mix the ingredients into a stiff dough and chill it in the refrigerator. Lightly flour a board and roll the dough very thin. Sprinkle with caraway seeds and roll these in. Now transfer the thin pastry to an oiled cookie sheet. Cut in squares and prick with fork tines. Bake at 350 degrees about 20 minutes. Makes about 3 dozen.

Sesame Chips

In blender:

3 eggs, blended well

Mix 3 tablespoons of unflavored gelatin with 1 cup of sesame seeds thoroughly. Add the blended eggs and stir. Keep stirring and let set awhile to thicken. After it is thick form into a ball with a rubber scraper. Roll well in sesame seeds. Sprinkle cutting board or table heavily with sesame seeds. Roll out a piece about 6″ by 8″ at a time. If the rolling pin sticks, keep sprinkling sesame seeds over. Cut these with cookie cutters, or any shape you want. Oil the cookie sheet to keep the chips from sticking to it. Bake until brown clear through at 350°. You might have to remove the outside ones if they are done sooner. The flavor seems to improve after a day or more of storage.

Cheese

The variety of cheeses available to us helps to make this high-protein food a popular between-meal snack. In general, cheese is made by coagulating the casein, or protein, of milk, skimmed milk or milk enriched with cream. The coagulation is accomplished by means of rennet or some other suitable enzyme, souring, or a combination of the two.

Sometimes sour milk is used for cheese. The curd, or solid, coagulated mass that results is then altered by heat, pressure, molds or other special treatment, depending on what kind and flavor of cheese is wanted.

Processed cheese is, as its name implies, a product that has gone through several more processing steps. It involves mixing several kinds of cheese with an emulsifying agent to produce the intended consistency. Artificial coloring is commonly added to factory-made cheese, and an acidifying agent may also be used.

The processing through which many modern dairy products go—pasteurization, homogenization, emulsifiers, stabilizers, preservatives, dyes, possibly toxic wrapping materials, insecticides—must be taken into account when the health-seeker shops for them. It is worth whatever added costs are involved to search out the small retailers who can supply the natural, unadulterated product if cheese is on your shopping list.

Yogurt

Yogurt is one dairy product that has found a place among the most popular of the so-called health foods. Supermarkets sell large quantities of it to people who are not at all health conscious. They simply like the taste of yogurt without regard for nutritional value.

And why not? Yogurt *is* delicious and looks appetizing. It is served cold and has the appearance and texture of very firm whipped cream. The taste is tangy and smooth, on the order of satiny buttermilk. When served with raw fresh fruit or vegetables, it is a gourmet course. It can also be combined with chopped onions or chives to make an excellent spread or dip. And it is low in calories—about 330 calories per pint.

In some form or another yogurt has been a familiar food in many parts of the world since Biblical times. There's nothing new about yogurt but the bright-colored containers it is packaged in nowadays. However, to avoid the excessive sweetening in some of the flavorings added by commercial manufacturers, buy plain yogurt and add the fruit or vegetables at home.

The digestive problems presented by ordinary milk for some babies and older people are absent in yogurt. Another of the less wholesome effects of regular milk is the allergic reaction experienced by some who drink it. A large percentage of the people who show an allergy to milk are able to tolerate yogurt with no ill effect whatsoever.

Contrary to popular belief, yogurt is easily made and requires only simple equipment. You will need ½ cup yogurt starter, 1¾ pints of milk, a thermometer, a quart fruit jar, a pail of hot water and a blanket. You can get the starter from any of the advertised places, or use ½ cup from the commercial yogurt on sale at the dairy counter in most any supermarket.

Heat the 1¾ pints of milk to 118 degrees. Stir the ½ cup of starter smooth and blend it thoroughly with the hot milk. Pour this into the quart jar, seal it tight, and immerse the jar in the pail of water which has also been heated to 118 degrees. Cover the pail and wrap it in a thick blanket. Let stand for 2 hours, after which the yogurt should be congealed. Refrigerate the can of yogurt, keeping out ½ cup to use as a starter for the next batch.

Fancy Yogurt Recipes

Vanilla Yogurt: Add ½ cup honey and 1 teaspoon vanilla to 2 cups of yogurt, blending carefully. Use as dessert.

Date, Fig or Prune Yogurt: Soak the dried fruit until soft, remove pits or stems, mash, add honey to taste and stir into yogurt; any proportions desired. This is a fine breakfast dish as it aids elimination.

Berry Yogurt: Mash fresh or frozen (and thawed) berries and add enough honey to sweeten—about half berries and half yogurt. This makes a fine dessert or TV snack.

Molasses Yogurt: Add 2 tablespoons of blackstrap molasses and a pinch each of ginger and cinnamon to 2 cups of yogurt. Blend and use as dessert or stir thin and drink.

Yogurt Drinks: Add all kinds of fruit and vegetable juices from the blender or juicer to yogurt, using herbs to season the vegetable drinks and mint to season the fruit drinks. Add supplements with both as needed.

Yogurt Salad Dressing (Vegetables): 1 cup yogurt, ½ cup home-made mayonnaise, 1 teaspoon wine or pure cider vinegar, 1 pinch of tarragon herb, minced onion or garlic, paprika and sea kelp.

Yogurt Salad Dressing (Fruit): 1 cup yogurt, ¼ cup honey, 1 teaspoon pineapple juice, shredded mint leaves.

Mattenitza: The Bulgarians, who originated yogurt, mix yogurt with pure water, half-and-half, and drink it like buttermilk.

Yogurt Custard: Blend gently 2 cups yogurt, ⅓ cup honey, 3 beaten egg yolks, 1 teaspoon vanilla, ½ teaspoon nutmeg. Put in custard cups and chill until time to eat. This is a fine dessert for invalids and children.

Menus for a Month

First Week

SUNDAY

Breakfast: Tomato Juice • Oatmeal with dates or raisins and nut milk • Scrambled Eggs and Mushrooms • Fenugreek Tea

Luncheon: Seedburgers • Zucchini Boats • Raisin Muffins • Raw Beet Salad • Fruit Cup • Peachy Fruit Flip

Dinner: Roast Stuffed Veal • Corn Bread Stuffing • Braised Leeks • Bean and Cabbage Salad • Fruit Bars • Strawberry Mint Nectar

MONDAY

Breakfast: Apple Juice • Muesli • Buckwheat Pancakes & Maple Syrup • Alfalfa Tea

Luncheon: "Mock" Chicken Salad (made with veal) served on Lettuce leaves and surrounded by tomato slices • Corn Bread • Applesauce • Soybean Coffee

Dinner: Broiled Steaks (with mushrooms & onions if desired) • Fluffy Brown Rice • Minted Carrots • Broccoli Salad • Southern Spoon Bread • Indian Pudding • Sweet Port "Wine"

TUESDAY

Breakfast: Sliced Peaches with berries • Oatmeal, topped with Wheat germ and Sunflower Milk • Peanut Corn Sticks • Avocado Spread • Mint Tea

Luncheon: Vegetable Soup • Crackers • Egg Salad • Ambrosia • Oat Tea

Dinner: Herbed Pot Roast • Sweet Potatoes cooked in jackets • Cardinal Salad • Cauliflower with Yogurt • Apricot Whip • Comfrey and Peppermint Tea

WEDNESDAY

Breakfast: Stewed Prunes • "Muffin" Poached Eggs • Raw Blackberry Jam • Tahini Milk

Luncheon: Cold Sliced Beef • Protein Bean Salad • Waikiki Muffins • Carob Brownies • Pineapple Tonic (Beverage)

Dinner: Baked Short Ribs of Beef • Mashed Potatoes • Mushroom Sauce • Avocado Stuffed Tomatoes on Lettuce • Blackberry Shortcake • Blender Benedictine

THURSDAY

Breakfast: Grape Juice • Griddle cakes with Honey • Eggs Minnetonka • Soymilk with Carob Syrup

Luncheon: Hamburger Puffs • Brussels Sprouts • Millet Bread • Tutti-Frutti Jam • Raspberry Ambrosia • Garden Cocktail (Beverage)

Dinner: Liver Loaf • Saffron Rice • "Sunday" Salad • Red Beets • Cranberry Muffins • Date Delight • Beverage

FRIDAY

Breakfast: Sliced Fresh Peaches • Millet Porridge with Coconut or Nut Milk and Honey • Hard Cooked Eggs • "Sunflower Fig Cookies" • Beverage

Luncheon: Liver Dumplings and Dill Sauce • Dixie Corn Bread • Cabbage and Green Pepper Slaw • No-cook Fudge • Raspberry, Pineapple Juice

Dinner: Fish and Cabbage Casserole • Green Bean Salad • Molasses Custard • Hot Spearmint Tea

SATURDAY

Breakfast: Fresh Pineapple Juice • Eggs Foo-Yung • Popcorn Cereal • Herb Tea

Luncheon: Mushroom Soup • Saturday Beans • Corn Flour Buns • Avocado Salad • Bananas Plus • Delicious Health Drink

Dinner: Chicken Pie with Corn Topping • Sprout Salad • Spinach with hard-cooked chopped eggs • Peanut-Raisin Cookies • Fenugreek Tea

Second Week

SUNDAY

Breakfast: Fresh or Frozen Berries with Honey and Wheat Germ • Kidney Omelet • Corn Sticks • Raw Fruit Cookies • Peanut Milk

Luncheon: Almond Loaf with Spiced Apple Halves • Muffins • Raw Carrot and Celery Sticks • Cherry Cobbler • Beverage

Dinner: Baked Chicken • Kasha (Groats) and Mushrooms • Gravy (thickened with Arrowroot) • Squash cups • Herbed Broccoli • Cabbage and Raisin Salad • Carob-Peanut Clusters • Apple-Grape Juice Drink

MONDAY

Breakfast: Dish of cherries or grapes • Carrot Muesli • Peanut Corn Sticks • Avocado Spread • Soy Milk flavored with honey, vanilla and blackstrap Molasses

Luncheon: Chicken Livers and Mushrooms • Chopped Asparagus • Salad • Sesame Treats • Grape-Yogurt Drink

Dinner: Meat Loaf with Herbs • Soy Noodles with Poppy seeds • Waxed Beans • Dandelion or Endive Salad • Mock Pecan Pie • Sweet Port "Wine"

TUESDAY

Breakfast: Cranberry Juice • Wheat Germ with Strawberries, honey and soy or nut milk • Sunflower Seed Omelet • Rose Hips Tea

Luncheon: Cold Sliced Meat Loaf • Roasted Green Peppers • Sesame Chips • Celery Stuffed with Peanut Butter • Comfrey Tea

Dinner: Honey of A Lamb • Broiled Tomatoes • Green Salad with French Dressing • Asparagus • Date Dandies • Peachy Fruit Flip

WEDNESDAY

Breakfast: Plums—fresh or home-canned • Hot Cornmeal Mush with Nut Milk • Fruit Omelet • Spearmint Tea

Luncheon: Lamb on Brown Rice • Stuffed Beets • Raw Carrot and Celery Sticks • Crusted Honey Almond Cream • Blackstrap "Coffee"

Dinner: Tenderized Beef and Gravy • Mashed Sweet Potatoes • Almondine Green Beans • Pickled Red Beets • Apple Dessert • Pineapple Tonic

THURSDAY

Breakfast: Apple Juice • Buckwheat Pancakes with Honey or Maple Syrup • Soft Boiled Egg • Rose Hips Tea

Luncheon: Irish Stew • Tomato Aspic • Bran Muffins • Soy Spread • Uncooked Taffy • Beverage

Dinner: Broiled Chicken Halves • Baked Potatoes with Yogurt • Bean Surprise • Celery Root Salad • Icebox Cookies • Oat Tea

FRIDAY

Breakfast: Honeydew Melon Slice • Scrambled Eggs • Potato Pancakes • Nut Milk Yogurt • Coconut Milk

Luncheon: Salmon-Spinach Casserole • Corn Puff • Raw Tomato Slices with Russian Dressing • Peanut Cookies • Mint Tea

Dinner: Jellied Fish • Potato-Carrot Souffle • Herbed Zucchini Squash • Green Soy Salad • Corn Squares • Dewberry Jam • Papaya Date "Ice Cream" • Purple Cow (Beverage)

SATURDAY

Breakfast: Fresh Cantaloupe • Oatmeal Muffins • Herbed Omelet • Blackstrap "Coffee"

Luncheon: Fish Chowder • Green Bean Salad • Caraway Millet Muffins • Peachy Prunes • Herb Tea

Dinner: Broiled Hamburgers • Sweet Onion Slices • Surprise Pepper Buns • Special Green Beans • Stuffed Tomatoes • Fresh Fruit Bowl • Fenugreek Tea

Third Week

SUNDAY

Breakfast: Apple Juice • Wheat Germ Pancakes with Honey • Poached Eggs • Carob Milk

Luncheon: Bouillabaisse • Corn Sticks • Peanut Hootenannies • Artichoke Flip (Beverage)

Dinner: Roast Leg of Lamb • Creole Lima Beans • Applesauce with Mint • Honey-Glazed Carrots • Sprouted Lentil Salad • Strawberry Yogurt Freeze • Peppermint Tea

MONDAY

Breakfast: Sliced Mixed Fruit • Oatmeal, Maple Syrup • Beanburgers • Nuts, Sunflower Seeds • Beverage

Luncheon: Lamb Ragout • Persian-American Rice • Crunchy Apple Salad • Fruit Drink

Dinner: Vegetarian "Nutty" Loaf • Tossed Green Salad with Tripled Health Dressing • Herbed Wax Beans • Hard Cooked Eggs • Millet Bread • Uncooked Date Pie • Oat Tea

TUESDAY

Breakfast: Fresh Pear Slices with Yogurt and Honey • Mung Bean Omelet • Oat-Corn Crumbles • Banana-nut Milk

Luncheon: Beef Chop Suey • Parsleyed Brown Rice • Peanut Muffins • Raw Grape Butter • Garbanzo Salad • Apricot Ice • Strawberry Mint Nectar

Dinner: Fruited Pot Roast • Sesame Potatoes • Watercress Salad with Mayonnaise Dressing • Young Beets and Greens • Berry Bowl • "Nutty" Confections • Herbed Tomato Punch

WEDNESDAY

Breakfast: Kadota Figs • Muesli • Best Buckwheat Cakes with Honey • Herb Tea

Luncheon: Beef Curry • Crackers • Green Beans • Banana Sherbet • Apple Juice

Dinner: Baked Liver and Onions • Scalloped Tomatoes • Broccoli Marinated in Oil and vinegar on Salad Greens • Muffins • Peanut Butter Pudding • Beverage

THURSDAY

Breakfast: Cantaloupe with Berries • Corn Popovers with Nut Butter • Baked Herb Omelet • Nut Milk

Luncheon: Chopped Beef Liver • Sesame Chips • Baked Eggplant Slices • Harvard Honey Beets • Fresh Fruit Cup • Apricot Shake

Dinner: Herbed, Baked Veal Chops • Stuffed Baked Potatoes and Peas • Steamed Cabbage • Grated Carrot-Raisin Salad • Prune Whip • Manchurian Milk Drink

FRIDAY

Breakfast: Stewed Prunes • "Scrapple" • Hard Cooked Eggs • Dates and Nuts • Soy Carob Milk

Luncheon: Tomato Soup • Jellied Meat Salad • Fruit Bread (Sun-baked) • Green Beans and Baby Onions • "Little Imp" Cake • Peach Nectar

Dinner: Broiled Short Ribs • Broiled Tomato Slices • Corn Chapatties • Pear Conserve • Fresh Spinach Salad with Carrot Curls and Onion Slices (Italian Dressing) • Raspberry Ice • Fenugreek Tea

SATURDAY

Breakfast: Apple Juice • Garbanzo Omelet • Assorted Fruit and Nut Plate • Herb Tea

Luncheon: Chili Con Carne • Corn Caraway Gems • Green Peas with Celery Slices • Coconut Custard • Grape Punch

Dinner: Hot Lettuce Soup • Pressed Chicken • Irish Potato Salad • Brussels Sprouts • "C" Salad on Tomato Slices • Carrot Relish • Coconut Banana Meringue Pie • Rose Hips Tea

Fourth Week

SUNDAY

Breakfast: Apple-Grape Juice • Broiled Breakfast Steaks • Hashed Brown Potatoes • Sunflower Seeds • Soyafig Shake

Luncheon: Egg Salad • Corn Sticks • Sliced Raw Vegetables with Yogurt • Carob Brownies • Garden Cocktail

Dinner: Roast Prime Ribs of Beef • Oven-Browned Potatoes • Steamed Cauliflower • Dieters' Delight Artichokes • Bean Sprout Salad • Banana Pudding Cake • Herb Tea

MONDAY

Breakfast: Hot Fruit Peppo • Soy Corn Flour Waffles with Orange Honey • Porcupines • Peppermint Tea

Luncheon: Cold Sliced Beef • Kidney Bean Salad • Tomato and Lettuce • Muffins • Cranberry Sherbet • Apricot Shake

Dinner: Soybean Roast • Shredded Potato Casserole and Sesame Seeds • Zucchini Squash • Molded Green Salad • Maple Pears Under Glass • Mint Tea

TUESDAY

Breakfast: Pineapple Chunks • Artichoke Pancakes • Mushroom Omelet • Herb Tea

Luncheon: Broiled Hamburgers • Succotash • Spring Onions • Oatmeal Crackers • Cranberry-Apple-Grape Fruit Punch

Dinner: Steak and Kidney Casserole • Fresh, Tender Raw Broccoli Stalks with Avocado Dip • Minted Carrots • Angel Food Cookies • Soybean Coffee

WEDNESDAY

Breakfast: Tomato Juice • Soya Chops • Dandelion Coffee

Luncheon: Herbed Omelet • Lentil Salad • Muffins • Berries • Coconut Milk

Dinner: Baked Beef Heart • Mushroom Stuffing • Lettuce with Hot Soy Mayonnaise Dressing • Green and Wax Beans • Apple Custard Pie • Floral Punch

THURSDAY

Breakfast: Fruit Juice • Brown Rice Griddle Cakes • Scrambled Eggs in Asparagus • Plumped Dried Apricots and Almonds • Almond Milk

Luncheon: Sliced Cold Heart • Jellied Vegetable Salad • Muffins • Peanut Patties • Nuts and Raisins • Fresh Apple Juice

Dinner: Roast Chicken with Millet Stuffing • Baked Eggplant Slices • Cole Slaw • Oatmeal Bread • Avocado Dessert • Oat Tea

FRIDAY

Breakfast: Stewed Prunes • Polynesian Scrambled Eggs • Corn Muffins • Nut Milk

Luncheon: Broiled Lamb Chops • Potato Pancakes • Corn Relish • Sliced Bananas topped with chopped nuts • Herb Tea

Dinner: Baked Haddock • Broiled Stuffed Peppers • Steamed Cauliflower • Pineapple-Green Pepper Slaw • Soy Custard • Rose Hips Tea

SATURDAY

Breakfast: Hot Tomato Tonic • Soft Boiled Eggs • Oven Fried Potatoes • Fiji Fruit Cocktail • Blackstrap Coffee

Luncheon: Corn Chowder • Millet Bread with Peanut Butter • Vegetable-Fruit Dessert Ice • Frosty Fruit Shake

Dinner: London Broil • Stewed Tomatoes and Onions • Rice Colorful • Sauerkraut and Apple Combo (Salad) • Sliced Peaches and Ginger Snaps • Fenugreek Tea

Holiday Menus

EASTER

Breakfast: Almond Milk-Berry Shake • Spanish Omelet • Mexican Tortillas • Arabian Makoud

Luncheon: Djuvece (Lamb and Vegetables from Yugoslavia) • Salata—Mixed Salad (from the Balkans) • Baked Mushrooms • Waikiki Muffins • Tropical Milk Shake

Dinner: Russian Steak • Corn Fritters • Easter Lily Salad • Easter Basket Fruits • Coconut-egg Custard • Hawaiian Dash (Beverage)

THANKSGIVING

Breakfast: Fresh Cranberry Juice • Peanut Pancakes • Eggs Minnetonka • Squash or Pumpkin Seed Milk

Dinner: Holiday Roast Turkey • Plymouth Dressing • Baked Sweet Potatoes • Brussels Sprouts • Corn Pudding • Baked Squash • Raw Apple-Cranberry Relish • Harvest Vegetable Tray (served with yogurt) • November Punch • Fruit Cornucopia (Centerpiece)

Supper: Cold Sliced Turkey • Lettuce • Protein Bean Salad • Cranberry Sauce • Indian Corn Bread • Walnut Spread • Beverage

CHRISTMAS

Breakfast: Honeyed Pears • Waffles with Maple Syrup • Eggs • Santa Claus Cookies

Dinner: Roast Goose • Holiday Dressing • Peanut Honey Yams • Red and Green Vegetables • Red and Green Pickles • Cranberry Muffins with Raspberry Jam • Holly Berry Fruit Cake • Holiday Punch

Supper: Cold Sliced Goose • Apple Cranberry Relish • Christmas Tree Salad • Christmas Cookies • Carob Drink

PASSOVER

Breakfast: Sliced Bananas with Nut Milk • Matzo Meal Pancakes • Bowl of Fruit • Nuts • Mint Tea

Luncheon: Baked Fish • Baked Potatoes • Carrot and Celery Sticks • Kosher Dill Pickles if desired • Egg Salad • Applesauce • Fruit Juice

Dinner: Chopped Beef Liver • Matzo Meal Muffins • Frozen Berries (thawed) • Baked Eggplant Slices • Pickled Beets • Baked Sweet Potatoes & Prunes • Herb Tea

Seder Meal: Soup • Gefillte Fish with Beet Flavored Horseradish • Roast Chicken with Matzo Meal Stuffing • Mixed Green Salad • Fruit Compote • Honey Cake • Herb Tea

Index

℗